The "How To" Grants Manual
Successful Grantseeking Techniques for Obtaining Public and Private Grants

Fourth Edition

by
David G. Bauer

AMERICAN COUNCIL ON EDUCATION ★
ORYX PRESS ★
Series on Higher Education
1999

The rare Arabian Oryx is believed to have inspired the myth of the unicorn. This desert antelope became virtually extinct in the early 1960s. At that time, several groups of international conservationists arranged to have nine animals sent to the Phoenix Zoo to be the nucleus of a captive breeding herd. Today, the Oryx population is over 1,000, and over 500 have been returned to the Middle East.

© 1999 by The American Council on Education and The Oryx Press
4041 North Central at Indian School Road
Phoenix, Arizona 85012-3397

Published simultaneously in Canada
Printed and bound in the United States of America

∞ The paper used in this publication meets the minimum requirements of American National Standard for Information Science—Permanence of Paper for Printed Library Materials, ANSI Z39.48, 1984.

Library of Congress Cataloging-in-Publication Data
Bauer, David G.
    The "how to" grants manual : successful grantseeking techniques for obtaining public and private grants / by David G. Bauer. — 4th ed.
        p. cm.
    Published simultaneously in the United States and Canada.
    Includes bibliographical references (p.) and index.
    ISBN 1-57356-326-9 (alk. paper)
    1. Fund raising. 2. Grants-in-aid. 3. Nonprofit organizations.
I. Title.
    HG177.B38   1999
    658.15'224—dc21
                                                        99-31057
                                                        CIP

CONTENTS

LIST OF EXHIBITS, FIGURES, AND TABLES

PREFACE

I t is an honor to provide you with the fourth edition of *The "How To" Grants Manual.* There have been many changes in grantmaking since the third edition of this manual was released. The challenges that grantseekers face are daunting. The fiercely competitive environment coupled with rapidly changing advances in technology force the successful grantseeker to keep current. Therefore, this edition incorporates the techniques and strategies I developed over the past 30 years with the newest changes in grantmaking and the latest grant-related technological advances. While those of you who are familiar with other editions of this book will find that many of the basic constructs remain the same, even the tried and proven strategies that have been retained in this edition have been augmented with current examples.

Since the third edition was released, I have had the opportunity to instruct 10,000 more grantseekers, who have provided me with feedback on techniques that work and information on how they have adapted certain techniques to further assure their success. The information I have gleaned from them and my work with major nonprofit organizations has allowed me to try new techniques and discover what works and what doesn't. All of this and more has been incorporated into this book.

The "How To" Grants Manual will increase your knowledge of the grants marketplace and show you how to locate and secure grant funds. It also outlines a systematic approach for organizing proposal efforts that will save you hours of precious time and increase your monetary return by thousands of dollars. By applying the techniques presented in this book, you will increase your success rate while projecting a more professional image to funding sources.

The arrangement of this book follows the recommended grantseeking pattern. Part 1, "Getting Ready to Seek Grant Support for Your Organization," will show you how to view your proposal from the perspective of the potential grantor. Part 2, "Government Funding Sources," is devoted to understanding the federal grants process and includes strategies for improving the quality of your federal proposal. Part 3, "Private Funding Sources," takes a comprehensive look at the foundation and corporate grants marketplace. Part 3 assists the grantseeker in researching and selecting private funding sources and preparing a letter proposal to a foundation or corporation. The focus in both parts 2 and 3 is on how to select prospective grantors and increase your chances of success through pre-proposal contact. You will learn how to create a tailored approach designed to meet the grantor's needs as well as those of your organization.

No matter what your level of grantseeking expertise, this book will help promote *your* system for grants success. While this manual does not come with a guarantee, surveys of its users consistently demonstrate success rates of 70 to 80 percent.

A software package entitled *Grant Winner* is available to help you organize the grantseeking techniques outlined in this manual. (For ordering information, see the list of resources available from Bauer Associates at the end of the book.)

If you are involved in evaluating and improving your organization's grants effort, you will find the book *Administering Grants, Contracts, and Funds— Evaluating and Improving Your Grants System* (Phoenix: American Council on Education/Oryx Press, second edition, 2000) particularly helpful. If you are interested in learning more about the grantseeking process, you may find the videotape training program *Winning Grants 2* useful. If you are interested in instructing others in grantseeking, you may find the videotape training program *How to Teach Grantseeking to Others* invaluable. (See the Bauer Associates ordering information at the end of the book for both of these resources.)

Special thanks must be given to the American Council on Education, the SUNY Institute of Technology, the University of Rochester School of Medicine, Department of Pediatrics, and the University of Alabama, Birmingham, School of Education and Center for Educational Accountability for providing me with opportunities to develop many of the techniques shared in this manual.

INTRODUCTION

W hy seek grants? Your immediate response may be—for the money. However, research and my experiences have repeatedly demonstrated that money is not the prime motivator for grantseekers. Take the 78-year-old retired scientist working diligently on a proposal to fund a program to get young girls interested in pursuing his much-loved profession. Is money his motivation? Definitely not. He will not receive remuneration for his efforts, and yet he still devotes his time and energy to the task. Or what about our society's countless volunteers? What motivates them? Could it simply be that they value the contributions that a grant-funded project or research provides? And finally, consider the over 654,000 501(c)3 nonprofit organizations that utilize the grants mechanism to provide benefits to our world that reach far beyond any one person's gain of money.

As long as there are needs and interests that require more support than nonprofit organizations can provide through their normal allocation processes, there will be a demand for grant funds. And as long as there are wealthy individuals and profitable companies looking for ways to impart their values and demonstrate their concerns, as well as governments willing to fund scientific research and efforts to find new and better solutions to social problems, there will be grantseekers.

For many faculty members at universities and research centers, grantseeking is a necessity. The ability to attract grant funding is a requirement for their continued appointment and tenure. Many faculty members, however, continue seeking grants even after they have secured their position. Why? They pursue grant funding for many of the same reasons that those of you in nonacademic fields do, and it's not for money!

Do grantseekers get paid extra to write proposals? While a few may, most nonprofit organizations (including universities and research centers) do not pay their staff extra for writing proposals. In fact, they do not even provide release time or reduced work loads to help individuals who are seeking grants. In actuality, the legal and ethical requirements that govern grantseeking do not allow proposal developers or consultants to be paid for efforts or costs incurred before the grant award date and the idea of paying a grant writer a percentage of the awarded grant is out of the question. Why individuals pursue grant funding is not a mystery. The quest for a grant in the nonprofit world is equivalent to efforts in the for-profit world that are associated with superior performances and super achievers. In fact, findings in studies on motivation and achievement in the for-profit world are similar to those documented in a study by Sharol Jacobson and Mary Elizabeth O'Brien on the satisfying and stressful experiences of first-time federal grantees.[1] Some of the satisfying experiences reported by the respondents in this study included

- praise and personal recognition
- satisfaction from working with a research team
- satisfaction from immersion in research
- satisfaction from commitment of subjects
- salary, space, travel, and equipment
- speaking opportunities
- opportunity to review proposals
- familiarity with federal agency personnel
- recognition in university publications
- increased awareness of research among students and colleagues
- increased responsiveness from campus research officials

Grantseekers want and deserve recognition and support from their organizations and peers for dedicating their spare time and extra efforts to the pursuit of grant funding. While payment for successful grantseeking may be illegal and unethical, recognition and appreciation are acceptable anytime. In fact, after reading and applying the techniques described in The "How To" Grants Manual, you may want to look further into how your organization can employ the latest management techniques to build a grant system that promotes superior performance. Suggested reading includes Administering Grants, Contracts, and Funds—Evaluating and Improving Your Grants System (Phoenix: American Council on Education/Oryx Press, second edition, 2000).

The "How To" Grants Manual contains many suggestions to help you integrate grantseeking into your busy professional life. Initially, you may think that some of the suggestions will direct you away from that special project that brought you to the grants marketplace, but this is not the case. All of the suggestions are aimed at helping you develop a wider perspective from which to view your project so that you can increase your chances for funding.

To those individuals and organizations who have made this world a better place through the use of the grants mechanism, I thank you. To you, the grantseeker who is trying to improve our collective lot, I applaud your efforts and dedicate this book to providing you with the best techniques I know for locating funds while using your time most efficiently.

REFERENCE

1. Sharol F. Jacobsen and Mary Elizabeth O'Brien, "Satisfying and Stressful Experiences of First-Time Federal Grantees," *IMAGE: Journal of Nursing Scholarship* 24, no. 1 (Spring 1992): 45-49.

PART ONE

• • • • • • • • • • • •

Getting Ready to Seek Grant Support for Your Organization

CHAPTER 1

Setting Yourself Up for Grants Success

Developing a Proactive Grants System

What is reactive grantseeking? When a grantseeker develops a grant proposal first and then searches for a possible grantor to submit it to, he or she is engaging in reactive grantseeking. Another example of reactive grantseeking is when a grantseeker locates or is presented with a potential grantor by a superior then scrambles to create an appropriate proposal before a looming deadline. The time constraint forces the grantseeker into a *reactive* mode that precludes being able to develop insight into the hidden agenda of the grantor, does not allow for pre-proposal contact, and makes it virtually impossible to prepare a proposal that is tailored to the grantor. Because of these factors, reactive grantseeking is fraught with rejection, as well as negative attitudes. To avoid these problems, grantseeking should be viewed as a quest to develop a relationship with a grantor who values the same outcomes that your proposal suggests, not as an opportunity to locate funding for what *you* want to do.

The ability to submit proposals electronically over the Internet has further enhanced the propensity to employ reactive grantseeking. Now, the hastily prepared, last-minute proposal can be transmitted at the very last minute. In this instance, the use of technology may actually result in a decrease in the quality of the proposal.

In contrast, proactive grantseeking is based on researching prospective grantors in order to match their grant interests with your projects and ideas. In many cases, reactive grantseekers and proactive grantseekers invest the same amount of time developing their proposals. What is different is *when* and *how* they invest their time and how these variables influence their success rate. Proactive grantseekers put in small amounts of time *throughout* the grantseeking process. The analogy to the age-old story of the rabbit and the turtle applies here. The reactive grantseeker (rabbit) makes a Herculean attempt at developing a proposal, racing against time (and the deadline), only to lose to the proactive grantseeker (turtle) who has been plodding along the grants trail using an energy-efficient and ultimately successful strategy.

The first step in taking a proactive approach to grantseeking is for you to extricate yourself from the notion that your proposal's approach is the only one (or at least the best) way to move ahead. In reality, there are many approaches that could result in the changes your proposal suggests. By neglecting to develop several approaches to discuss with the potential grantor during pre-proposal contact, grantseekers limit their ability to uncover any preferences or hidden agendas that the grantor may have. Those grantseekers who have fixed ideas about their projects and exactly how they will be carried out miss the opportunity to learn what the grantor is really looking for. In addition, their proposals often suffer from a narrow viewpoint, focusing on what the grantseeker wants instead of the needs of the prospective grantor. This myopic approach can be contrasted with the equally ill-fated general approach. General proposals are designed to fit any possible grantor's guidelines. Whether myopic or general, proposals resulting from these approaches are easily recognizable because of a preponderance of statements beginning with "We want," "We need," and so on.

Unfortunately, this self-focus has been aided by the use of computers for researching grantors. In many cases the overzealous and self-focused grantseeker will secure printouts of all the grantors who have funded projects even remotely related to theirs and then send the same proposal to every grantor on the list. What these grantseekers overlook is that the "shotgun" approach results in high rates of rejection and negative positioning with funding sources.

Whenever your proposals (or those of your nonprofit organization) result in failure, you risk positioning your organization in a negative manner. Of course, grantseeking will always result in a certain percentage of rejection. That is bound to happen. But how much rejection can you, the grantseeker, and your organization afford before the very appearance of your name on a proposal elicits a negative reaction from grantors? What is the success rate you need to achieve to avoid negative positioning? Anything less than a 50 percent success rate could result in negative positioning. A 70 or 80 percent failure rate could not possibly create a positive image for your organization.

Embracing a proactive approach to grantseeking means starting the process early. This in itself, enables the grantseeker to employ quality assurance techniques to increase success and avoid negative positioning. A proactive grantseeker has enough time to conduct a mock review of his or her proposal using the same review system that is ultimately to be used by the grantor. This technique helps to ensure that the submitted proposal represents the grantseeker's best effort. By starting early and finishing your proposal a few days before the grantor's deadline, you will be able to have your proposal read and scored by friendly role players who can pick up any errors before your proposal is submitted for its real review. While chapter 12 provides details on how to use a grants quality circle to improve a proposal, the simple fact is that you will not have enough time to use this invaluable technique unless you become a

---

APPLICATION NUMBER:

Technology Innovation Challenge Grant Program
Individual Technical Review Form: FY 1998 - <u>Tier 1</u>

<u>SUMMARY ASSESSMENT</u>

Please summarize your overall thoughts about the application in light of your previous comments on "significance" and "feasibility," and mention any important points on which the application is unclear so that these points can be raised with the applicant.

The conversational style was welcome and easy reading. For once there was an absence of educational "buzz words." However, watch out for too much informal style. (The phrase "parents don't have a clue.")
Don't forget to identify acronyms. GSAMS was only identified in a letterhead in the appendix.
It is extremely important to proofread your application. There were no less than nineteen grammar and punctuation errors. If simple details like these are not corrected as a matter of professionalism, can one reasonably be expected to properly manage several million dollars?

OVERALL GRADE   B
A=high, B=medium, C=low

SAMPLE REVIEWER'S COMMENTS

EXHIBIT 1.1

proactive grantseeker! Exhibit 1.1 shows what kind of reviewer comments are likely to be received when proactive grantseeking is abandoned.

Many reactive grantseekers resort to a "one proposal fits all grantors" strategy because they run out of time and mistakenly believe that the shotgun approach will be time efficient. Time efficiency means nothing, however, when proposal after proposal is rejected. In my early attempts at grantseeking I quickly learned that the best strategy for winning grants was to tailor each and every proposal to the perspective of the potential grantor. After a reactive grantseeking failure, I remembered a theory I learned as a psychology major and applied it to grantseeking. Thirty years later, I can say unequivocally that this theory has helped me develop millions of dollars in successful projects and research for nonprofit organizations. I share this theory with you to help you approach grantseeking from the grantor's perspective, and to provide you with the basis for developing a tailored proposal to each grantor.

FESTINGER'S THEORY OF COGNITIVE DISSONANCE

Leon Festinger developed the theory of cognitive dissonance[1] to explain how individuals learn and assimilate information. In brief, Festinger states that each of us sees, hears, and remembers what we already believe to be true. When we are presented with information that is contrary to what we believe to be true, dissonance or static is created in our information-receiving systems. To reduce this static and maintain homeostasis, we discount the new information. While Festinger was interested in how individuals learn, the theory of cognitive dissonance has great application to grantseeking.

VALUES-BASED GRANTSEEKING

By expanding Festinger's theory, I developed the "values glasses theory" and the concepts of values-based grantseeking. A common mistake of grantseekers is to write their proposals based on their own values. They assume that prospective grantors have similar values to themselves, and that they will read the proposals from their (the grantseeker's) point-of-view. This is a mistake. Using a proposal to try to change the values of a grantor or to show that the funding source's granting pattern is unenlightened is another mistake that usually results in dissonance and rejection. Some grantseekers also make the mistake of using their own vocabulary in proposals, forgetting that grantors will read and react to proposals based upon their (the grantor's) vocabulary.

Figure 1.1 illustrates the grantseeker's predicament. As a proactive, values-based grantseeker he or she must strive to get the facts through the lenses

VALUES-BASED GRANT SEEKING

FIGURE 1.1

(filters) of the grantor over to the brain of the grantor which controls the hand, arm, and money (check) the grantseeker wants.

The ensuing chapters in this book are all based upon uncovering the information you need to understand the values of the grantor so that your proposal can be written and presented in such a way that it reinforces your prospective grantor's values. Values-based grantseeking entails uncovering information about the grantor that will help you develop an appreciation and understanding of the grantor's values glasses. Once you have this information, you can use it as a guide to your approach, helping you select the "right" needs data and vocabulary to include in your proposal and ensuring that you present a compelling case for funding.

Successful grantseekers avoid jeopardizing their chances at being funded by being sensitive to the values of the grantor. They do not pander to the reviewer, or wrap a wolf in sheep's clothing, but their approach to proposal preparation does reflect their knowledge of the grantor and ultimately, respect for the grantor's values.

If you follow this theory through, it will be obvious to your prospective grantor that you know what the grantor values and that rejecting your proposal would be a repudiation of their (the grantor's) own values. In fact, not funding you would be unpleasant, create internal static, and produce dissonance!

This theory does not apply just to private funding sources (foundations and corporations). Proposals to federal and state grantors are read by staff and peer reviewers who are also likely to give the best scores to proposals tailored to their beliefs. In fact, reviewers selected by government bureaucrats are likely to be professionals who have perspectives and values similar to those of the government bureaucrats.

To be truly successful, your proactive grants system should be based upon a triple win—meeting the needs of the grantor, your organization, and you, the proposal developer. You need not invest more time in the process than the reactive grantseeker; you just need to invest your time earlier and more wisely. Instead of a 72-hour, last-minute, Herculean proposal effort, invest 10 hours per month for seven months. This will give you plenty of time to research the grantor, make pre-proposal contact, and construct a tailored proposal—all without the stress of a last-minute effort!

REFERENCE

1. Leon Festinger, A *Theory of Cognitive Dissonance* (Stanford, CA: Stanford University Press, 1962).

CHAPTER 2

Developing and Documenting the Need for Your Project

Creating Urgency

B efore you become overly involved and focused on your project or research, step back and look at the larger picture. Your proposal will be evaluated against hundreds, sometimes thousands, of others. Yours must cause the grantors/reviewers to motivate themselves to select it over the others. Your proposal must present a clear vision of what exists now compared to what ought to or could be. The motivation for funding your proposal over another's is directly related to how well you document the gap that exists and how compelling you make the case for closing or reducing the gap.

Failure to document need most often results from the self-focus of the proposal writer. Committed proposal writers frequently believe that grantors are as motivated as they are to solve a particular problem, so they move directly to presenting the project/solution before ever establishing the need for a solution. Do not assume that the grantor knows the need in your field. Even if the proposal reader is an expert, your efforts to describe the most relevant advances demonstrate *your* expertise and command of the most current data and provide the motivation for the grantor to reduce the gap.

To begin developing the need statement for your proposal, answer the following questions:

- What is the problem that requires a solution?
- What will happen if this needs area is not addressed?
- What is the gap between what exists now and what ought to be or would be if the knowledge existed to solve the problem?

- Why should grant funds be used *now* to solve the problem and reduce the gap?

Many grantseekers make a fatal error when answering these questions. While they are well intended, they often are so overzealous that they look at the problem in a myopic manner. For example, a grantseeker who sought funds for computers to bring technology and the Internet to her school felt she had documented the gap and developed a compelling need by stating the age of her school's existing equipment and mentioning how other schools already had the computers her school needed. What she didn't realize is that she couldn't possibly show a compelling need by simply documenting what kind of and how many computers her school currently had and what kind of and how many they wanted. In brief, equipment is a means to an end, not the end. The gap was not what her school didn't have compared to what it needed. The true need for the computers and for technology should have been documented through an explanation of how the equipment and technology would allow her school and its students to function in improved ways. The end should not have been presented as a room full of equipment, but rather as increased reading or math scores or better preparation for the job market.

While the above example may seem obvious, the same problem often occurs when the prospective grantee desires a building. Architecture plans and the documentation of a leaky roof in the existing building are not reasons enough for a grantor to fund a new building. In this instance the gap should be created by documenting the difference between what can be done in the existing facility and what more a new facility would enable the organization to do. In other words, how would a new building facilitate increased programs and services and better solve the problems of the organization's clients? The building is not the problem (or lack of it). It is the means to an end, and the end is what needs to be documented.

Even a grant for playground equipment can fall prey to mistaken needs documentation. The need is not the absence or condition of existing equipment. Again, equipment is a means to an end—whether it's playground equipment or computers. What needs to be demonstrated is what the new playground equipment will allow children to do that they cannot do now. To create a compelling need the grantseeker must demonstrate things like how many children will be affected and for how many hours, and what alternatives for their time exist now.

Researchers are faced with a similar dilemma. The need is not the research they propose to accomplish, but rather the benefits of their research and the problems it can be used to solve. Even pure bench research must seek to close a gap of knowledge in the field. The documentation of the need must include a cohesive explanation of how current research has driven the researcher to ask other questions, seek to test other relationships, and advance the field so that new and even more poignant questions can be asked.

Researchers may focus on studies to document need, while those seeking project grants may look beyond facts and statistics to case studies. In either instance, needs documentation should be gathered before contacting a funding source or writing a proposal.

Researchers should be wary of becoming so impassioned in the documentation of their project that they run the risk of being perceived as arrogant or disrespectful of their fellow scientists. Imagine you are writing a proposal for a research project, and you have decided to document the need by citing relevant research in the field (search of the relevant literature). This is not difficult for you to do because you consistently read the journals and major publications in your field and you actually set aside a specific time each week to review them. After performing a thorough search of the studies and articles in your field and gathering many resources, it is now time to select the citations to include in your proposal. You want to select only the best citations (those that present a clear, concise, and current picture of the problem) and be careful not to include so many that you overwhelm the reader and cloud or confuse the real issue or problem. Besides making sure that your search documents both the urgency of the problem and your command of the current knowledge in the field, you also have to decide which of the following two statements to include.

- Statement 1—Smith and Jones overlooked the importance of "X" and failed to explore its relevance to "Y."
- Statement 2—Smith and Jones's pioneer work brought a focus to the field and advanced the understanding of "ABC." As a result of their work it now appears that "X" is a critical variable to explore in relationship to "Y."

The first statement tends to minimize the work of Smith and Jones and even makes them appear ignorant because they either didn't see the variable or understand its importance. The second statement tries to depict the work of Smith and Jones as advancing the field and ultimately allowing other researchers to push forward. Before you make your decision, remember that the real Smith and Jones, or one of their graduate students, doctoral students, or friends, may be on the grantor's review committee. Keep sight of the fact that the last thing you want to do is cause dissonance in the reviewers.

Be aware also that you could cause dissonance by citing references, researchers, or data that the reviewers do not favor. While the reviewers' reactions to specific information is not totally in your control, the more you know about the values and background of the reviewers and decision makers, the better able you will be to avoid this problem.

NEEDS ASSESSMENT APPROACHES

There are six basic approaches for assessing and documenting need:

1. Key informant: Quotes from people who know about the problem or are experts in the field.
2. Community forum: Public meetings to get testimony on the problem.
3. Case studies: Examples of clients in a need population.
4. Statistical analysis: Use of data from public records.
5. Survey: Random selection of population to answer questions related to the need.
6. Studies: Literature search of published documents on the subject.

The needs assessment table and needs assessment worksheet (see table 2.1 and exhibit 2.1) will help you decide which approach to adopt for your project. Corporate and foundation grantors may respond to best case studies or examples of the human side of the need, while government funders usually prefer a needs statement based on facts and studies. By having a variety of needs assessment techniques at your disposal, you will enhance your ability to tailor your proposal to a specific grantor.

Whether the potential grantor understands the importance of addressing the problem and ultimately enacts your solution is a function of how compelling your needs documentation is.

After you, the grantseeker, document a need, ask yourself the following question: Would you dedicate your own money to closing this gap between what we know now and what we could know or do?

NEEDS ASSESSMENT GRANTS

If it becomes difficult to locate studies, literature, or data to document the problem you seek funds to solve, you may find that you need to attract a small foundation or corporate grant to help you. Yes, it is possible to locate a funding source that will value the fact that its modest investment will allow you to develop an excellent needs statement and ultimately make it possible for you to attract larger grants from other funding sources for conducting your project. A needs assessment grant can also help to position you as the resident expert in your field and provide you with valuable insights into the problem. Since you only are able to measure the success of your project on how much of the gap is closed due to your intervention, a needs assessment grant may also provide you with an improved tool to use in the measurement of the need. See chapters 19 and 20 for information on how to locate potential funding sources for small needs assessment grants.

TABLE 2.1

NEEDS ASSESSMENT TABLE

Type of Approach	Advantages	Disadvantages
Key Informant—Solicit information from individuals whose testimony or description of what exists for the client population or state of affairs is credible because of their experience and/or expertise. Includes elected officials, agency heads (police chiefs, juvenile delinquency case workers, parole officers, etc.). Funders may value their opinions/insights.	· Easy to design. · Costs very little. · You control input by what you ask and whom. · Excellent way to position your organization with important people (shows you're working on common problems/concerns).	· Most funding sources know you have selected and included comments from those individuals sympathetic to your cause. You may be leaving out parts of the population who have not been visible and caused problems that were noticed and commented on.
Community Forum—Host or sponsor public meetings. You publicize the opportunity to present views of the populace and invite key individuals to speak. Funder may like the grassroots image this creates.	· Easy to arrange. · Costs very little. · Increases your visibility in the community. · Promotes active involvement of the populace.	· Site of forum has profound effect on amount and type of representation. · You can lose control of the group and have a small vocal minority slant results or turn meeting into a forum for complaints.
Case Studies—An excellent approach to assist the funder in appreciating what representative members of the client population are up against. Select individuals from the needs population or client group and provide an analytical, realistic description of their problem/situation, their need for your services, etc.	· Easy to arrange. · Costs very little. · Increases sensitivity to the client's "real world." · Very moving and motivating.	· Your selection of a "typical" client may be biased and represent a minority of cases. · You must describe one "real" person—not a composite of several. The anonymity of the person must be ensured.

TABLE 2.1

Needs Assessment Table *(continued)*

Type of Approach	Advantages	Disadvantages
Statistical Analysis—Most funders like to see a few well-chosen statistics. With this approach you utilize existing data to develop a statistical picture of the needs population: · Census data/records · Govt. studies/reports · Reports and research articles	· There is an abundance of studies and data. · Little cost to access data. · Allows for flexibility in drawing and developing conclusions. · Analysis of data is catalytic in producing more projects and proposals as staff "sees" the need.	· Can be very time-consuming. · Bias of staff shows up in studies quoted. · Feelings on funder's part that you can prove anything with statistics. · If original data have questionable validity, your extrapolation will be inaccurate.
Survey—Very commonly used approach to gathering data on the needs population, this approach is useful even when the survey is carried out with volunteers and has limited statistical validity. Accurate surveys may entail control groups, random samples, and computers and statistical analysis. However, acknowledgment by you that the results of your survey cannot be extrapolated beyond the sample group will prove more than adequate in most situations.	· High credibility with funders. · Excellent flexibility in design of survey to get at problem areas and document exactly what you want to document. · Demonstrates local needs. · Provides proof of your concern for the problem well in advance of proposal preparation. · Small sample size and identified needs population provide for an inexpensive means of assessment.	· Takes time to do survey properly. · Small sample size and nonrandom sample make it impossible to extrapolate to the entire needs population.

TABLE 2.1

NEEDS ASSESSMENT TABLE *(continued)*

Type of Approach	Advantages	Disadvantages
Studies—Citing of relevant research in the field or area of need. This is a commonly used approach to document the gap between what is and what ought to be for research projects. However, it can also be used for model projects. The literature search should focus on articles, books, and papers that resulted from a controlled study or use of a scientific approach to increasing information.	· Citing studies demonstrates the proposal developer's thoroughness and expertise in the area and command of the subject data. · Studies provide an unbiased approach to documentation of need.	· Unless properly organized, the literature search may seem disjointed and overwhelming to the reader. · Time-consuming.

What information do we need to document the problem?	Which approaches to needs assessment are best for us and/or preferred by the funder? Key Informant: _____ Community Forum: _____ Case Studies: _____ Statistical Analysis: _____ Survey: _____ Studies: _____				
Data to be gathered	How data will be gathered	Who will do it	Date due	Cost	Consortium agencies involved

NEEDS ASSESSMENT WORKSHEET

EXHIBIT 2.1

CHAPTER 3

Finding Time to Write Grant Proposals

Organizing a Proposal Development Workbook

M ost grantseekers prepare proposals in their spare time. After working with nonprofit organizations for 30 years to increase staff involvement in grantseeking, I have determined that the two major obstacles to grantseeking are finding the time to get involved and developing a proactive approach.

Many creative and well-intentioned grantseekers develop innovative approaches to solving problems. They often can cite the literature that documents their command of the current state of knowledge in the field, but they have a problem putting the need and their idea together in a proposal. When asked why, they often say they cannot find the time.

The steps necessary to produce a grant application are logical and follow a definite order. Many people are overwhelmed by their perception of the work involved. Because of this, they procrastinate and avoid approaching proposal development until it is too late to do an adequate job.

Allen Lakein was one of the early leaders in time management. In his book *How to Get Control of Your Time and Your Life*, Lakein presents a technique that you can use to get your grant writing process under control and organized.[1] His "Swiss cheese" concept suggests dividing a difficult task into smaller, less overwhelming parts. Lakein's example of a mouse confronted by the job of carrying away a huge piece of cheese is analogous to a grantseeker presented with the prospect of creating a grant proposal. Both the mouse and the grantseeker feel overwhelmed! To avoid this feeling, Lakein suggests that the mouse should divide the big piece of cheese into smaller parts. By eating small pieces of cheese at a time, making the cheese into "Swiss cheese," the mouse can divide the task into manageable parts so that final task of carrying the cheese away is less onerous (see figure 3.1).

THE SWISS CHEESE CONCEPT

FIGURE 3.1

I have applied this concept to grantseeking and created a set of tabs of making a "Swiss cheese" book, referred to professionally as the proposal development workbook (see exhibit 3.1).

Suggestions for tabs are given later in this section, or sets of tabs are available for purchase from Bauer Associates. I have divided the task of developing a proposal into 25 steps. By addressing each step in the grantseeking process, you, the proposal developer, can organize your approach, control the process, and lower your anxiety level. By nibbling at your proposal a piece at a time, you will not be overwhelmed by the process and you will ultimately save time and increase your success rate.

I have found the "Swiss cheese" concept a great help in making the grants process more understandable and manageable. In fact, I suggest that you construct a proposal development workbook for each of the major problem areas for which your organization is planning to seek grant funding.

For example, imagine that your nonprofit organization is working with senior citizens. You might construct four proposal development workbooks: one for the elderly and transportation, one for the elderly and health, one for the elderly and nutrition, and one for the elderly and recreation. Each proposal development workbook would be placed in a three-ring binder with each tab acting as a divider for one of the tasks involved in developing a full-scale proposal. When you read a research article on nutrition and the senior citizen, you would make a copy of the article, abstract, or summary and place the copy under the tab for "Documenting Need." To avoid making this section of your workbook too voluminous, place the summary or abstract of the article in your workbook instead of the entire article, but be sure to include a reference as to where the entire article has been filed.

When politicians or community leaders visit your organization and express their concern for the elderly, you could ask them for a letter of support for your group's work and whether they would be willing to serve on your advisory committee. Copies of their letters of support would be filed under the tab labeled "Advisory Committees and Advocacy," as would their names, addresses, and telephone numbers.

As you can see, proposal development workbooks act as files for proposal ideas. Most potential funding sources would be very impressed by a prospective grantee who responds to a question by referring to a proposal development workbook instead of fumbling through a tattered pile of file folders and loose pages of notes.

One grantseeker using this process called our offices to tell us how helpful her proposal development workbook was during a visit with a funding source. When asked why the funding source should give the money to her organization instead of one of the hundreds of other applicants, she opened her proposal development workbook to the tab on uniquenesses and presented a list of 50 reasons why her organization was uniquely suited to carry out the proposed project, with the top five reasons circled. The grantor was quite impressed.

The proposal development workbook is one step in the process of making your grants effort more cost- and time-efficient. If you thought that proposal preparation was a Herculean task—a last minute, 72-hour miracle—think again. You will find that the application of the "Swiss cheese" concept and the development of proposal development workbooks will provide you with an organized approach to proposal preparation, an approach that makes effective use of your time. In addition, this approach will help you improve your organization's image with funding sources (known as "positioning" in marketing talk) by enabling you to present your organization as an honest, organized, well-planned agency.

Those grantseekers who prepare proposals overnight run the risk of damaging their organization's image in the eyes of funding sources. One hastily written proposal with budget transpositions and typographical errors can affect your organization's image for many years.

The construction of proposal development workbooks is a proactive process that can work for you and your organization. Once this approach is initiated, I

INTRODUCTION TO YOUR
PROPOSAL DEVELOPMENT WORKBOOK
(SWISS CHEESE BOOK)

The grants mechanism is one method to unlock the world's largest reserve of collective and specific genius and it pits that reserve against the multitude of problems that plague the modern world.

By supplying monies to solve a problem, funding sources, be they federal, foundation, or corporate, benefit from competition amongst the best minds and groups that seek their funds and ultimately create innovative solutions and new research techniques, and apply their methodology to the test of reality.

Funding sources exist because individuals have created them by acts of commission that represent various motivations and bias views of what the needs are. **Each funding source has a certain perspective** on what it **wants for its money**—a perspective based on its values and how it interprets its charge as a granting entity. Each funding source (corporation, foundation, or government agency) has determined that there is a **NEED** to invest the money entrusted to it in ways that reflect the goals of the organization.

You, as a grantseeker, have a **NEED** for financial resources to support projects aimed to address specific and critical problems. The key to successful grantseeking is matching up your particular need for financial resources with the need(s) of funding sources to invest their financial resources in projects such as yours and produce the mutual desired results. Successful grantseeking requires that you carry out your "homework" **before** your write your proposal. All too often, grantseekers begin the process with a proposal outlining **what they want**! Successful grantseekers know that the writing of the proposal occurs much later in the process—after they know the funding source **wants**.

Your grant Proposal Development Workbook is your Swiss Cheese Book. The steps involved in preparing for and producing a grant application or proposal are simple and follow a definite order. The design of this notebook is based upon a systematic approach to grantseeking described by **David G. Bauer** in his *"How To" Grants Manual.*

The "Swiss Cheese" Concept
Many individuals find the grantseeking process complex, tedious, and difficult to deal with. They just want the grant money to do what they want! They get overwhelmed with the enormity of the total task and the time and planning required. They frequently delay starting the application process until it is too late to do an adequate job.

One way of approaching the task of applying for grants is to be proactive. Allen Lakein, the author of *How to Get Control of Your Time and Your Life* uses the analogy of a mouse confronted with a large piece of cheese. The mouse does not attempt to eat or move the cheese in one large piece. Instead, it eats holes in the cheese, devouring a little at a time until it is all gone. The same applies to grantseeking. **APPROACH EACH PART OF THE GRANTSEEKING PROCESS A LITTLE AT A TIME AND BEFORE YOU KNOW IT, THE PROCESS WILL BE COMPLETED!**

PROPOSAL DEVELOPMENT WORKBOOK

EXHIBIT 3.1

am sure you will find it invaluable for promoting the development of project ideas, locating funding sources, and writing proposals.

Review the list of suggested proposal development tabs after you have read this manual. You may want to change, eliminate, or add some areas to tailor the concept to your organization. The following are suggested tabs:

- Introduction
- Documenting Need
- Organizing the Process
- Developing Ideas
- Redefining Ideas
- Uniquenesses
- Advisory Committees and Advocacy
- Choosing the Marketplace

In addition, you will want tabs to organize the research and contacts in the marketplace you choose. For government funding sources, consider the following additional tabs:

- Researching Government Marketplace
- Characteristics: Government Grants
- Contacting Government Sources
- Planning Federal Proposals
- Improving Federal Proposals
- Submission: Public Sources
- Decision: Public Sources
- Follow-Up: Government Sources

For private funding sources, you may also include the following tabs:

- Differences: Public versus Private Sources
- Recording Research
- Foundation Research Tools
- Researching Corporate Grants
- Contacting Private Sources
- Letter Proposal
- Submission: Private Sources
- Decision: Private Sources
- Follow-Up: Private Sources

The following chapters include worksheets, letters, and forms that could be placed behind each of the tabs in your proposal development workbook. These materials also are available on the software program *Grant Winner*. (For ordering information see the list of resources available from Bauer Associates at the end of the book.)

Grantseekers can also create a computer file for each of their proposal development tabs. While some may prefer to do this, a computer disk may be difficult to use with a potential funding source during a visit. You will still need a hard copy of your proposal development workbook. In addition, some proposal developers may find that arranging hard copies of certain sections of their workbook, like the studies to be included under the "Documenting Need" tab, will help them develop their approach.

REFERENCES

1. Allen Lakein, *How to Get Control of Your Time and Your Life* (New York: New American Library, 1996).

CHAPTER 4

Developing Grant-Winning Ideas

From Research to Model Projects

The underlying theme of this manual is that when you ask a funding source for grant support you must look at your organization and your request from the funding source's perspective. This concept supports the "golden rule of grantseeking"—he or she who has the gold—rules. The least the prospective grantee can do is try to determine what the grantor values, likes, and dislikes, avoiding those areas that are potentially negative and highlighting those that appeal to the grantor's interests and make the prospective grantee look competent.

The process outlined in this chapter recommends that you develop several alternative approaches to the problem you have documented. There is usually more than one way to perform your research or develop your model project. To increase your chances of selecting the "right" approach for inclusion, you should be able to discuss more than one way of solving the problem with the prospective funding source before submitting your proposal. Even the briefest pre-proposal contact could give you the insight necessary to tailor your approach to the funding source. In addition, discussing several approaches with the prospective funding source before selecting one for your proposal will increase your credibility and demonstrate that your favored approach is based on careful analysis, not the personal biases and preferences of you or your staff. The worksheets in this chapter will help you

- generate ideas by brainstorming your approaches with colleagues and key individuals on your grants advisory committee
- develop a system to summarize your best ideas and assess organizational commitment to the project
- conduct a cost-benefit analysis of your best ideas that highlights the differences, strengths, and weaknesses of each approach

BRAINSTORMING

One of the best techniques for developing sound proposals and alternative solutions to problems is to brainstorm proposal ideas with staff and peers. Inviting others to share in idea generation taps the collective genius of the group and builds support for your proposal. In fact, the brainstorming process can even promote the feeling that your project is "everyone's" project, so that colleagues and volunteers will be more willing and eager to work at night and on weekends to beat the deadline.

Many researchers are reluctant to share their ideas and creative solutions because they fear that they will be stolen by colleagues. In the majority of cases this fear is unwarranted. Most colleagues can be trusted, and discussing proposal ideas and solutions with them can help eliminate the development of narrow, self-focused grant ideas.

Brainstorming is a simple technique for quickly generating a long list of creative ideas. To obtain maximum benefit from the process

1. Break your participants into groups of five to eight.
2. Appoint a neutral group leader to facilitate the process (encouraging and prodding other members, checking the time).
3. Appoint a recorder.
4. Set a time limit (10 minutes will be plenty).
5. State one question or problem (e.g., reducing the number of high school dropouts, nutritional needs of pregnant adolescents, reducing alcoholism in the elderly, increasing awareness of wildlife preservation).
6. Ask group members to generate and present as many possible solutions to the problem as they can within the time limit.
7. Encourage group members to "piggyback" on each other's ideas (suggesting a new idea that adds to one already given).
8. Record all answers, combining those that are similar.
9. Avoid any evaluation or discussion of ideas until the process is over; this rule is critical for productive brainstorming. The recorder can ask to have an idea repeated but should allow no comments, negative or positive (e.g., "We can't do that!" "That's stupid!" or "I love your thinking") from others.

COST-BENEFIT ANALYSIS WORKSHEET

An important aspect of any fundable idea is its economic feasibility. Funding sources want to know that you have chosen methods that will produce the best results for the least amount of money. The cost-benefit analysis worksheet (see exhibit 4.1) will help you demonstrate economic accountability.

Column One

Place brief descriptions of each approach you are considering in column one. For example, a project to feed senior citizens could range from a meals-on-wheels program, to group meals, to a food cooperative of the elderly. Choose two or three possible approaches that will meet the goals of the project from your brainstormed list of ideas.

Column Two

Record the estimated price or cost of each idea or set of methods in column two. This figure can be taken off of your pre-proposal summary and approval form and is intended to be an estimate of the cost of the approach, not a final budget. One way to ensure variety in the approaches and in the amount of funds required is to select the approach you favor and determine how you would have to alter if you could have only one-half of the amount requested.

Column Three

Use this column to estimate the number of people who will be affected by a particular approach. Remember to roll out the benefits over several years and over the life of the equipment.

Column Four

Enter the estimated cost per person or client served. This is essential because funding sources are apprehensive about sponsoring projects that possess an unrealistic cost per individual served. Projects with a high cost per person are considered a waste of money by many funders, so grantseekers may have great difficulty securing continued or follow-up funding for such projects.

Column Five

Summarize the advantages of each idea or set of methods in this column. By having this information on hand, some funders may actually consider supporting a more costly approach because they can see how the outlined advantages outweigh the expense.

1 Summary of Idea and Methodology	2 Cost	3 No. of Persons Served	4 Cost per Person Served	5 Positive Points	6 Negative Points	7 Rating

COST-BENEFIT ANALYSIS WORKSHEET

EXHIBIT 4.1

Column Six

In this column outline the disadvantages or drawbacks to each approach. This demonstrates your honesty, which will increase both your credibility with funders and their confidence in you. Funders know that each approach has pitfalls or variables that must be controlled.

Column Seven

The seventh column is used to rate each approach. Your objective is to present the problem and several alternative solutions while allowing funding sources to

- feel confident that you have analyzed the situation carefully
- observe your flexibility and see the pros and cons of each approach
- identify the approach they favor (giving you the advantage of knowing which approach is most likely to result in funding)

You may prefer not to place your preferences on the cost-benefit analysis worksheet, but rather to rate the approaches based upon the funder's comments.

Use this worksheet each time you refine your project ideas and bring completed cost-benefit analysis worksheets to preliminary meetings with funding officials. They will be impressed by the fact that you considered their financial interest while designing your project.

Remember that many grant officials are executives of profit-making companies. They are very sensitive about maintaining cost efficiency in all of the investments they make. Take this into account when refining your project ideas; it will help you win more grants.

PRE-PROPOSAL SUMMARY AND APPROVAL FORM

The pre-proposal summary and approval form (see exhibit 4.2) could be subtitled "The Grant Seeker's Insurance Policy." When you have an idea for which you would like to seek funding, fill out this form before writing your full-scale proposal. Have the form reviewed by your proposal review committee, staff, or administrators and returned to you with their criticisms and suggestions. The purpose of the pre-proposal summary and approval form is to elicit comments from your organization's leaders and to have them endorse your solution. Make sure the form is reviewed by those people who must sign the final proposal; this ensures that the individuals who are required to sign your proposal at submittal time know (in advance) that the proposed project is coming. The form actually provides a vehicle to test the acceptance of your idea or project with your superiors. This is important because they should agree on the use of institutional resources before you invest hours of your time on proposal development. This is especially important when the grant will require matching funds. You need to get a "go ahead" before you invest your valuable time. There are many benefits to using the pre-proposal summary and approval form:

- Projects can be quickly summarized, so more ideas for projects are generated.
- The increase in the number of ideas lends itself to an increase in the number of fundable projects.
- By generating a number of ideas you may enhance your ability to see the advantages of combining several good ideas into one great one. Comments from those reviewing the form may also lead the proposal writer in this direction.
- Because at this point in the proposal development process project designers have not invested a great deal of time in writing a proposal for their idea, they are less defensive when their project summary is criticized and suggested improvements are easier to make.

Many organizations find it useful to make the pre-proposal summary and approval form available electronically to the appropriate individuals via e-mail. I recommend that you have key people comment on the areas they question or may object to in the right-hand margin of the form. Then ask them to initial the form, giving their consent or approval to proceed. This ensures that the time, money, and resources spent in your proposal preparation process will not be met with a negative response internally and result in failure to have your proposal signed when ready for submittal.

This pre-proposal summary and review process also allows decision makers to comment on important issues and requirements relative to

- matching funds commitment
- space, equipment, personnel, and resource allocations

Your grantseeking efforts are more likely to receive support and to provide a basis for matching funds and other resource allocations when you appraise your administration of your entrepreneurial grants effort and seek their endorsement.

Problem Area: _____

Possible Solution: _____

_____

1. Total Estimated Dollar Cost: $_____

	Comments	Signature
2. Matching/In-Kind Commitment: $_____ 3. Estimated Time Needed for Proposal Process: _____ Pre-Proposal Contact Date(s): _____ Proposal Submission Date: _____ Project Start-Up Date: _____ 4. Individual(s) in Charge—Project Director: _____ Co-workers: _____ 5. How This Project Relates to the Mission or Goal of Our Organization: _____ 6. Summarize the Objectives: 7. Summarize the Methods: 8. Estimate of Non-Personnel Resources Needed Travel: _____ Supplies: _____ Printing: _____ Equipment: _____ Other: _____ 9. Estimated Equipment Costs: _____ 10. Facilities Needed: _____ Square Feet: _____ Desired Location: _____ Special Considerations: _____ 11. Project Personnel Needed Title Salary Range Name (If Known) 		

PRE-PROPOSAL SUMMARY AND APPROVAL FORM

EXHIBIT 4.2

CHAPTER 5

Redefining Proposal Ideas to Find More Funding Sources

Many grantseekers have a myopic view of their proposal ideas. They are so self-focused that they develop tunnel vision and as a result, define their idea narrowly. What these grantseekers fail to see is that they could make their project appeal to many more funding sources by just broadening their perspective.

To expand your funding horizons, think of your project in as many ways as possible. This will help you uncover potential funding sources that may not be obvious when you think of your project in only one way. Consider your project or research in terms of at least the following five categories to determine how you could change or alter your idea so that it appeals to different grantors:

1. Subject area: What subject areas can you relate your project/research to?
2. Constituency group: What constituencies or target groups could benefit from the project/research?
3. Type of grant: Could your proposal be considered a needs assessment? Pilot project? Model project? Research?
4. Project location: What are the geographic boundaries of your project as currently conceived? Could they be expanded to attract more or different funding sources?
5. Partners: Could you change your proposal's focus by adding "partners" who will share in the proposed work? Would another organization's involvement add depth to your project and increase your credibility with the funding source?

Carefully examine each of these categories. Each time you look at your project from another subject area, constituency group, grant type, geographic boundary, or potential partner you may uncover additional funding sources interested in supporting your work.

Remember, you are in control here. You must decide how far you want to go in your attempt to uncover additional funding sources. It is not necessary for you to redefine your project in ways that ultimately alter the basic concept of what you want to do. Also, do not make the same mistake as one overzealous grantseeker I worked with. He redefined his project so much that he couldn't remember how it related to his original idea!

Your ability to locate a funding source for your project depends on how well you can relate your project to the funding source's interests and needs. However, what is equally important is that the funding source gets what it wants out of the project, while you and your field also derive benefits. The concept is one of win-win-win. There is no subterfuge implied. If, for example, your project could provide benefits for individuals in your city, but could also be performed as a two-site study involving another city that contains a grantor who is interested in the field and would be highly motivated if the project involved its workers or hometown, why not redefine your geographic perspective and work with a colleague in that city?

The same concept applies to subject area and to constituency groups. If you are working on a project related to alcohol addiction and you expand your search to those funding sources who have a stated interest in projects related to drug addiction, you may uncover many more potential grantors. However, you must then ask yourself if altering your project to include addiction to other drugs as well as alcohol will still provide you with the end you want to achieve.

COMPUTER SEARCHES, KEY WORDS, AND REDEFINITION

The key to efficient utilization of the computer databases on government and private grantors is in this chapter. The fastest, most comprehensive, and current databases all require the same ingredient for locating the "right" grantor—key words. Key words are basically the subject areas and constituency groups you can relate your project to, and are used when working with the indexes in grants research books such as *The Foundation Directory* as well as computer databases. In computer searches, your key words are matched to the key words grantors use to describe their interests. How successful your computer search proves to be will have much to do with your creativity and ability to extrapolate. The more key words you use, the more ways you redefine your project. The more ways you redefine your project, the more potential funders you uncover. By expanding your universe of funders and selecting your best choices for pre-proposal contact, you will have a better chance of locating the grantor who is most likely to be attracted to your proposal.

In chapter 9 there is a description of database services you can subscribe to on which you or the service can run a comparison of your key words to current grant opportunities on a daily or weekly basis. Grantseekers often complain that computer searches such as these yield the wrong grantors. This is because many grantseekers do not update their list of key words or use too few key words. Due to advances in fields of study, new key words are developed every day and likewise, old words are used less frequently. Therefore, it is crucial that grantseekers periodically review the key words they employ in their searches. Successful grantseekers recognize the need to change their key words if they are coming up with inappropriate grantors. In fact, they try different words, omit old ones, and adjust their lists of key search words constantly.

DEVELOPING YOUR KEY WORDS WORKSHEET

Taking the time to redefine your project through the development of a key words worksheet will pay dividends when you begin your search to locate the best possible funding source for your project. The first step is to list the words that describe the subject area your project/research is directly related to. Step two involves listing the changes you could make in your project/research that would allow you to relate it to other subjects areas. And the final step is to develop a list of key words for your general area of interest. There are several ways to come up with a list.

1. Review the subject index in any of the research tools described in chapter 19. Record the key words (subject areas) that you can relate your project to.
2. If you are working through a database searching service, ask to see the total key word index it uses to code grant opportunities. Again, record the key words that relate to your project.
3. Record key words from the titles of relevant literature and journal articles in your field.

After you have developed your tailored list of key words, review it for its relevancy to corporate interests. Even though corporations can be powerful sources of funding, their interests are not always obvious or included in indexes or databases. Look at your list and see if it includes any words related to how your project could be of use to a corporation. Consider the following:

- employee benefits (including benefits to family and children)
- employee productivity, motivation, and quality of future employees
- employee training
- company products and product development
- company sales and positioning of products
- company expansion, product expansion, and patents

In addition, always consider how your project can relate to corporate profits.

It is also important to consider project location when developing your key words worksheet. Is it possible to conduct your project in another city or to make it statewide, regional, national, and/or international? By incorporating another city, state, region, or country in your project, you can uncover a whole new list of potential grantors.

Exhibit 5.1 is an example of a key words worksheet. The general field of interest is education. The worksheet has been expanded to include some education-related subcategories and areas and other potentially relevant fields outside of education. Please note that space has been provided on the worksheet to put checkmarks next to the subcategories, areas and fields that might apply and to explain how the project could be related to the checked items. This format should be followed when developing your own tailored worksheet.

Field of Interest: General Education

Subcategories:

—   Early Childhood   _____
—   Preschool   _____
—   Elementary   _____
—   Middle School/Junior High   _____
—   Secondary/High School   _____
—   Higher Education   _____

Areas:

—   Adult   _____   —   Alcohol Education   _____
—   Bilingual   _____   —   Curriculum   _____
—   Drop-Out   _____   —   Drug Abuse Education   _____
—   Gifted/Talented _____   —   Literacy   _____
—   Math   _____   —   Reading   _____
—   Science   _____   —   Vocational   _____
—   Technology   _____   —   Research   _____
—   _____   _____   —   _____   _____

KEY WORDS WORKSHEET

EXHIBIT 5.1

Other Potentially Relevant Fields:

___ Aging	___ ___ Medicine	_____
___ Child Development	___ ___ Mental Health	_____
___ Computers	___ ___ Music	_____
___ Disabled	___ ___ Natural Resources	_____
___ Dispute Resolution	___ ___ Nursing	_____
___ Domestic Violence	___ ___ Parks/Playgrounds	_____
___ Economics	___ ___ Poverty	_____
___ Employment	___ ___ Religion	_____
___ Environment	___ ___ Social Services	_____
___ Engineering	___ ___ Telecommunications	_____
___ Family	___ ___ Voluntarism	_____
___ Health	___ ___ Women	_____
___ Human Services	___ ___ Youth	
___ _____	___ ___ _____	_____

Constituency Groups:

___ Children _____

___ Youth _____

___ Teachers _____

___ Parents _____

___ Grandparents _____

___ Teenagers _____

___ Professors _____

___ _____ _____

Corporate Considerations:

___ Employee Benefits _____

___ Employee Productivity, Motivation, Quality of Future Employees _____

___ Employee Training _____

___ Company Products, Product Development _____

___ Company Sales, Product Positioning _____

___ Company Expansion, Product Expansion, Patents _____

___ Corporate Profits _____

___ _____ _____

KEY WORDS WORKSHEET *(continued)*

EXHIBIT 5.1

Location: Place a check mark next to the areas your project/research could have a significant impact on.

——	City/Community	——	Region
——	County/Borough/Parish	——	Nation
——	State	——	International

Type of Grant: Review your project in relation to the different types of grant funds.

——	Model/Demonstration Project	——	Training Grant
——	Research Project	——	Construction
——	Needs Assessment Grant	——	Discretionary
——	Planning Grant	——	Equipment Grant

Potential Partners: List organizations whose involvement would add to your project and increase your credibility with funding sources.

Partner   Advantage

_____   _____

_____   _____

KEY WORDS WORKSHEET *(continued)*

EXHIBIT 5.1

CHAPTER 6

Why Grant Funds to You and Your Organization?

Capitalizing on Your Capabilities

Many grantseekers lose sight of the fact that funding sources must select a few grant winners from many applicants. The successful grantee must stand out from the rest of the competition. Therefore, it is important for you to project an image that puts you a cut above the rest. One way to do this is to demonstrate to the funding source that you are different from the others in your field and that because of these differences you are their best choice for funding.

Grantseekers often have difficulty articulating why a grantor should choose them over others. Many grantseekers see themselves as just another college, hospital, school district, association, or nonprofit organization. A closer look, however, inevitably yields a number of very positive differences between them and others. A little time spent developing a list of your organization's special qualities or uniquenesses will go a long way toward convincing a grantor that yours is the right organization to fund.

Start by examining what you do differently from the others and then look at how you do it. Consider your staff, location, buildings, and special areas of interest. In some cases, being similar to other organizations could even be presented as a feature that makes you particularly suited for funding. For example, if your organization is similar to many others in the United States, you might suggest to the funding source that your proposal be viewed as a pilot project that could be replicated throughout the country.

UNIQUENESS EXERCISE

Use the following brainstorming exercise to develop a list of your organization's unique features. This exercise will add a little excitement and flavor to meetings and can be done with a variety of groups such as staff, volunteers, clients, board members, and grants advisory committee members. Keep the information you develop in your proposal development workbook, where it will be ready for use in proposals, endorsement letters, and pre-proposal contact.

Please note that you may encounter some initial reluctance to this exercise because some individuals think it promotes bragging. However, these same individuals probably believe that humility and occasional begging will move grantors to take pity on your organization, and fund your proposals. They are wrong! From the grantor's point of view, the humble approach does not highlight the reasons a prospective grantee should be funded.

To combat this problem, just remind all those participating in the exercise of its positive results. After the exercise, you will have a list of factors that make your organization unique, from which you will be able to select those uniquenesses that may appeal to a particular funding source. Also, the exercise will refocus those participating in the activity on the positive attributes of your organization and away from the negative.

1. Distribute the uniquenesses worksheet (see exhibit 6.1) to the group, remind the group of the rules for brainstorming (outlined in chapter 4), and set a time limit for brainstorming.
2. Use question one or two from the worksheet, and record the group's answers.
3. Give each individual 10 points, and ask them to rank the group's answers from a potential grantor's perspective. Each person should allocate his or her 10 points over the entire list.
4. Add the totals for each answer, and you will have a weighted list.

Our organization has many unique qualities. These positive qualities can be used to convince funding sources that they are investing wisely when they grant our organization money.

This exercise will result in a combined list of qualities that make us stand out from the competition for grant funds.

Your leader will tell you whether to answer question one or two and when to begin recording your responses.

1. What makes our organization good at what we do?

_____

_____

_____

_____

2. Why would a funding source give a grant to us instead of some other organization in our field? (What makes us a good investment? What are the advantages of funding us?)

_____

_____

_____

_____

UNIQUENESSES WORKSHEET

EXHIBIT 6.1

If you do this exercise with several different groups, combine all of the lists and distribute the combined list to all of the groups. All the group members will then be aware of your organization's unique qualities.

Use the final list to select uniquenesses that will convince funders that their money will go farther with you than with any other prospective grantee. For example, a particular funding source may be impressed with your total number of years of staff experience, central location of buildings, special equipment, and broad needs populations and geographic coverage.

Your uniquenesses list will also prove valuable in

- recruiting and training staff, board members, and volunteers
- developing case statements
- using other fund-raising techniques such as direct mail and wills and bequests

Do not forget to include yourself, the proposal initiator, project director, or principal investigator, as a uniqueness. Your previous work, publications, collaborative efforts, awards, and recognition are important components of your organization's overall uniqueness.

One culminating activity is to have half of your group role-play a grantor and the other half role-play a prospective grantee. Review one of the problems or needs your organization is planning to address and your organization's proposed solution. Then have the individuals playing the grantor ask those playing the prospective grantee why the grantseeker's organization should be the one selected to implement the proposed solution. Have the grantee group start by saying, "Our organization is uniquely suited to implement this solution because . . ."

Another strong reason to review and record your organization's and your personal uniquenesses relates directly to the section of your proposal in which you will be required to record the rationale for funding your project. Depending on the funding source, the section can be referred to by a variety of terms and requested in differing sections. The information the funding source is requesting may or may not be outlined, and may or may not be scored by specific criteria. However, one thing is for certain, uniquenesses are an important part of both government and private funding. Exhibit 6.2 outlines the "quality of key personnel" and the "adequacy of resources" sections of the Department of Education's proposal evaluation process. These areas are directly related to uniquenesses and, as you can see, they are weighted heavily. In fact, they alone total 25 points out of a possible 100. This means that 25 percent of why you may be selected as the recipient is based upon your positive qualities and how these qualities enhance your image as the "right" grantee.

USING YOUR ORGANIZATION'S CASE STATEMENT TO SUPPORT YOUR PROPOSAL

Your case statement is another key ingredient in convincing the grantor that your organization should be selected for funding. When you submit your application for funding, your approach should be based on the following three important factors:

Quality of Key Personnel   (15 pts)

1)   Do the job descriptions adequately reflect skills needed to make the project work?

2)   Are the duties of personnel clearly defined?

3)   What relevant qualifications do the proposed personnel possess, especially the Project Director? (Focus on their experience and training in fields related to the objectives of the project, though other information may be considered.)

4)   Will proposed personnel need to be trained for the project?

5)   How much time will the proposed personnel actually devote to the project?

6)   To what extent does the applicant encourage employment applications from members of traditionally underrepresented groups (ethnic or racial minorities, women, handicapped persons, elderly persons)?

Adequacy of Resources   (10 pts)

1)   Are the proposed facilities adequate for project purposes?

2)   Is the proposed equipment adequate for project purposes?

3)   Does the applicant have access to special sources of experience or expertise?

DEPARTMENT OF EDUCATION PROPOSAL EVALUATION PROCESS

EXHIBIT 6.2

1. There is a compelling need for the project.
2. Your organization is uniquely suited to carry out the project.
3. The project supports your organization's stated purpose or mission.

The third factor is especially important. Your case statement should demonstrate your organization's predetermined concern for the project area. If yours is a joint or consortia proposal, the mission or case statements of all the participating organizations should provide a documental concern for the problem you will address. In short, your case statement should give the funding source written documentation that the purpose of your organization (its reasons for existing), your project, and the grantor's values and concerns are a perfect match.

Elements of a Case Statement

Your case statement should consist of how and why your organization got started, what your organization is doing today, and where your organization is going in the future.

How and Why Your Organization Got Started. Explain the original societal problems or needs that resulted in the formation of your organization. Most funding sources will find societal need today more important than the number of years your organization has been in existence. In fact, some funding sources actually have the greatest doubts about those nonprofit organizations that have been around the longest. These funders believe that such organizations generally are bureaucratic, have a tendency to lose sight of their mission, and have more "deadwood" on their payrolls than "younger" nonprofit organizations.

What Your Organization Is Doing Today. Describe your organization's activities. What are its current priorities, programs, resources, and uniquenesses? Who are its clients? How has the passage of time affected its original mission and reason for being?

Where Your Organization Is Going in the Future. Because funding sources look at their support as an investment, they want to be sure they invest in organizations that will be around when their funding runs out. In other words, they want the organizations they invest in to have a 5-year, 10-year, or even longer plan for operation. By demonstrating to funding sources that your organization has a long-range plan and the ability to secure future funding, you will show grantors that you are worthy of their funding and that the project they invest in will continue to benefit people for many years to come.

Use the case statement worksheet (see exhibit 6.3) to determine what should be included in your case statement. If you already have a case statement, review it to see whether it needs updating or tailoring to the grants marketplace. If your existing statement is long, use the case statement worksheet to help you edit it to one concise page.

Remember, most potential grantors are more interested in how funding your proposal will move both of your organizations (theirs and yours) toward each of your missions than in your actual project methods. Funding sources consistently work to separate applicants who sought them out simply as a source of money from applicants who can demonstrate that the direction outlined in their proposal is predetermined and an important component of their organization's overall mission.

In a recently funded grant from the Bell South Foundation for over $250,000, the successful grantee told Bell South that it was their organization's goal and priority to approach the very same problem that the Bell South funding was designed to impact. In fact, the successful grantee told Bell South it could show them over five years of meeting minutes and budget expenditures that demonstrated its commitment to dealing with the problem. The grantee also went so far as to suggest that it would be committed to the same course of action even without Bell South's grant. Yes, the grantee told Bell South that it was so much a part of their goals, priorities, and case statement that the organization would move ahead with the project anyway! Naturally they also let Bell South know it would take 10 years without their money instead of three years with it. The Bell South money would be the catalyst in the equation for change and would hasten the result.

The importance of relating your proposal to your organization's mission cannot be overemphasized. Before soliciting a potential grantor, be sure to ask yourself whether you are going to the funder just because you heard it had money and you want some, or because your proposal can serve the missions you both value.

1. How and Why Your Organization Got Started: _____
   Year: _____ Primary Movers/Founders: _____
   Original Mission: _____

2. *Today*—Where Your Organization Is Now:

   Changes from the Original Mission: _____
   _____
   _____

   Societal Need Changes: _____
   _____
   _____

   Current Priorities: _____
   _____
   _____

   Clients: _____
   Staff: _____
   Buildings: _____

1. *Future*—Where Your Organization Will Be Five Years from Now:

   Changes in Mission: _____
   _____
   _____

   Changes in Need: _____
   _____
   _____

   Changes in Facilities and Staff: _____
   _____
   _____

2. Opportunities that Exist or Will Exist to Move Your Organization Toward
   Its Plans/Goals:
   • _____
   • _____

CASE STATEMENT WORKSHEET

EXHIBIT 6.3

CHAPTER 7

Involving Volunteers through Advisory Committees and Advocacy Groups

One of the most important resources in a successful grants effort is the involvement of volunteers. When grantors are faced with volunteers who believe so strongly in a project that they are willing to work to further it with no personal benefit, the parent organization's credibility is greatly enhanced.

Involving others in increasing your potential to attract funding suggests that *who* you know may be more valuable than *what* you know and how you write your proposal. But a poorly developed idea and proposal will need much more than just "friends" and the suggestions presented here. If you have a great idea or proposal, however, you owe it to yourself to take advantage of every possible edge in your quest for funding. This includes involving individuals who can help ensure that your proposal receives the attention it deserves. One foundation director told me that approximately one-third of her foundation's grants went to the board members' favorite organizations and projects, one-third to the board members' friends' favorite projects, and the remaining one-third to the most skilled grantseekers.

While this may sound like politics, hold your condemnation just one more minute. The politics of grantseeking is a fascinating area that spells M-O-N-E-Y for those who master the art. Do not be frightened or disgusted by the word *politics*. The politics of grantseeking is a very understandable process that enables individuals to become advocates for what they value and believe in.

Those people who know your organization and identify with your cause or mission deserve to know how they can be of service to you and the cause or field you represent. When asked to become advocates for your project, individuals are free to say no or that they are too busy, but you should not make this decision for them by assuming that they would not want to be involved. There is no harm in asking, and you will be surprised by how many individuals welcome your invitation.

Consider exploring the area of advocacy and how you can help others help you. The worksheets in this chapter will assist you in determining who your advocates are and how they can best serve you. You will probably discover that there are more supporters for your project than you realized.

GRANTS ADVISORY COMMITTEES

One highly effective method for involving volunteers in your grants quest is to develop a grants advisory committee focused on the need or problem your grant proposal will address. For example, while working for a university-affiliated hospital, I initiated one grants advisory committee on health promotion and wellness for children and another on research for children's diseases with different individuals on each committee. Think of your grants advisory committee as an informal affiliation of individuals you invite to take part in attracting grant funds to the problem area you have chosen. These individuals will be surveyed to determine their willingness to supply resources, as well as play an advocacy role.

Invite fellow professionals, individuals from other organizations and the community, and corporate members who are interested in the area you have identified. By inviting a cross section of individuals to join your committee, you develop a wider base from which to draw support. Ask yourself who would care if you developed grants resources to solve a particular problem. The one common denominator for all the committee members should be their concern for positive change in the identified area of need. Develop a list of individuals, groups, and organizations you think would volunteer a little of their time to be instrumental in making progress in the problem area. Be sure to include

- individuals who might know foundation, government, or corporate grantors
- colleagues who may have previously prepared a proposal for the grantor you will be approaching or who may have acted as grant reviewers

Also consider current and past employees, board of trustees members, and former clients.

GRANT RESOURCES

After you have identified individuals or groups who would be interested in seeing change in the area identified, make a list of skills and resources that would be helpful in developing your proposal. Match these with the types of individuals who might possess them. Your list of skills and resources may give you some ideas about who you should recruit for your grants advisory committee. Consider the skills and resources and the types of individuals that could be useful in

- preparing your proposal (writers, experts in evaluation design or statistics, individuals with skills in the areas of computer programming, printing, graphics, or photocopying)
- making pre-proposal contact (individuals with sales and marketing skills, people who travel frequently, volunteers who could provide long-distance phone support)
- developing consortia or cooperative relationships and subcontracts (individuals who belong to other nonprofit groups with similar concerns)

Review the grants resources inventory (see exhibit 7.1) for those resources and skills your volunteers may be able to provide.

Please indicate the resource areas you would be willing to help with. At the end of the list, provide more detailed information. In addition, if you are willing to meet with funding sources, please list the geographic areas you travel to frequently.

___ Evaluation of Projects
___ Computer Equipment
___ Computer Programming
___ Layout and Design Work
___ Printing
___ Budgeting, Accounting, Developing Cash Flow, Auditing
___ Audiovisual Assistance (equipment, videotaping, etc.)
___ Purchasing Assistance
___ Long Distance Telephone Calls
___ Travel
___ Writing/Editing
___ Searching for Funding Sources
___ Other Equipment/Materials
___ Other

GRANT RESOURCES INVENTORY

EXHIBIT 7.1

Description of Resources: _____

_____

_____

_____

Areas Frequently Visited: _____

_____

_____

_____

GRANT RESOURCES INVENTORY *(continued)*

EXHIBIT 7.1

HOW TO INCORPORATE ADVOCATES TO INCREASE GRANTS SUCCESS

Specific activities to consider in relation to advocacy roles of individuals on your list are

- writing endorsement letters
- talking to funding sources for you and setting up appointments
- providing expertise in particular areas (finance, marketing, and so on)
- accompanying you to meetings with potential funders or even visiting a funding source with you

Use the advocate planning sheet (see exhibit 7.2) to organize your approach.

Endorsement Letters

One very effective way to use advocates is to request that they write endorsement letters related to your organization's credibility and accomplishments. Without guidance, however, many advocates will develop endorsement letters that focus on inappropriate aspects of your project or organization. To prevent this, spell out what you are looking for. Provide advocates with a draft endorsement letter that suggests what you would like them to consider including in their letters, such as

- pertinent facts or statistics that you may then quote or use in your proposal
- the length of time they have worked with you and/or your organization (e.g., number of hours, consortia, or cooperative work relationships)
- a summary of their committee work and their major accomplishments

Project Title: _____   Project Director: _____

Select from the following list the ways you can use advocates to advance your project.

- Endorsement letters
- Testimonials
- Letters of introduction

- Set appointments
- Accompany you to see funding sources
- Go see funders for you

Techniques for This Project	Advocate to Be Used	Who Will Contact Advocate and When	Desired Outcome	Date Completed

ADVOCACY PLANNING SHEET

EXHIBIT 7.2

Advocates should almost be able to retype your draft on their stationery and sign it. If the grantor has any special requirements concerning endorsement letters, make sure they are followed.

Contacts

Another way to involve your advocates is to present them with the names of potential grantors and their board members, and to ask whether they know any of the grantors' key individuals. This approach is particularly useful if your advocates are reluctant to reveal all of their contacts and are holding back to see how serious you are in researching potential grantors.

If your advocates are trusting, you can ask them outright for a comprehensive list of their contacts. This includes asking your grants advisory committee members to reflect on their ability to contact a variety of potential grantors that may be helpful in your grants effort. To take this proactive approach, follow these steps:

1. Explain the advocacy concept to the individuals you have identified and how the information they provide will be used. Ask each participant to complete an advocacy/webbing worksheet (see exhibit 7.3) and return it to you. Some organizations find they have better results in introducing the advocacy concept when they relate the concept to a major project of the organization that has widespread support.
2. Distribute the advocacy/webbing worksheet to the individuals you have identified as possible advocates. This may be done in a group or individually.
3. Input the advocacy information you collect from the completed worksheets to your computer, or file it.
4. When a match between a potential funder and advocate is made, call your advocate and discuss the possibility of having him or her arrange a meeting for you with the funding source. Ask the advocate to attend the meeting with you to add credibility to your presentation.

Keep all completed advocacy/webbing worksheets on file and update them periodically. This is a good activity for volunteers. Be aware, however, that care should be taken to safeguard advocacy data. Advocacy data should be considered personal information that is privileged; you must not allow open access to the data or you will be violating your advocates' trust. Using a large central computing facility to store this information greatly reduces security. Instead, use a personal computer system, and store a copy of your program in a safe place. This approach will ensure the privacy of this confidential information. An inexpensive software program designed especially for storing and using advocacy information entitled *Winning Links* is available from Bauer Associates. (For ordering information, see the list of resources available from Bauer Associates at the end of the book.)

If possible, computerize your advocacy information using *Winning Links* or other software. When a potential funding source is identified, search your advocacy database to determine whether any of your advocates have a relationship to the potential funding source. You may have an advocate who

- is a member of both your organization and the funding source's board
- can arrange an appointment to get you in to talk to the funder
- can write a letter to a "friend" on the funding source's board
- has worked for the grantor or been a reviewer for the funder's grant program

Community Support

Advocacy can also play a valuable role in developing and documenting community support for your project. Some funding sources require that you demonstrate community support in the form of advisory committee resolutions and

Our organization's ability to attract grant funds is increased substantially if we can talk informally with a funding official (or board member) before we submit our formal proposal. However, it is sometimes difficult to make pre-proposal contact without having a link to the funding source. We need your help. By completing this worksheet, you will identify any links that you may have with potential grantors and possibly open up an oasis of opportunities for our organization.

If you have a link with a funding source that our research indicates may be interested in supporting one of our projects, we will contact you to explain the project and discuss possible ways you could help us. For example, you could write an endorsement letter, arrange an appointment, or accompany us to see the funding source. Even a simple phone call could result in our proposal actually being read and not just being left in a pile. No matter what the case may be, you can rest assured that we will obtain your complete approval before any action is taken and that we will never use your name or link without your consent.

Links to foundations, corporations, and government funding sources are worth hundreds of thousands of dollars per year, and your assistance can ultimately help us continue our vital mission. Thank you for your cooperation.

Your Name: _____   Phone No.: _____

Address: _____

1. What foundation or corporate boards are you or your spouse on?

2. Do you know anyone who is on a foundation or corporate board? If so, whom and what board?

3. Does your spouse know anyone on a foundation or corporate board? If so, whom and what board?

4. Have you served on any government committees? If so, please list.

5. Do you know any government funding contacts? If so, please list.

6. Please list any fraternal groups, social clubs, and/or service organizations to which you or your spouse belong.

ADVOCACY/WEBBING WORKSHEET

EXHIBIT 7.3

copies of the minutes of meetings, and more grantors are encouraging the development of consortia when applying for funding. Whether you are looking at a joint submittal for your proposal or just endorsement and support, it is important to start the process of applying for a grant early so that deadlines do not interfere with your ability to document your advisory committee's involvement and valuable work. To deal creatively with the area of community support:

- put together a proposal development workbook (see chapter 3) to focus on your problem area
- organize an advisory committee to examine the problem area
- involve the advisory committee in brainstorming project ideas, examining needs assessment techniques, writing letters of endorsement, and providing links to funders

Review the worksheet on developing community support (see exhibit 7.4) to help you determine how to use community support to increase your fundability.

Organize your supporters and maximize your chances for success by working through and with your volunteers. Involve those individuals who can be of service to your cause, from enhancing your resources to helping identify links to funders.

INVOLVING EXISTING BOARDS, ADVISORY GROUPS, VOLUNTEERS AND STAFF

Do not overlook the advantages of using the linkages that your existing organizational groups may have. These groups have already demonstrated an affinity for your organization and your programs. Participation in this opportunity should be voluntary, and while some administrators may express concern over asking paid staff to contribute names of friends and relatives who have connections to funding sources, they will be surprised over the voluntary response they receive. Involve your employee associations and unions, and initiate the idea by relating it to strong needs and well accepted programs and projects that many people want to see developed or expanded.

Many nonprofit organizations already have boards and standing committees that can be invited to become involved in this webbing and linkage process. Most corporate people will be happy that they have been asked to participate in a "game" that the corporate world plays all the time. From my experience at universities, I have also found that department chairs, deans, and members of boards of institutes and centers usually respond favorably to the concept.

The key to acceptance of the webbing and linkage process is to assure those participating that linkages will not be contacted without their knowledge or approval and in most cases, their assistance.

HOW TO USE WEBBING AND LINKAGE INFORMATION

To help you get the most out of your newly discovered linkages, list them by linkage type. For example, foundation, corporate, federal, state, etc. Then use the funding source research tools described in chapters 9 and 19 to look up the interest areas of the grantors you have a link to. Review your organization's needs and projects and look for potential matches with the grantors. When a match is found, make pre-proposal contact through your linkage.

Project Title: _____   Project Director: _____
                                        Date: _____

#	Techniques	Applicability to This Project	Who Will Call Meeting	Members of Committee	Dates
1	Use advisory committee to brainstorm uniquenesses of your organization (chapter 6).				
2	Use advisory committee to work on setting up needs assessment.				
3	Use advisory committee to brainstorm project ideas.				
4	Use your committee to develop a public relations package and produce it (printers, media reps.), including newspaper coverage for your organization (press releases, interviews) and television coverage (public service announcements, talk shows).				
5	Have an artist perform or have an open house for key people* in the community.				

*Public officials, congresspeople, potential advocates, and others.

HOW TO DEVELOP COMMUNITY SUPPORT WORKSHEET

EXHIBIT 7.4

CHAPTER

Choosing the Correct Marketplace

Proactive grantseeking involves assessing your grants potential, selecting the basic marketplace (government, foundation, or corporate) for your proposal idea, and researching the best prospects within the chosen marketplace.

Many prospective and oftentimes overzealous grantseekers launch their efforts to research possible grantors too quickly. To maximize your grants potential, you must do the kind of planning described in the preceding chapters. Developing a proposal effort that will promote a professional image of your organization requires an approach to research that has the following characteristics:

- Reflects a win-win attitude. Your research must be in-depth enough to ensure that your project will meet the funding source's interests, needs, and values while moving your organization toward its mission and providing benefits to your clients or field of interest. In this case the funder wins, your organization wins, and your clients win.
- Provides you with the confidence to present yourself as worthy of funding. You have taken the time to find the "right" funder by doing your research, and this will become apparent to the prospective grantor. The funder will hear the confidence in your voice and see it in your proposal.

After you have redefined your project, begin to narrow down your search for the correct funding source. How do you know which funding marketplace is the "right" one for your project? Each marketplace has different types of funding sources and distinct funding characteristics. Certain factors predetermine how a funding source will "view the world," so you must match your proposal idea with those grantors most likely to find your proposal appealing.

Start by reviewing the distinct characteristics of each marketplace. After you select the right marketplace for your project, you may start researching individual funding sources within that marketplace.

GENERAL GRANTS MARKETPLACE INFORMATION

I have administered a grants marketplace quiz as a pretest assessment instrument to over 25,000 grantseekers since 1975. These grantseekers attended one of my training seminars and, therefore, were not randomly selected and may not represent all grantseekers. However, they do vary widely in grants expertise and background. What is interesting and surprising is that more incorrect answers are given to the quiz today than 25 years ago. Why is this, when today's grantseekers are exposed to an abundance of information about grants and funding sources through the general media, professional journals, newsletters, and conferences? I believe that news sources may in fact contribute to current misconceptions about the grants marketplace.

Grantseekers, and the administrators they work for, read announcements about nonprofit groups that attract large, above-average grant awards, but the awards that make the news are usually exceptions to the rule. These awards, unfortunately, are often interpreted by well-meaning, motivated grantseekers and their administrators as the norm or average. Nonprofit leaders use these large award to shape their view of the marketplace. Judging the marketplace by what makes the headlines thus creates and reinforces misconceptions about grant giving and influences expectations about the level of grant support from each sector of the marketplace. As a result, many grantseekers end up basing their strategic decision making on fantasy rather than fact.

To choose the correct marketplace for your proposal, you need to base your choice on knowledge. The two main sources of support for nonprofit organizations and their grant requests are government and private philanthropy.

In the late 1970s, the Filer Commission Report estimated that government grant support was equal to support from private philanthropy (grants from foundations and corporations, bequests, and individual giving). This figure was estimated to be about $40 billion from each marketplace. Since that time, the marketplace has changed significantly.

- Federal funding through grants declined from a 1980 high of $40 billion, to a 1984 low of between $22 billion and $25 billion, to a 1987 level of $30 billion, to a 1999 estimate of $90 billion.

- Private philanthropy grew from a 1979 level of $43.69 billion to a 1997 level of $143.5 billion. What most grantseekers fail to realize, however, is that only 15 percent of the $143.5 billion in the private marketplace is disbursed through the grants mechanism by foundations and corporations.

Grantseekers must look beyond these figures to determine what these changes really mean and how to adapt their grantseeking strategies.

In the public arena, the decrease in government grant funding in the mid 1980s created an initial overreaction on the part of nonprofit organizations. Because many grantseekers knew that government funding was cut, they did not even bother to apply for government funds, and the applications for government grants declined substantially. The same phenomenon reoccurred in the mid 1990s. Well-publicized cuts in a few government program resulted in minimal increases in applications to federal sources and large increases in requests to foundation and corporations.

The late 1990s saw an historic event—the balance of the federal budget. In past years when budget cuts had to be made, the grants area was a convenient place to make them. This is due in part to the fact that most budget allocations are for fixed areas of expenditures such as social security and medicaid, and no politician or federal bureaucrat wants to be associated with cuts to these programs. It is also due to the fact that the grants area is one that does not have a political action committee or strong lobby. The grants area experienced cuts or no increases for many years, and only a few professional organizations appealed for no cuts or more funding. But with the balancing of the budget and the actual 1998 budget surplus, politicians could increase grant dollars to popular programs. Added to the balanced budget was Congress's zeal to get out of Washington, DC, in the fall of 1998 and the subsequent passing of the 1998-99 federal budget that contained billions more for grant-related research and model projects.

The turn of the century is bringing with it the potential for still more increases in the federal grants marketplace. However, even with these expected increases, the federal grants marketplace will not return to the equal status it held with private philanthropy in 1979. Estimates are that private philanthropy will exceed $150 billion while federal grants will do well to break $100 billion in the beginning of the next century. Even though private giving by individuals will continue to exceed federal grants, marketplace-savvy grantseekers knows that they should go to the federal grants marketplace first. This is because private philanthropy is driven by individuals who give smaller amounts of money and who do not accept applications.

Remember that

- foundation and corporate grants only account for 15 percent of the $143.5 billion in private philanthropy
- the federal grants marketplace is approximately $90 billion

Although private philanthropic support of nonprofit organizations encompasses individual giving, gifts made through bequests, and foundation and corporate giving, these components have not shared equally in the increase from $40 billion to $143.5 billion. Corporate grant funding has actually lost ground, while individual donations have grown. The actual percentage of private funds distributed through the grants mechanism has remained relatively stable over the years and is much less than most individuals realize. In fact, the total grants marketplace for corporate and foundation grants has only grown from $9.67 billion in 1986 to approximately $15 billion in 1994 to $21.6 billion in 1997.

Many executive directors, presidents, and board members of nonprofit organizations do not know or understand the marketplace facts. When your organization's leaders base their resource-development strategies on misconceptions about the marketplace, you, the grantseeker, may not receive the resources you need for a successful grantseeking effort nor the recognition you deserve for doing an exemplary job.

THE GOVERNMENT MARKETPLACE

Seek federal funds first. The marketplace facts have already substantiated the basis for this deduction. The federal government is the largest single grantor in the world (estimated $90 billion in 1999). Foundations and corporations together only grant $21.6 billion annually, and some of these private grantors will fund only those grantseekers who have exhausted the possibility of a federal grant. In other words, foundations and corporations know who has the most grant funds to give away and may only consider requests from those who have been rejected by or have discussed their projects with federal grantors.

Historical Perspective

The federal government has used the grants mechanism in one way or another since the United States was founded. The term *land grant college* refers to the federal government's early attempts to encourage states to develop a system of higher education that would link education and agriculture by granting them funding. The grants mechanism was utilized sporadically until World War II. The federal government developed much of its current role as a grantor during the post-Korean War period. The Russian accomplishment in space, *Sputnik*, encouraged the U.S. government to make grants available to foster education and research.

Use of the government grants mechanism increased with the Kennedy and Johnson administrations. Most grants under their New Frontier and Great Society programs were administered on the federal level. Early grant programs supported projects and research related to specific problems. For example, when national concern centered on the social issues of the 1960s, the grants mechanism was employed to encourage research and develop model projects that focused on the disadvantaged, the elderly, minority groups, people with disabilities, and so on. In the 1970s the grants mechanism was used to support advances in health care and to address such problems as drug and alcohol abuse, smoking, and cancer. Grants such as these, aimed at specific categories or problem areas, came to be known as categorical grants.

In the 1970s, however, there began a growing trend toward local, regional, and state distribution of federal government grant dollars. This trend was based on federalism, or the belief that local and state governments know best what they need. This "New Federalism," or revenue-sharing perspective, moved the grants marketplace from categorical grants, in which the federal government allocated to selected categories, to formula and block grants, which allowed the state and local governments to combine categorical funding and pool federal funds to address problems. The Reagan administration encouraged this trend by signaling a decline in government's use of the grants mechanism to initiate, direct, and sustain change in American society.

First, the Reagan administration called for a reduction of $40 billion in domestic grants. Although there were repeated attempts to virtually eliminate grants altogether, Congress did not allow cuts below the $20 billion to $22 billion level. However, grant funds were cut almost in half.

Second, the Reagan administration attacked the categorical grants funding mechanism. The administration's philosophy of "the government governs best which governs least" could not support a categorical grants system controlled by Washington bureaucrats. Instead, the Reagan administration capitalized on "New Federalism" concepts and growing conservatism to institute the most dramatic change in the history of the U.S. grants mechanism—the block grant.

Block Grant

The block grant concept was founded on the premise that it was not the purview of the federal government to force the states to follow categorical grant program priorities. The categorical programs were "blocked," or synthesized into groups of related programs, and the funds were sent directly to the states. The states could set their priorities and "grant" the federal funds to high-priority areas and projects.

The block grant movement caused mass confusion in the grants world because grantseekers had to figure out who had the funds and what would be funded. In most cases the states received more decision-making power but less money than they did under categorical grants. The block grant mechanism allowed the federal government to reduce staff formerly used to administer categorical grant programs. Decreases in staff were limited, however, because the federal government still had to direct the research component of categorical programs to avoid duplication and to coordinate research efforts.

Because of the federal government's continued involvement in the administration of grants, along with Congress's desire to deal with problems in education, employment, and crime, the late 1980s marked the decline of the block grant mania of the early Reagan years, and the use of categorical funding mechanisms increased. Virtually all of the new grant programs introduced after 1986-87 were categorical grants.

Project, Categorical, and Research Grants

Project, categorical, and research grants are designed to promote proposals within defined areas of interest. These grant opportunities address a specific area with which a federal program is concerned, such as arts, humanities, drug abuse, dropout prevention, nutrition for the elderly, or research on certain types of diseases. The government, through hearings and appropriation of money, selects the problem to be corrected, and prospective grantees design approaches to solve or reduce the problem, or to increase knowledge in the area through research.

Project and research grants are awarded by various agencies under congressionally authorized programs. Ideally, grants are awarded to the organizations (and individuals) whose proposals most clearly match the announced program guidelines. Most federal grant programs use nongovernment review panels (often referred to as peer review panels) to evaluate the projects. Peer review helps ensure that the "best" proposals are selected for funding. Because project design is left to the grantseekers, there is room for a wide variety of creative solutions, making the project grants approach very popular among grantseekers.

Government granting agencies usually require grantseekers to complete long applications. As categorical grants have increased, each federal agency that controls funds has developed its own grants system. Grants applications and the administration of grants differ in format from agency to agency. Generally, the applications are tedious, complicated, and time-consuming to complete. They can make it very challenging to tailor your proposal content to meet the needs of the granting agency as well as your own needs. There is usually a three- to six-month review process, which may include a staff review by federal agency personnel and a peer review. Successful grantees are required to submit frequent reports, maintain accurate project records, and, in some cases, agree to federal audits and site visits by government staff.

To be successful in research and project grants, grantseekers must be mindful of the constant changes in emphasis and appropriations. Hidden agendas and shifts in focus result from the funding agency's prerogative to interpret and be sensitive to changes in the field of interest.

Formula Grants

The term *formula grants* refers to granting programs under which funds are allocated according to a set of criteria (or a formula). The criteria for allocation of these grant funds may be census data, unemployment figures, number of individuals below the poverty level, number of people with disabilities, and the like, for a state, city, or region. Formula grant programs are generally specific to a problem area or geographic region and have historically been used to support training programs in the fields of health, criminal justice, and employment.

The formula grant funds must pass through an intermediary, such as a state, city, or county government or a commission, before reaching the nonprofit grantee. The formula grants mechanism is another example of the "New Federalism" that started developing in the early 1970s. While the general rules for formula grants are developed at the federal level, the rules are open to interpretation, and local input can significantly alter the federal programs. To encourage local control and input into how federal funds are spent, the formula grants mechanism requires a mandated review by local officials.

Contracts

No discussion of federal support to nonprofit organizations would be complete without a discussion of government contracts. In recent years the differences between a grant and a contract have become more difficult to discern. Indeed, after hours of negotiation with a federal agency on your grant, you may end up having to finalize your budget with a contract officer.

In theory, the basic difference between a grant and a contract is that a contract outlines precisely what the government wants done. You are supplied with detailed specifications and the contract is awarded on a lowest-bid basis. With a contract, there is decidedly less flexibility in creating the approach to the problem. To be successful in this arena, you must be able to convince the federal contracting agency that you can perform the contract at an acceptable level of competency and at the lowest bid. Contracts are also publicized or advertised in different ways than grants. Grant opportunities are published in the *Catalog of Federal Domestic Assistance* and the *Federal Register* (see chapter 9), while contracts are advertised in a daily government publication known as *Commerce Business Daily* (see chapter 9).

There are several types of contracts, including fixed cost, cost reimbursable, and those that allow the contractor to add additional costs incurred during the contract. The grants statistics quoted in the chapter do not include government contract monies. The variety, number, and dollar value of government contracts are staggering and go far beyond the $90 billion in grants cited earlier. Scandals over inflated prices for parts in government contracts highlight the problems in administering contract bids and are leading to changes aimed at simplifying government purchasing and reducing paperwork.

Contracts have been increasingly pursued by nonprofit groups in recent years. The contracts "game," however, requires a successful track record and documentable expertise. The best way to break into this marketplace is to identify a successful bidder and ask whether you can work for them as a subcontractor. This way, you gain experience, confidence, and contacts with the contractor.

Many nonprofit groups have found that they can reduce the problems they routinely encounter in bidding on contracts by developing separate profit and nonprofit agencies for dealing with such issues as security agreements, academic freedom, patents, and copyrights.

Shifts away from domestic grant program funds have led some nonprofit organizations to look at Defense Department contract opportunities for implementation of their programs and research. But please note that bidding on government contracts is a task for the experienced grantseeker only.

State Government Grants

It is difficult to estimate how many grant dollars are awarded through individual state program initiatives. Many of the federal government grantseeking techniques in this book also apply to accessing state grant funds. Many states develop their own initiatives in the social welfare and health areas, and few states deal in research funding. Many state grant funds are federal funds that must pass through the state to you, the grantseeker.

There are some advantages to state control of grants. Because states distribute federal block and formula grants, these grants are easier to access. They require less long-distance travel and allow you to use your state and local politicians to make your case heard. These advantages are counterbalanced, however, by the fact that some states develop their own priorities for federal funds. States may add additional restrictions and use a review system similar to the federal peer review system, or use a system made up of state bureaucrats and political appointees. Although states have their own monies, granting programs, and rules, if they distribute grant monies obtained from the federal government, they must guarantee that the eventual recipient of those funds will follow all federal rules and circulars.

THE FOUNDATION MARKETPLACE

In 1997, there were approximately 41,588 private foundations in the United States with $268 billion in assets. These foundations made awards totaling $13.37 billion. Though these figures may seem staggering to the novice grantseeker, there is some consolation in the fact that you do not need to keep track of all of them since less than 2 percent of all foundations control more than 65 percent of all foundation assets and award nearly half the country's foundation grants.

News coverage of large grant awards made by the bigger foundations leads to misconceptions about this marketplace. Many grantseekers and their boards would be shocked to learn that there were only 226 grant awards in excess of $2.5 million in 1997 and only 86,203 grants of $10,000 or more. Grantseekers hear about the big grants and may not want to deal with the reality that only a small number of all foundations—approximately 450—have a relatively high grant size (from tens of thousand into the millions). The 41,138 other foundations have a much lower average grant size, but collectively award hundreds of thousand of grants including many for less than $10,000.

Foundations increased their grant giving by 11.4 percent between 1996 and 1997. This increase was due to an overall increase in foundation assets of 18.0 percent. Foundations by law must give away 5 percent of the market value of their assets each year or pay a tax. Most do not have a plan for what to do if they experience a dramatic increase in their stock portfolios, so the Internal Revenue Service allows a grace period of one year to adjust to the compulsory 5 percent payout. This results in many foundations granting monies from their last year's plus their current year's assets as long as the stock market and their assets continue to increase.

Whether your nonprofit organization is a research institute or a small community agency, you need to know the basic facts about the foundation marketplace. Not only are the grant award sizes very different from what you may expect, so are the purposes for which foundations grant money.

Most grantseekers mistakenly believe that foundations grant the majority of their funds for building and renovation projects (capital grants). This is not true. While the average size of capital grants is $174,048 and likely to make the news, less than 25 percent of foundation grant dollars go toward capital support. A closer look reveals that foundations break down capital support as follows:

- 4.8 percent for capital campaigns
- 11.0 percent for building/renovation
- 1.7 percent for equipment
- 1.6 percent for computer systems/technology
- 3.7 percent for endowments
- 1.3 percent for other capital support

The astute grantseeker can now see why so many uninformed grantseekers make major strategic errors when they go after foundation grants for capital campaigns! Their board members may be aware of the fact that 1,529 grants were given for capital campaigns in 1997 by 1,016 of the larger foundations and that the average dollar value of these capital campaign grants was almost $250,000, but what they neglected to consider is that this accounted for only 1.8 percent of all foundation grants—hardly an exception to generalize from.

In the same way, failure to synthesize this data results in schools and other nonprofit organizations sending proposals to foundations for computer systems and technology. The odds of getting a foundation grant for these purposes is slim since this type of support accounts for only 1.6 percent of foundation grant dollars.

A whopping 43.3 percent of foundation grant dollars supports program development. What's interesting is that most colleges and universities separate their grants effort into a federal grants office to serve the academic side of the institution and a development office to serve the other. The development office controls access to foundations, yet the programs that garner 43.3 percent of foundation support usually emanate from the academic side of higher education. The faculty and staff are the source of the ideas for program development, faculty/staff development, and curriculum development—the three categories that make up the bulk of the 43.3 percent of foundation support for programs. Also, faculty and staff are the source of the research projects that account for an additional 10.1 percent of foundation dollars. The reason that most development offices usually give for controlling foundation access is that they need to apply for capital campaigns which in reality only accounts for 4.8 percent of foundation giving! It is only recently that many of the more advanced development efforts are teaming up with the academic side to create proposals for the greatest opportunities rather than the smallest.

Knowledge of the foundation marketplace requires that grantseekers be more flexible in their approach to funding. For example, just because your organization would like to acquire computer equipment does not mean you should apply for an equipment grant. You will be more likely to obtain the desired equipment by attracting foundation grant support through a model project or research proposal that proposes to make a difference in the foundation's stated areas of interest and by including the computer equipment in the proposal as a necessary means to the desired outcome.

Researchers should take note of the potential of foundation funding as a means to developing the preliminary data and publications that are essential for winning a federally funded research proposal. Prospective federal grantees require preliminary data to substantiate their approach. With a small foundation grant, you can develop preliminary data and possibly publish an article to position you for acquiring a federal grant.

One other important consideration is that foundation grants can provide a source of matching funds. While only a small percentage of foundation funds are awarded for matching contributions, the mere possibility of pursuing a grant for this purpose can be significant to those organizations that find that matching requirements place some valuable federal sources out of their reach.

Selecting the right segment of the foundation marketplace and requesting an appropriate grant size from a potential funder require knowledge of the types of foundations and their specific characteristics. The five basic classifications of foundations are:

1. Community
2. National general purpose
3. Special purpose
4. Family
5. Corporate

Community Foundations

Community foundations, a group of 500 plus foundations, represent the newest and fastest growing area in the foundation marketplace. The main purpose of community foundations is to provide a grants mechanism to address problems and interests that affect the geographic area the foundation was created to serve.

Community foundations use a variety of geographic parameters to define *community*. Some use state boundaries, while others use city boundaries and zip codes. In any case, community foundations are easy to identify because their name denotes the area they serve (e.g., San Diego Foundation, Cleveland Foundation, North Dakota Foundation, Oregon Foundation).

Most community foundations have little connection with United Way fund drives and usually are not in competition with their community's United Way or its supported organizations. In actuality, community foundations are frequent grantors to agencies supported by the United Way. While both groups seek to enrich the community and address its problems, the community foundation usually builds its funding base through bequests. Local citizens make a bequest to the community foundation to ensure that the interest proceeds from the bequest stay in the community. Donors may even restrict grants to their specific areas of interest in the community. The bequest method of fund-raising is very different from the United Way approach of payroll deductions, cash contributions, and corporate solicitation. In some communities the United Way has begun to incorporate a more aggressive bequests program to build an endowment fund. In these communities, conflicts may arise as both the community foundation and the United Way seek the same donors. In some communities, these organizations have developed ways to work together.

The assets of community foundations are growing daily, reaching $17.1 billion in 1996, a 28.6 percent increase over 1995. The primary beneficiaries of community foundation grants are health, social welfare, education, and arts and culture. Community foundations are concerned with what works and are more interested in supporting the replication of successful projects than in taking chances with experimental approaches or research.

Most community foundations have been initiated by public-spirited citizens who leave money in a bequest to the foundation for specific types of local projects. Since the monies may be held separately according to donor interests or for general purposes, these foundations are classified as public charities. Community foundations exist to deal with local needs. They will fund causes that other foundations would not think of funding.

If your organization's purposes relate to local need, community foundations may even be willing to fund your organization to cover last year's deficit if it means keeping you in business to serve your target population. You can even acquire funding from your community foundation for a needs assessment if you approach the foundation with the rationale that a good needs assessment will result in attracting monies from other sources. In other words, you must convince a community foundation that a needs assessment grant will help you produce a higher quality proposal and will ultimately be responsible for all other funds that you generate.

If you are not sure whether there is a community foundation in your area, write or call

The Council on Foundations
1828 L St NW, Ste 2200
Washington, DC 20036
(202) 467-0427

If you find that there is not a community foundation in your area, invite some community leaders and wealthy, long-standing citizens together to consider initiating one. As a matter of fact, you can even get a grant to start a community foundation. You will never be sorry. Your community will benefit and you will gain another prospective funding source for your proposals.

National General Purpose Foundations

When asked to name a general purpose foundation, most people would give the name of a large foundation like the Rockefeller Foundation or Ford Foundation. Although large foundations like these number less than 100, they have two-thirds of all assets among the 41,588 foundations and account for over 50 percent of the grant dollars.

To be designated as a national general purpose foundation, a foundation does not need to fit a hard-and-fast definition. *National general purpose* refers to the foundation's scope and type of granting pattern. Foundations in this group have a philanthropic interest in several subject areas and make grants for proposals that will have a broad-scale impact across the United States and, more recently, the world. They prefer model, creative, innovative projects that other groups can replicate to solve similar problems. Since national general purpose foundations like to promote change, they do not usually fund deficits, operating income, or the many necessary but not highly visible or creative functions of organizations.

Special Purpose Foundations

Several hundred foundations fall into the special purpose category. How *special purpose* is defined could increase this number by thousands. For our purposes, this group of several hundred special purpose foundations includes those foundations whose funding record consistently supports a specific area of concern and whose funding represents a significant contribution in that specific area. For example, the Robert Wood Johnson Foundation is a special purpose foundation focusing on the area of health. These foundations are well financed by unusually large asset bases.

The key to success in this marketplace is to match your project with the special purpose foundation's specific area of interest. Your grant request will be evaluated according to the potential impact your project will have on the foundation's special area of concern.

Family Foundations

There are over 38,000 foundations in this category. Because their granting patterns represent the values of the family members whose interests have been memorialized by the creation of the foundations, granting patterns of family foundations vary widely from foundation to foundation. Most family foundations do have well-defined geographic preferences and specific interests, so they may seem to act as small-scale, special purpose foundations. True special purpose foundations, however, represent large-scale efforts and long-term commitments to a field, while family foundations change their giving patterns and funding priorities frequently.

The family foundation is the type of foundation most susceptible to the influence of board members, friends, and popular causes. In fact, linking your organization to friends of a family foundation will ensure that your proposal at least receives attention. Since many family foundations periodically change their priorities, it is helpful to have a contact who keeps you informed of the foundation's current funding interests. Even when you have a link to the board and access to the foundation, you must research the foundation thoroughly to keep abreast of changes in interests and commitment.

Corporate Foundations

Corporate foundations account for only approximately 20 percent of the $8.2 billion that corporations report as tax-deductible contributions on their tax returns. Historically, corporate foundations use foundation assets to maintain their giving pattern when corporate profits are down. With recent increases in corporate profits corporations have been able to maintain their granting programs without invading foundation assets.

The main distinction between corporate foundations and other corporate philanthropy vehicles is that corporate foundations must follow the same federal rules that the other four types of foundations must follow. The establishment of a foundation for public good requires that all foundations list the benefactors of their grants and make their tax returns available for public viewing. This requirement can become a problem for corporations when their corporate stockholders object to the types of organizations or specific projects that the corporate foundation supports. In addition, the public scrutiny to which the corporate foundation is subject allows for social activists and leaders of particular causes to research a company's giving pattern and arrange for demonstrations, which could result in negative public relations. To avoid such problems, many corporations only make noncontroversial grants through their foundation; they make all other grants through a corporate grants program that does not require public disclosure.

The main reason for initiating a corporate foundation is to stabilize a corporation's philanthropy program. Corporate foundations lead to a more uniform and stable approach to corporate social philanthropy than giving programs that rely solely on a percentage of company profits. Programs tied to company profits are subject to the "seesaw" effect, because profits can vary widely from year to year.

Since corporate foundations are an extension of a profit-making company, they tend to view the world and your proposal as any corporation would. They must see a benefit in all of the projects they fund. Many of these foundations fund grants only in communities where their parent corporations have factories or a special interest. For the most part, every grant made by a corporate foundation must benefit either the corporation or its workers or enhance the corporation's ability to attract high-quality personnel to the community.

CORPORATE PHILANTHROPY

There are approximately 5 million for-profit corporations in the United States, and many misconceptions about their giving patterns exist. A small percentage of corporate grants are well publicized, so grantseekers mistakenly think there are many more corporate grants than there really are and that the grants are large. In actuality, a minority of corporations make any grants at all, and fewer still make the large grants that get the publicity that most grantseekers unfortunately generalize from.

- Corporate contributions (noncorporate foundation) account for approximately 80 percent of all corporate grants.
- Only 35 percent of all corporations make tax-deductible contributions to nonprofit organizations.
- Of those corporations that do contribute, only a small percent give grants of over $500 a year.

You must do extensive research before applying for a grant from a corporation. This will help you avoid the embarrassment of asking for a grant from a corporation that has never given one or has never given one for the size you are requesting or the type of project you are proposing.

Although corporations contributed $8.2 billion in 1997, tax-deductible corporate contributions reported have shown little growth in recent years. The most widely accepted index used to measure corporate philanthropy is the percentage of pretax income donated to nonprofit organizations as a tax deduction. Consider that in 1987 pretax income donated by corporations was 1.8 percent, while in 1997 the amount declined to 1.1 percent. In the past, corporate profits were directly related to corporate philanthropy, but this is no longer true. While corporate profits are increasing, giving as a percentage of profit is declining. Clearly there are forces acting on this source of grant funds that need to be explored.

First, many companies are cutting employees and are under pressure to show the greatest dividends and returns. Second, employee loyalty and community image are not as great a concern to corporations as they have been in the past. Mergers and acquisitions have removed corporations from their original ties with the community. Significant decreases in corporate philanthropy have been particularly apparent in merged companies that have moved their corporate headquarters to Europe, Asia, and Australia.

Why do corporations give tax-exempt gifts of money and products? Some give out of feelings of social philanthropic responsibility. Others give to help themselves improve relationships with employees, the community, and unions or to gain marketplace advantages through product research opportunities and the positioning of products in lucrative marketplaces.

Corporate giving is usually a "this-for-that" exchange. Corporations do not usually *give away* money; they *invest* it.

- For the first time in more than a decade, health and human services is receiving more corporate contributions than education—34 percent. (Health and human services provide direct benefits to employees and have the potential to lower health costs and services.)
- Education receives 30 percent of corporate contributions. (Education provides trained workers for the companies and raises the purchasing power of the population.)
- Civic and community affairs receive 12 percent. (By investing in these areas, corporations provide visible support to communities.)
- Culture and the arts receive 10 percent. (These areas create and sustain quality of life.)
- Unallocated accounts for 8 percent. (This is up substantially from previous years primarily because giving programs are decentralized and company headquarters may not know where its other company sites are directing their giving.)
- Other receives 5 percent. (Within this category is a 69 percent increase in giving to U.S.-based international organizations and a 200 percent increase in giving to public policy research organizations.)

The mechanisms that corporations use to invest in nonprofit organizations can all be traced back to the basic need of the company to continually develop profits. Some corporate contributions officers refer to this as *enlightened corporate self-interest*. This "quid-pro-quo" philosophy is best understood by looking at the world through the values glasses of a corporate official. Stockholders invest in a company in order to get a return on their investment—profits. They seldom purchase the company's stock to reinforce social causes. The concept that a grant is similar to an investment pervades corporate philanthropy. Hence, the bottom line relates to the return on the investment. With this investment/return philosophy as a guiding principle, corporations use five basic contributions vehicles. Keep in mind that many corporations use a variety of these vehicles, so if your research reveals that a corporation employs one of these mechanisms, keep searching to determine whether it employs any of the others.

1. Employee Matching Contributions Program—The company matches gifts made by employees to certain approved 501(c)3 tax-exempt groups. A recent survey by the Council for Advancement and Support of Education (CASE) reported that 30 percent of companies will match contributions to education and that 15 percent will match employee gifts to other nonprofit organizations. In addition, some companies provide a greater than one-to-one match. Some actually double the amount given by the employee.

2. Corporate Contributions Committee—The company makes a certain amount of money available to make grants to nonprofit organizations that it values. It may be a percentage of its profits (i.e., 1 percent) or a fixed dollar amount. Interests vary from company to company but generally fall within the categories listed above (education, health and human services, civic and community, culture and arts). The committee members may be corporate executives and/or representatives of employee groups or unions. One overriding factor is whether any of the corporation's employees are volunteers for the prospective grantee. The idea behind this is that if the nonprofit organization (the prospective grantee) is a valued asset in the community, corporate employees will donate their time. No volunteers equates to no or little value to what the corporation does and hence, no corporate grant.

3. Corporate Foundations—Many corporations make a corporate tax-deductible gift from the company to its foundation. This allows the company some flexibility in making grants. If profits are down one year, the corporate contributions program can be supported by expending some of the assets that have built up in the foundation.

4. Marketing—Corporations are using this mechanism more and more, but data on its use is difficult to collect and analyze. The basic concept is that by providing a contribution to a certain nonprofit group the company has the right to associate its name with the nonprofit's name or cause and has the potential to benefit through product positioning and ultimately, increased sales and profits. The benefits of product positioning are well documented through work with schools. Many of us have heard of the large chain supermarket that has allowed customers to select a school to receive contributions representing a percentage of its (the supermarket's) sales receipts. This type of activity is called *cause related marketing*. These gifts are generally not listed as a tax-charitable deduction on a company's tax return. However, it is estimated that this technique brought in $2.5 billion for nonprofit organizations in 1997 and that this figure will double to $5 billion over the next three years.

5. Product Development—Some corporations contribute to nonprofit organizations based on the nonprofit's ability to contribute to the testing, improvement, or creation of a new product.

Many corporations' giving patterns are related to the geographic concerns of their workers and factories. You can learn far more about the profitability of the publicly held corporations in your area and their contributions potential by purchasing a share or two of their stock than by buying expensive resource books on corporate philanthropy. Begin your search for corporate grants by asking your chamber of commerce for a list of corporations in your area. From this list, identify those companies that might be interested in your project because it could benefit their workers or product development. Then purchase shares of their stock and watch how much information will be sent to you. In no time at all you will learn about their parent firms, officers, proxy statements, and dividends.

To approach corporate funding sources, you must relate your request to

- their attainment of corporate goals (e.g., programs that will provide manpower training or increase the availability of resources)
- employee or management benefits (e.g., health programs, cultural programs, recreation facilities)
- improvement of the environment around the corporation (e.g., programs that affect transportation, communication, or ecology)
- improved corporate image (e.g., programs that will give the corporation a better reputation in the community)

When you evaluate your potential for getting corporate grants, determine what the "returns on the investment" are, and emphasize these in your presentations to corporate funding officials.

Do not automatically assume that all corporations want to be publicly recognized for their grants. In some cases, what they really want is anonymity. A survey by the Conference Board of 410 corporations that granted $2.25 billion to nonprofit organizations uncovered $100 million that the companies did not even claim as tax deductions. Although it is not clear what motivates corporations to award grants they do not claim as tax deductions or receive public recognition for, grantseekers should be careful about assuming they know why corporations make grants.

Another interesting aspect of corporate philanthropy is what might be called the "school of fish syndrome." Corporations do not like to be the first to fund a project because there is an element of risk involved. They are afraid to leave the protection of the "school" and are extremely sensitive to what their competition is doing. This can work in favor of the successful grantseeker. Once one corporation gives you a grant, others will tend to follow. In addition, if a corporation gives grants to another organization in your field, your chances of getting a grant from a competing corporation increase. Corporations do not want to be first to take a chance, but, then again, they do not want to get left behind. Risk reduction by association, however, may be on the decline as corporations seek new types of arrangements with nonprofit organizations.

SUMMARY OF THE GRANTS MARKETPLACE

Now you have a basic idea of the types of funding sources that make up the grants marketplace and the amount of grant support contributed by each. You know that the best strategy is to approach the federal grants area first. You must play the odds that favor this $90 billion marketplace and also explore the possibility of state and block grants. The greater the potential for developing a model that applies to a large area or a great number of people, the more interest you will generate from federal and state funding sources. After you have exhausted your funding potential with government sources, move to the private sector marketplace.

The $21.6 billion in contributions from foundations and corporations provide a distant second to the government's $90 billion, but the variety of project interests and ease of proposal preparation are definite pluses. After reviewing foundation and corporate opportunities, move to associations, service clubs, and other nonprofit groups for support.

THE GRANTS SUPPORT TABLE

The grants support table (see table 8.1) will give you an idea of the strengths and weaknesses of your project in relation to the various funding sources and will help you choose the correct marketplace for your project.

Record your project title and a brief description on the top of the table. Then evaluate how closely your project meets the criteria for each of the funding sources.

Criterion A: The Need

What is the need for your project or research? On whom will it have an impact? How large is the target population? Can the needs population be defined as "special"?

Criterion B: Project Methods/Approach

The information provided in this section is for general use only. There will always be exceptions to the categories presented here, but funding sources generally prefer a specific approach or type of project. For example, some grantors like to fund replication grants, while others prefer research proposals.

Criterion C: Friends/Contacts/Links with Funders

Having friends, contacts, and others who can talk with a funding official or board member or set up an appointment for you is valuable in all grantseeking, but is particularly critical when you are applying close to home.

Criterion D: Grants Experience

Your organization's grants track record is an important credibility builder with state and federal funding sources, corporations, and national foundations. You can still attract funding from community and family foundations, however, even if your organization does not have a track record. Having a solid board whose names are recognized by grantors will help you.

Criterion E: Personal Contact with Officers or Board Members

Personal contact is important with community, national, special purpose, and family foundations, and is essential with corporate, state, and federal sources.

TABLE 8.1

GRANTS SUPPORT TABLE

Project Title: _____

Project Description: _____

Criteria	Community Foundation	National Foundation	Special Purpose Foundation	Family Foundation	Corporate Source	State Source	Federal Source
A The Need	Local needs only	National needs, widespread	Need in their specialty	Geographic concerns usually	Needs of workers or products and marketing concerns	Local and statewide need	National need
B Project Methods/ Approach	No experiments; interested in time-tested, proven approaches that can be replicated	Unique, cost-effective, research, model and demonstration	Viewed as special to this area, projects, models, research	Depends on what the Board likes and has funded in the past	Proven safe project methods, unique research protocols related to corporate interests	Replication and model approaches	Mostly model, innovative and research
C Friends/ Contacts/Links with Funders	Very important, local contacts	Important	Important, especially in field of interest	Very important, gives you hidden agenda	Very important, give money to those they trust	Important to have endorsement/ support of bureaucrats, politicians	Same as state

TABLE 8.1

Grants Support Table (continued)

Criteria	Community Foundation	National Foundation	Special Purpose Foundation	Family Foundation	Corporate Source	State Source	Federal Source
D Grants Experience	Credibility and need can overcome lack of experience	Important, likes to work with grantees who are proven	Not as important as potential contribution to field	Not critical, will overlook experience in favor of making a difference	Important, expert experience	Credibility in your state important	Credibility important, as are experience of project director or P.I., publications, and past grants
E Personal Contact with Officers or Board Members	Very important, especially with board members	Important with staff and program officials	Important with staff and program officials	Important with board members	Essential to contact corporate officials and involve their workers	Essential to contact program officers	Same as state

PART TWO

• • • • • • • • • • • • •

Government Funding Sources

CHAPTER 9

Researching the Government Marketplace

The government grants marketplace comprises

- federal funds—grants and contracts received directly from federal agencies
- state funds—funds from (a) state grant program that distribute funds generated from state revenues other than federal revenue-sharing monies, and (b) state grant programs that distribute federal grant funds
- county, borough, and city funds—funds consisting of everything from parking-meter monies to dollars passed down from the state and federal government, for grants to specific geographic or political boundaries

FEDERAL GRANTS

Federal granting programs are created by Congress though the enactment of public laws and the appropriation of funds. The actual disbursement of these funds follows a systematic progression based on publicly announced rules. Many grantseekers are unaware of how this federal funding system works and, therefore, are unable to take advantage of grant-related announcements and rules published early in the funding process.

When you do not know the system, you are forced to react to a Request for Proposals (RFP) announcement and develop your proposal in a few short weeks. Grantseekers who know the system, however, can develop a proactive approach to seeking funds that alerts them to a deadline four to six months or more in advance.

Since many federal grants have matching funds and other requirements, use the pre-proposal summary and approval form in chapter 4 (see exhibit 4.1) to ensure you will have the support of your administration before you invest your time. Almost all federal funding documents use key words and subject areas to categorize granting programs. Therefore, your worksheet on redefining your project (see chapter 5, exhibit 5.1) will be useful in your research.

FEDERAL GRANTS RESEARCH FORM

Gathering the information necessary to choose your best federal grant prospect requires persistence. You must make personal contacts, gather data, and analyze the data. Without careful attention to detail, the information you were sure you would remember can easily get lost. As one grantseeker reported in a grants seminar, "The only way I can extort my unusually high salary from my boss is to keep all my grants research and contacts in my head. Nothing is written down, and my board prays that nothing will ever happen to me!" This is not a good idea because all those contacts and bits of information could be lost.

The key to providing your organization with federal funding is a combination of determination, hard work, and homework. The homework consists of systematic research, record keeping, and follow-up. The federal grants research form (see exhibit 9.1) will allow you to keep track of the grant programs you investigate (i.e., those that seem like your most logical grant sources) and will prevent your contacts and projects from being lost if anything happens to you. Copy this form and pass out a sufficient number of copies to your grants researchers so that your data gathering will be consistent and complete. Each of the areas on the form will be explained in this chapter. (This form and many of the others in this book are included in Bauer Associates software package entitled *Grant Winner*. For ordering information, see the list of resources available from Bauer Associates at the end of the book.)

As you look at examples of the resources available on funding opportunities, you will see that information necessary to complete the federal grants research form is readily available. Do not stop with the first few funding sources that sound or look good. Remember, your goal is to locate the best funding sources for your project. Complete your research, then review and rate those funding sources you have identified using the federal funding source evaluation worksheet in chapter 10 (see exhibit 10.2).

For *(Your Project Reference or Title)*: _____

CFDA No. _____ Deadline Date(s): _____

Program Title: _____ Gov't. Agency: _____

Create a file for each program you are researching and place all information you gather on this program in the file. Use this Federal Grants Research Form to

- keep a record of the information you have gathered
- maintain a log of all telephone and face-to-face contacts made with the government agency
- log all correspondence sent to and received from the agency

Agency Address: _____ Agency Director: _____

Telephone Number: _____ Program Director: _____

Fax Number: _____ Name/Title of Contact Person: _____

Place a check mark next to the information you have gathered and placed in the file.

    ❑ Program description from CFDA
    ❑ Letter requesting to be put on mailing list
    ❑ List of last year's grantees
        ❑ Sent for   ❑ Received
    ❑ List of last year's reviewers
        ❑ Sent for   ❑ Received
    ❑ Application package   Expected availability date _____
        ❑ Sent for   ❑ Received
    ❑ Comments on rules/final rules from *Federal Register*
    ❑ Notice of rules for evaluation from *Federal Register*
    ❑ Grant Scoring System—Point allocation for each section
        Source: _____
    ❑ Sample funded proposal
    ❑ Federal Funding Source Staff Profile (exhibit 10.5)
    ❑ Written summary of each contact made

FEDERAL GRANTS RESEARCH FORM

EXHIBIT 9.1

FEDERAL RESEARCH TOOLS

How do you research and track federal grants? The federal research tools worksheet (see table 9.1) outlines some of the more useful resources for locating government funds.

TABLE 9.1

FEDERAL RESEARCH TOOLS WORKSHEET

Name	Description	Where to Get It	Cost	Where to Use it Locally
Catalog of Federal Domestic Assistance (202)512-1800 Fax (202)512-2250	The official information on all government programs created by law (see sample entry)	Mail Orders: Supt. of Documents P.O. Box 371954 Pittsburgh, PA 15250-7954 On-line at: www.gsa.gov/fdac/default.htm	Printed Copy: $72/year Online: Free access	
Federal Assistance Programs Retrieval System (FAPRS) (202)708-5126 (800)669-8331	A retrieval system that uses key words to search CFDA programs that are related to the desired grants area.	Federal Domestic Assistance Catalog Staff (MVS) General Services Administration 300 7th St., S.W. Room 101 Washington, DC 20407 Or call your congressperson.	Ask your congressperson how to do a FAPRS search. He or she may do it for you at no cost.	
Federal Register (202)512-1800 Fax (202)512-2250	Official news publication for the federal government; makes public all meetings, announcements of granting programs, regulations, and deadlines (see sample entry).	Mail Orders: Supt. of Documents P.O. Box 371954 Pittsburgh, PA 15250-7954 Online at: www.nara.gov/fedreg/	Printed Copy: $607/year with indexes, $555/year without indexes Online: Free access	
U.S. Government (202)512-1800 Fax (202)512-2250	Official handbook government. Describes all federal agencies and gives names of officials.	Mail Orders: P.O. Box 371954 Pittsburgh, PA 15250-7954 On-line at: www.access.gpo.gov/	Printed Copy: $41 Online: Free access	

TABLE 9.1

FEDERAL RESEARCH TOOLS WORKSHEET *(continued)*

Name	Description	Where to Get It	Cost	Where to Use it Locally
Federal Directory (202)333-8620	Includes names, addresses, and phone numbers of federal government agencies and key personnel.	Carroll Publishing 1058 Thomas Jefferson St., N.W. Washington, DC 20007	$300.00 per year	
Commerce Business Daily (202)512-1800 Fax (202)512-2250	The mechanism to announce the accepting of bids on government contracts (see sample entry).	Mail Orders: Supt. of Documents P.O. Box 371954 Pittsburgh, PA 15250-7954 Online at: cbdnet.access.gpo.gov	Printed Copy: $275/year to $324/year depending on type of postage. Online: Free access	
Congressional Record (202)512-1800 Fax (202)512-2250	Day-to-day proceedings of the Senate and House of Representatives; includes all written information for the record (all grant program money appropriated by Congress).	Supt. of Documents P.O. Box 371954 Pittsburgh, PA 15250-7954 Online at: www.access.gpo.gov/ su_docs/aces/aces150. html	Mail Orders: $295/year Online: Free access	
Listing of Government Depository Libraries (202)783-3238	Locations of public and university libraries that allow free access to government publications like the CFDA.	Chief of the Library Dept. of Public Documents U.S. Government Printing Office Washington, DC 20402, or locate library in your area on the Internet at: www.access.gpo.gov/ su_docs/libpro.html	Free	
Agency Newsletters and Publications, RFPs, and Guidelines	Many federal agencies publish newsletters to inform you about the availability of funds and program accomplishments. You may also request application materials guidelines, and so on.	From agency. See "Regulations, Guidelines, and Literature" in CFDA entry.	Usually Free	

Catalog of Federal Domestic Assistance

The Catalog of Federal Domestic Assistance (CFDA), which is published by the federal government, lists over 1,300 granting programs that disseminate approximately $90 billion in grants annually. The catalog is provided free of charge to at least two federal depository libraries in every congressional district. If you prefer to work with a hard copy, consider locating and using one of these copies instead of purchasing your own. For those of you with Internet access, the *CFDA* is available in a free computer-accessible version.

Many colleges, universities, and large nonprofit organizations subscribe to grants databases to research federal grants opportunities. Subscribers pay a fee for access, but these databases often offer more user-friendly, faster ways to get to the best federal sources. Many have an automatic function that periodically scans the database for sources related to the grantseeker's key search terms and alerts the grantseeker of the most current opportunities. More information on these databases will follow. However, be aware that most of these databases provide abbreviated descriptions of the federal grant programs. Therefore, you will still need to access the *CFDA* to develop a full description of a prospective grantor's program.

Using the Hard Copy Version of the CFDA. If you choose to use the hard copy of the *CFDA* you should first familiarize yourself with its indexes. The following indexes are included:

- Agency Program Index: Although difficult to use to search for grant sources, provides information on the agencies administering programs in the catalog, including codes for the types of assistance each agency program provides.
- Applicant Eligibility Index: Allows you to look up a program to see whether you are eligible to apply. Because you must already know of the program to use this index, it is not a great help in identifying sources.
- Deadline Index: Enables you to look up the deadline dates for programs to see whether the programs have a single or multiple deadline system.
- Functional Index: Groups programs into 20 broad functional categories, such as agriculture and education, and 176 subcategories.
- Subject Index: The most commonly used index, since most people express their interests according to subject.

Users should also be aware of the following lists:

- Deleted Programs List: Identifies the programs that have been deleted since the previous edition of the catalog.
- Added Programs List: Identifies the programs that have been added since the previous edition of the catalog.

- Crosswalk of Changes to Program Numbers and Titles: Lists programs that have undergone a title or number change since previous edition of the catalog.

When using the print version of the CFDA compare your key words and redefinition sheets to entries in the agency index and the subject index, and select those programs that you believe will be interested in your project idea. Briefly outline the sources on your federal grants research forms. Be sure to write down the CFDA number that references the program, and make a copy of the full CFDA entry.

Accessing and Using the CFDA on the Internet. The CFDA can most easily be accessed on the Internet at www.gsa.gov/fdac/default.htm. Once you have gained access to the Web site click "Query the Catalog" to perform a search, then follow the instructions on the screen. In the sample search (exhibit 9.3) for programs interested in minority science and engineering the grantseeker has limited the number of documents to 50 and asked the program to sort by relevance. Search results are shown in exhibit 9.4. By clicking one of the programs listed on the search results, the grantseeker can retrieve a CFDA description of the program like that shown in exhibit 9.5.

Reading the CFDA. A sample CFDA entry (see exhibit 9.5) has been included to show the information provided in this valuable resource. In the sample, CFDA Number 84.120, Minority Science Improvement, the numbers that appear next to the left margin can be used as readers aids. These numbers appear in the actual online CFDA document.

:010 PROGRAM NUMBER AND TITLE

:030 FEDERAL AGENCY: This is the branch of government administering the program, which is not much help to you except as general knowledge or for looking up programs and agencies in the *United States Government Manual.*

:040 AUTHORIZATION: You need this information to fill out some program applications and/or to look up the testimony and laws creating the funding (for the "hard-core" researcher and grantseeker only).

:050 OBJECTIVES: Compare these general program objectives to your project. Do not give up if you are off the mark slightly; contact with the funding source may uncover new programs, changes, or hidden agendas.

:060 TYPES OF ASSISTANCE: Review and record the general type of support from this source, and then compare the information to your project definition.

:070 USES AND USE RESTRICTIONS: Compare your project to this description of eligible projects.

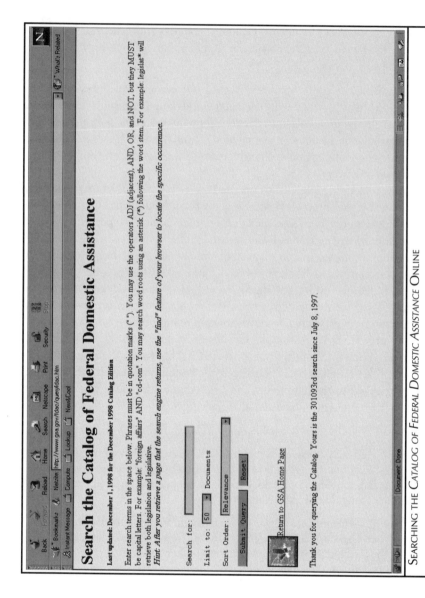

Search the Catalog of Federal Domestic Assistance

Last updated: December 1, 1998 for the December 1998 Catalog Edition

Enter search terms in the space below. Phrases must be in quotation marks ("). You may use the operators ADJ (adjacent), AND, OR, and NOT, but they MUST be capital letters. For example: "foreign affairs" AND "cd-rom". You may search word roots using an asterisk (*) following the word stem. For example: legislat* will retrieve both legislation and legislative.

Hint: After you retrieve a page that the search engine returns, use the "find" feature of your browser to locate the specific occurrence.

Search for:

Limit to: 50 Documents

Sort Order: Relevance

Submit Query   Reset

 Return to GSA Home Page

Thank you for querying the Catalog. Yours is the 301093rd search since July 8, 1997.

SEARCHING THE *CATALOG OF FEDERAL DOMESTIC ASSISTANCE ONLINE*

EXHIBIT 9.3

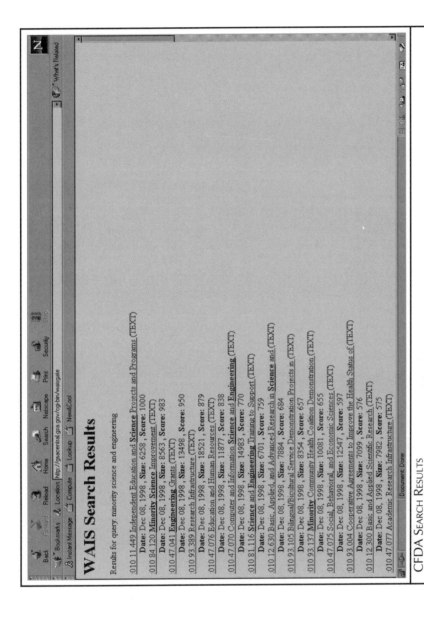

WAIS Search Results

Results for query: minority science and engineering

010 11.449 Independent Education and **Science** Projects and Programs (TEXT)
  Date: Dec 08, 1998 , **Size:** 6258 , **Score:** 1000
010 84.120 **Minority Science** Improvement (TEXT)
  Date: Dec 08, 1998 , **Size:** 8563 , **Score:** 983
010 47.041 **Engineering** Grants (TEXT)
  Date: Dec 08, 1998 , **Size:** 13498 , **Score:** 950
010 93.389 Research Infrastructure (TEXT)
  Date: Dec 08, 1998 , **Size:** 18521 , **Score:** 879
010 47.076 Education and Human Resources (TEXT)
  Date: Dec 08, 1998 , **Size:** 11877 , **Score:** 838
010 47.070 Computer and Information **Science** and **Engineering** (TEXT)
  Date: Dec 08, 1998 , **Size:** 14983 , **Score:** 770
010 81.116 **Science** and **Engineering** Training to Support (TEXT)
  Date: Dec 08, 1998 , **Size:** 6701 , **Score:** 759
010 12.630 Basic, Applied, and Advanced Research in **Science** and (TEXT)
  Date: Dec 08, 1998 , **Size:** 7884 , **Score:** 684
010 93.105 Bilingual/Bicultural Service Demonstration Projects in (TEXT)
  Date: Dec 08, 1998 , **Size:** 8354 , **Score:** 657
010 93.137 **Minority** Community Health Coalition Demonstration (TEXT)
  Date: Dec 08, 1998 , **Size:** 10081 , **Score:** 655
010 47.075 Social, Behavioral, and Economic Sciences (TEXT)
  Date: Dec 08, 1998 , **Size:** 12547 , **Score:** 597
010 93.004 Cooperative Agreements to Improve the Health Status of (TEXT)
  Date: Dec 08, 1998 , **Size:** 7099 , **Score:** 576
010 12.300 Basic and Applied Scientific Research (TEXT)
  Date: Dec 08, 1998 , **Size:** 7982 , **Score:** 575
010 47.077 Academic Research Infrastructure (TEXT)

Document: Done

CFDA SEARCH RESULTS

EXHIBIT 9.4

WAIS Document Retrieval   Page 1 of 3

:010   84.120 **Minority Science** Improvement

:020   (MSIP)

:030   FEDERAL AGENCY: OFFICE OF ASSISTANT SECRETARY FOR POSTSECONDARY
EDUCATION, DEPARTMENT OF EDUCATION

:040   AUTHORIZATION: Higher Education Act of 1965, Title X, Part B,
Subpart 1, as amended, 100 Stat. 1561, 20 U.S.C. 1135b, 1135c, 1135d.

:050   OBJECTIVES: To (1) effect long-range improvement in **science** and
engineering education at predominantly **minority** institutions and (2)
increase the participation of underrepresented ethnic minorities,
particularly **minority** women, in scientific and technological careers.

:060   TYPES OF ASSISTANCE: Project Grants.

:070   USES AND USE RESTRICTIONS: Grant funds may be used for paying
costs necessary for improving and maintaining high quality **science** and
engineering education programs in **minority** postsecondary institutions,
including salaries and wages, equipment and instructional materials and
supplies, travel related to the project activities, faculty
development, and other direct and indirect costs.

:080   ELIGIBILITY REQUIREMENTS:

:081   Applicant Eligibility: Private and public accredited two-and
four-year institutions of higher education whose total enrollments are
predominantly (50 percent or more) American Indian; Alaskan Native;
Black, not of Hispanic origin; Hispanic (including persons of Mexican,
Puerto Rican, Cuban, and Central or South American origin); Pacific
Islander; or any combination of these or other ethnic minorities who are
underrepresented in **science** and **engineering** may apply. Applications may
also be submitted by professional scientific societies, and all
nonprofit accredited colleges and universities which will render a
needed service to a group of MSIP-eligible institutions or provide
in-service training for project directors, scientists and engineers from
eligible **minority** institutions.

:082   Beneficiary Eligibility: Private and public accredited two-and
four-year institutions of higher education whose total enrollments are
predominantly (50 percent or more) American Indian; Alaskan Native;
Black, not of Hispanic origin; Hispanic (including persons of Mexican,
Puerto Rican, Cuban, and Central or South American origin); Pacific
Islander; or any combination of these or other ethnic minorities who are
underrepresented in **science** and **engineering** will benefit. Also
nonprofit **science**-oriented organizations, professional scientific
societies, and all nonprofit accredited colleges and universities will
benefit.

:083   Credentials/Documentation: Institutions must provide the
information necessary to establish their eligibility for participation
in MSIP. The data on enrollment furnished to the Office for Civil
Rights to satisfy requirements for the "Fall Enrollment and Compliance
Report of Institutions of Higher Education" are acceptable. Applications
must be signed by the project director(s), the relevant department
head(s), and by an authorized organizational official. This program is
excluded from coverage under OMB Circular No. A-87.

:090   APPLICATION AND AWARD PROCESS:

:091   Preapplication Coordination: The standard application forms as
furnished by the Federal agency and required by OMB Circular No. A-102
must be used for this program. This program is eligible for coverage
under E.O. 12372, "Intergovernmental Review of Federal Programs." An
applicant should consult the office or official designated as the single
point of contact in his or her State for more information on the process
the State requires to be followed in applying for assistance, if the
State has selected the program for review.

:092   Application Procedure: By submission of a formal application

http://gsacentral.gsa.gov/cgi-bin/waisgate?WAISconnType=&WAISdocID=4495410175+1+0+0&WAISaction=retrieve 2/21/99

SAMPLE CFDA ENTRY

EXHIBIT 9.5

describing the planned project and proposed amount of the grant. See 34
CFR 637 and the specific program guidelines. Application forms are
provided by MSIP. This program is subject to the provisions of OMB
Circular No. A-110.

:093 Award Procedure: Panels of outside experts with knowledge of the
fields covered by the application review all applications. Grants awards
are recommended to the Secretary by the program office, in the order of
merit.

:094 Deadlines: Deadlines are published in the Federal Register.

:095 Range of Approval/Disapproval Time: From three to six months.

:096 Appeals: None.

:097 Renewals: Not applicable.

:100 ASSISTANCE CONSIDERATIONS:

:101 Formula and Matching Requirements: The program suggests that some
institutional contribution be included as part of program support.
However, by law, this program has no matching requirements.

:102 Length and Time Phasing of Assistance: One to three years. Funds
are awarded annually and disbursed as required.

:110 POST ASSISTANCE REQUIREMENTS:

:111 Reports: The program requires interim performance reports from
directors of projects having duration of more than one year at the end
of each budget year's activities. A substantive performance and
financial report is required within 90 days upon completion of the
project for all funded projects.

:112 Audits: Compliance with standard Department of Education
requirements.

:113 Records: Grantees are required to maintain standard programmatic
and financial records. Records are subject to inspection during the life
of the grant and for three years thereafter.

:120 FINANCIAL INFORMATION:

:121 Account Identification: 91-0201-2-1-502.

:122 Obligations: (Grants) FY 97 $5,255,000; FY 98 est $5,255,000; and
FY 99 est $7,500,000.

:123 Range and Average of Financial Assistance: Average award in 1997
was: $140,000 for Institutional; $250,000 for Cooperative; $14,000 for
Design Projects; and $23,000 for Special Projects.

:130 PROGRAM ACCOMPLISHMENTS: In fiscal year 1997, approximately 68
awards were made.

:140 REGULATIONS, GUIDELINES, AND LITERATURE: Program regulations are
found in the Federal Register published October 16, 1981 (Vol 16, No.
200) amendments to the regulations are found in the Federal Register
published November 12, 1987 (Vol. 52, No. 218) and November 18, 1992
(Vol. 57 No. 223) respectively. Project abstracts for fiscal years
1990-1993, guidelines for preparation of applications and operation of
projects are available, at no cost, from the program.

:150 INFORMATION CONTACTS:

:151 Regional or Local Office: Not applicable.

:152 Headquarters Office: Institutional Development and Undergraduate
Education Service, Office of Postsecondary Education, Department of
Education, Washington, DC 20202-5251. Contact: Argelia Velez-Rodriguez.
Telephone: (202) 260-3261. Use the same number for FTS. Fax: (202)

http://gsacentral.gsa.gov/cgi-bin/waisgate?WAISconnType=&WAISdocID=4495410175+1+0+0&WAISaction=retrieve 2/21/99

SAMPLE CFDA ENTRY (continued)

EXHIBIT 9.5

401-7532; E-mail: Argelia-Velez-Rodriguez@ed.gov.

:160   RELATED PROGRAMS: 84.031, Higher Education_Institutional Aid;
84.116, Fund for the Improvement of Postsecondary Education.

:170   EXAMPLES OF FUNDED PROJECTS: (1) A project is supporting a
consortium of two historically Black institutions to substantially
increase the use and effectiveness of computer assisted instruction
(CAI) materials at the cooperating institutions and other **minority**
institutions nationwide. (2) Another cooperative project is supporting
two institutions, a historically Black college and a non-**minority**
university from the northeast, to develop a Comprehensive Interfaced
Computerized Instructional System for Mathematics, Statistics and
Computer Literacy. (3) A project is supporting a university in South
Texas with a predominantly Mexican-American student population to
implement an undergraduate student research apprenticeship/faculty
researcher mentorship program. (4) One project is assisting a Native
American institution to develop eighteen mobile **science** laboratory
experiences to deliver two basic **science** courses to students living in
the Standing Rock Sioux Indian reservation. (5) A project is supporting
a non-**minority** university in California to improve a pre-college
enrichment program for **minority** youngsters.

:180   CRITERIA FOR SELECTING PROPOSALS: Decisions are based primarily on
the scientific and educational merits of described activities and
conformance with the objectives of the program. Priority is given to
applicants which have not previously received funding from the **Minority
Science** Improvement Program and to previous grantees with a proven
record of success, as well as to proposals that contribute to achieving
balance among projects with respect to geographic region, academic
discipline and project type.

SAMPLE CFDA ENTRY *(continued)*

EXHIBIT 9.5

:080   ELIGIBILITY REQUIREMENTS: Be sure your organization is
designated as a legal recipient. If it is not, find an organization of the
type designated and apply as a consortium or under a cooperative
arrangement. Determine whether your project can benefit those that
the program is intended to benefit.

:090   APPLICATION AND AWARD PROCESS: Review this information and record it on your federal grants research form. Do not let
the deadline data bother you. If the award cycle has passed, you should
still contact the agency and position yourself for the following year by
asking for copies of old applications and a list of current grantees and
by requesting to be a reviewer.

:100   ASSISTANCE CONSIDERATIONS: Record any information
on any match you are required to provide. This will be useful in
evaluating funding sources. Matching requirements may eliminate
some funding sources from your consideration. In addition, assistance
considerations will help you develop your project planner (see chapter

11). When you know about matching requirements in advance, you can identify what resources your organization will be required to provide.

:110 POST ASSISTANCE REQUIREMENTS: This section provides you with performance report, audit and record requirements.

:120 FINANCIAL INFORMATION: This section gives you an idea of what funds the agency program may have received, but do not take the information here as the last word. One entry I reviewed said the funding agency had $3 million for research. When contacted, the agency had over $30 million to disseminate under the program described and similar ones in the CFDA. Refer to the entry, but investigate it further.

:130 PROGRAM ACCOMPLISHMENTS: This section provides you with information on how many and what types of projects were funded in the previous fiscal year.

:140 REGULATIONS, GUIDELINES, AND LITERATURE: Record and send for any information you can get on the funder.

:150 INFORMATION CONTACTS: Record and use to begin contacting funders as outlined in this book. If provided, note the name and phone number of the contact person. While the contact person or phone number may have changed, you at least will have a place to start.

:160 RELATED PROGRAMS: Some CFDA entries include suggestions of other programs that are similar or related to your area of interest. While these suggestions are usually obvious and you may have already uncovered the programs in your research, review this section for leads.

:170 EXAMPLES OF FUNDED PROJECTS: Compare your project with those listed and asked yourself how it fits in.

:180 CRITERIA FOR SELECTING PROPOSALS: Review and record the information here. Criteria are frequently listed with no regard to their order of importance and lack any reference to the point values that they will be given in the review. Therefore, you should also obtain the rules from the *Federal Register*, the agency publication, or a past reviewer.

After reviewing the CFDA entries, select the best government funding program for your project. Contact the federal agency by using the information listed under ":150 Information Contacts."

Federal Register

The *Federal Register* is the newspaper of the federal government. To make legal notices on a great variety of federal issues official, the government must publish notices in the *Federal Register*. Likewise, the creation of new government granting programs must be published in the *Federal Register*; rules to evaluate proposals are also printed there. The hard copy of this government publication is provided free of charge to at least two federal depository libraries in your congressional district. Locate your nearest source. It can also be accessed for free through the Internet at www.nara.gov/fedreg. Frequent and heavy users of the *Federal Register* may be interested in obtaining a CD-ROM version of the *Register*. The electronic CD-ROM versions allow for fast and easy searching by agency, title fields, and key words, and provides tables of contents and summaries of the last six months of rules and regulations. (See *Dialog OnDisc: Federal Register* in the list of resources for further information.)

Once you have used the *CFDA* to select the best government funding program for your project, phone, fax, or e-mail the contact listed in the *CFDA* entry to find out the day(s) the *Federal Register* published notices, proposed rules, and/or final rules and regulations regarding the program you are interested in. Ask for the volume(s), the number(s), the issue date(s), and the page(s). The more information you have, the easier it will be for you to locate the information you are looking for.

You can do a simple search of the *Federal Register* online for the information you need. In the sample search shown in exhibit 9.6 the grantseeker asked to search the December 29, 1998, *Federal Register* for notices related to minority science and engineering. Search results are shown in exhibit 9.7. By clicking on the first hit listed on the search results, the grantseeker retrieved the notice inviting applications for new awards for fiscal year 1999 under the Minority Science and Engineering Improvement Program, CFDA Number 84.120A (see exhibit 9.8). This particular notice describes the purpose of the program, eligibility criteria, and applicable regulations. However, contents of notices do vary.

"Notices" is not the only section of the *Federal Register* that can be searched. Grantseekers can also look at "Contents and Preliminary Pages," "Final Rules and Regulations," "Proposed Rules," "Presidential Documents," "Sunshine Act Meetings," "Reader Aids," and "Corrections."

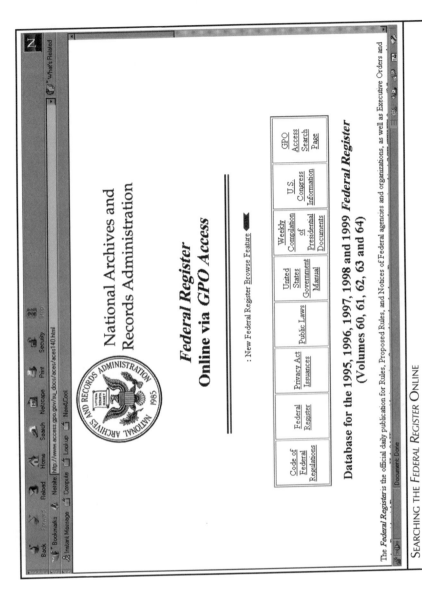

SEARCHING THE *FEDERAL REGISTER* ONLINE

EXHIBIT 9.6

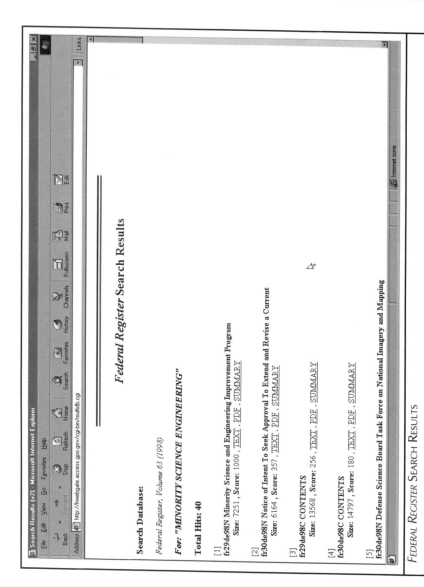

Federal Register Search Results

Search Database:

Federal Register, Volume 63 (1998)

For: "MINORITY SCIENCE ENGINEERING"

Total Hits: 40

[1]
fr29de98N Minority Science and Engineering Improvement Program
Size: 7251 , Score: 1000 , TEXT , PDF , SUMMARY

[2]
fr30de98N Notice of Intent To Seek Approval To Extend and Revise a Current
Size: 6164 , Score: 357 , TEXT , PDF , SUMMARY

[3]
fr29de98C CONTENTS
Size: 13568 , Score: 256 , TEXT , PDF , SUMMARY

[4]
fr30de98C CONTENTS
Size: 14797 , Score: 180 , TEXT , PDF , SUMMARY

[5]
fr30de98N Defense Science Board Task Force on National Imagery and Mapping

FEDERAL REGISTER SEARCH RESULTS

EXHIBIT 9.7

WAIS Document Retrieval

[Federal Register: December 29, 1998 (Volume 63, Number 249)]
[Notices]
[Page 71625-71626]
From the Federal Register Online via GPO Access [wais.access.gpo.gov]
[DOCID:fr29de98-42]

===

DEPARTMENT OF EDUCATION

[CFDA No. 84.120A]

Minority Science and Engineering Improvement Program

AGENCY: Department of Education.

ACTION: Notice inviting applications for new awards for fiscal year
1999 under the Minority Science and Engineering Improvement Program.

Purpose of Program

    The Minority Science and Engineering Improvement Program (MSEIP) is
designed to effect long-range improvement in science education at
predominantly minority institutions and to increase the flow of
underrepresented ethnic minorities, particularly minority women, into
scientific careers.

Eligibility for Grants

    With the October 7, 1998 enactment of the Higher Education
Amendments of 1998, Pub. L. 105-244, the criteria for eligibility for
grants under MSEIP were amended. Congress also relocated MSEIP from
Title X to Title III of the Higher Education Act of 1965 (HEA). Under
section 361 of the HEA, as now amended, eligibility for grants is now
defined as follows:
    Eligibility to receive grants under this part is limited to--
    (1) Public and private nonprofit institutions of higher education
that:
        (A) Award baccalaureate degrees; and
        (B) Are minority institutions;
    (2) Public or private nonprofit institutions of higher education
that:
        (A) Award associate degrees; and
        (B) Are minority institutions that:
        (i) Have a curriculum that includes science or engineering
subjects; and
        (ii) Enter into a partnership with public or private nonprofit
institutions of higher education that award baccalaureate degrees in
science and engineering;
    (3) Nonprofit science-oriented organizations, professional
scientific

[[Page 71626]]

societies, and institutions of higher education that award
baccalaureate degrees, that:
        (A) Provide a needed service to a group of minority institutions;
or
        (B) Provide in-service training for project directors, scientists,
and engineers from minority institutions; or
    (4) Consortia of organizations, that provide needed services to 1
or more minority institutions, the membership of which may include:
        (A) Institutions of higher education which have a curriculum in
science and engineering;
        (B) Institutions of higher education that have a graduate or
professional program in science or engineering;

http://frwebgate2.access.gpo.gov/cgi-bin/waisgate.cgi?WAISdocID=9975823185+0+0+0&WAISaction=retrieve 2/23/99

SAMPLE FEDERAL REGISTER NOTICE

EXHIBIT 9.8

(C) Research laboratories of, or under contract with, the Department of Energy;

(D) Private organizations that have science or engineering facilities; or

(E) Quasi-governmental entities that have a significant scientific or engineering mission.

Section 365(4) was also amended to include behavioral sciences in the definition of science programs that can be supported.

Deadline for Application Transmittal: March 5, 1999.

Applications Available: January 5, 1999.

Eligible Applicants: (a) For institutional, design, and special projects described in 34 CFR 637.14 (a), (b), and (c)--public and nonprofit private minority institutions as defined in section 361 (1) and (2) of the HEA.

(b) For special projects described in 34 CFR 637.14 (b) and (c)-- non-profit organizations, institutions, and consortia as defined in section 361 (3) and (4) of the HEA.

(c) For cooperative projects described in 34 CFR 637.15--groups of nonprofit accredited colleges and universities whose primary fiscal agent is an eligible minority institution as defined in 34 CFR 637.4(b).

Note: A minority institution is defined in 34 CFR 637.4(b) as an accredited college or university whose enrollment of a single minority group or combination of minority groups, as defined in 34 CFR 637.4(b), exceeds 50 percent of the total enrollment.

Estimated Range and Average Size of Awards: The amounts referenced below are advisory and represent the Department's best estimates at this time. The average size of an award is the estimate for a single-year project or for the first budget period of a multi-year project.

Institutional

    Estimated Range of Awards: $100,000-$200,000.
    Estimated Average Size of Awards: $120,000.
    Estimated Number of Awards: 22.

Design

    Estimated Range of Awards: $15,000-$20,000.
    Estimated Average Size of Awards: $18,000.
    Estimated Number of Awards: 4.

Special

    Estimated Range of Awards: $20,000-$150,000.
    Estimated Average Size of Awards: $25,000.
    Estimated Number of Awards: 11.

Cooperative

    Estimated Range of Awards: $20,000-$500,000.
    Estimated Average Size of Awards: $280,000.
    Estimated Number of Awards: 4.

Applicable Regulations

Regulations applicable to this program are (a) The Education Department General Administrative Regulations (EDGAR) in 34 CFR parts 74, 75, 77, 79, 83, 85, and 86; and (b) The regulations in 34 CFR part 637, except for 34 CFR 637.2 which has been superseded by section 361 of the HEA, as amended.

Note: The regulations in 34 CFR part 86 apply to institutions of higher education only.

Project Period: Up to 36 months.

For Application or Information Contact: Mr. Kenneth Waters or Ms. Deborah Newkirk, Institutional Development and Undergraduate Service, U.S. Department of Education, 600 Maryland Avenue, SW (Portals CY-80), Washington, DC 20202-5335. Telephone: 202/708-9926 or by Internet to deborah__newkirk@ed.gov. The government encourages applicants to FAX

SAMPLE FEDERAL REGISTER NOTICE (continued)

EXHBIT 9.8

WAIS Document Retrieval

requests for applications to 202/401-7532.
    Individuals who use a telecommunications device for the deaf (TDD)
may call the Federal Information Relay Service (FIRS) at 1-800/877-8339
between 8:00 a.m. and 8:00 p.m., Eastern Time, Monday through Friday.
    Individuals with disabilities may obtain this document in an
alternate format (e.g., Braille, large print, audiotape, or computer
diskette) on request to the contact person listed in the preceding
paragraph. However, the Department is not able to reproduce in an
alternate format the standard forms included in the application
package.

Electronic Access to This Document

    Anyone may view this document, as well as all other Department of
Education documents published in the Federal Register in text or
portable document format (pdf) on the World Wide Web at either of the
following sites:

http://ocfo.ed.gov/fedreg/htm
http://www.ed.gov/news.html

    To use the pdf you must have the Adobe Acrobat Reader Program with
Search, which is available free at either of the previous sites. If you
have questions about using the pdf, call the U.S. Government Printing
Office toll free at 1-888/293-6498.

Program Authority

    Sections 301 (a), (b), and 307 of the Higher Education Amendments
of 1998, Public Law 105-244, 112 Stat. 1581.

    Dated: December 22, 1998.
David A. Longanecker,
Assistant Secretary for Postsecondary Education.
[FR Doc. 98-34332 Filed 12-28-98; 8:45 am]
BILLING CODE 4000-01-P

SMALL *FEDERAL REGISTER* NOTICE *(continued)*

EXHBIT 9.8

Commerce Business Daily (CBD)

The *Commerce Business Daily* provides information regarding government procurement through contracts. Published daily Monday through Friday, *CBD* lists all available contracts in excess of $25,000. Thousands of separate contracting offices and countless grant programs advertise over billions in government contracts each year. The successful bidders are listed in the back section of each issue.

Many successful nonprofit organizations have used the list of successful bidders to develop subcontracts and form consortia. Through subcontracts and consortia, these organizations are able to build a track record and gain familiarity with both the contracts process and federal contract offices. The *CBD* also advertises notices of meetings that assist bidders in developing insight into upcoming contracts. To subscribe to the printed *Commerce Business Daily* contact Superintendent of Documents, P.O. Box 371954, Pittsburgh, PA 15250-7954, (202)512-1800, Fax (202)512-2250. Each congressional district has at least two libraries designated as federal depositories that receive the *CBD* daily at no charge. The *CBDNet* is the government's official free electronic version of *CBD*. *CBDNet* is provided through an alliance of the U.S.

Department of Commerce and U.S. Government Printing Office, and can be accessed at http://cbdnet.access.gpo.gov.

GRANTS DATABASES

Federal Assistance Programs Retrieval System—(FAPRS).

The Federal Assistance Programs Retrieval System (FAPRS) is an online, menu-drive system that offers complete text searching of the CFDA. FAPRS can be accessed through a personal computer with a Hayes-compatible modem and communications software. FAPRS is provided on a cost-reimbursable basis, and registration for online searching is required. Online searches of FAPRS also are performed by public access points. All states have designated access points where FAPRS searches may be requested. In addition, bulletins on FAPRS are available from the system to inform users of the addition or deletion of programs, changes to program numbers from one edition of the CFDA to the next, and enhancements and changes to the system. A packet of information which lists the public access points and describes the system is available from the Federal Domestic Assistance Catalog Staff at the General Services Administration, 300 7th St., SW, Ground Floor, Reporters Bldg., Washington, DC 20407, (202) 708-5126, http://www.gsa.gov/fdac. Your congressperson can also assist you in finding out where you can obtain an FAPRS search in your area.

GrantSelect

GrantSelect is a complete grants database available on the World Wide Web. Updated daily, it provides information on more than 10,000 funding programs available from over 3,400 federal, state, and local agencies; nonprofit organizations; foundations; and corporations in the U.S. and Canada. Grantseekers can subscribe to the entire research grants database or to any of five special segments: children and youth, health care and biomedical, arts and humanities, K-12 schools and adult basic education, and community development. The database also features an alert service that searches the database nightly and notifies the grantseeker via e-mail of any new funding opportunities within his or her area of interest. This service is available by itself or can be purchased with database access. *GrantSelect* has a flat fee, regardless of the size of purchasing institution. To preview excerpts from the *GrantSelect* database visit http://www.grantselect.com. For further information, call the Oryx Press at (800) 279-6799.

GrantScape CFDA

GrantScape CFDA is an electronic edition of the *Catalog of Federal Domestic Assistance* and includes the full text of all federal grant programs included in the CFDA. The material has been built into a special personal computer format called an information database or infobase. Users simply load the disks into their hard drives and search for the information. The database is available in Windows, Mac, or DOS. It can be purchased for a flat fee in either a single-user version or a multi-user version (up to 8 users). There are no fee-per-minute or additional charges. For more information contact Aspen Publishers, Inc. at (800)638-8437 or visit http://www.aspenpub.com.

Sponsored Programs Information Network (SPIN)

Originally developed by the Research Foundation of the State University of New York (SUNY), SPIN is a database that contains profiles on thousands of national and international funding opportunities from government and private sources. This fee-based system is used by over 700 institutions worldwide. Also available is SPIN.PLUS, which is composed of three modules: SPIN (funding opportunities database), GENIUS (searchable expertise profile system that currently contains faculty CVs and will eventually be expanded to contain facilities and institutional profiles), and SMARTS (a program that matches the profiles with the funding opportunities and delivers automatic daily updates). The SMARTS service is aimed at helping investigators keep current on new funding opportunities, new and approaching deadlines, and sponsor updates, and administrators on who is getting what "hits." Contact InfoEd International by calling (800)727-6427 or find out more about their products by visiting http://www.infoed.org/products.stm.

Illinois Researcher Information Service Database (IRIS)

Compiled by the University of Illinois at Urbana-Champaign, the IRIS database contains records on over 7,700 federal and nonfederal funding opportunities in the sciences, social sciences, arts, and humanities. The database is updated daily and is available in WWW and Telnet versions. It is available to colleges and universities for an annual subscription fee. The IRIS Alert Service and IRIS Expertise Service are also available. The alert service allows subscribers to create personal IRIS search profiles and receive funding alerts automatically. The expertise service enables users to create detailed electronic CVs and post them to the WWW for perusal by colleagues at other institutions, program officers at federal and private funding agencies, and technology transfer departments in private companies. You can arrange a free trial period for your institution, by contacting the IRIS office at (217)333-0284 or visiting http://www.library.uiuc.edu/iris/

Community of Science (COS)

The Community of Science (COS) is a global registry of information about scientists and the funding of science, and is designed to meet the needs of the research and development community. The COS system includes

- the COS *Expertise* database that connects academic and corporate researchers via the Internet
- the COS *Funding Alert* that provides the user with weekly e-mail updates concerning funding opportunities in the user's area of interest
- the COS *Funding Opportunities* database that includes sources of funding from government, foundations, corporations, and other organizations.

COS *Funding Opportunities* is included with fee-based membership in the Community of Science. Other institutions may purchase unlimited COS *Funding Opportunities* access for a fixed annual subscription fee. Subscription pricing is determined by the amount of external research funding your institution manages. To receive more information about the Community of Science and its products call (410)563-2378 or visit http://www.cos.com.

Federal Information Exchange Database (FEDIX)

FEDIX is a free online database of federal grant and research opportunities for the education and research communities. Other online services provided by the Federal Information Exchange in cooperation with the U.S. Department of Energy include the FEDIX *Opportunity Alert*, an e-mail alert service that allows users to automatically receive announcements of opportunities within their area of interest, and *MOLIS*, an online database of 164 minority institutions that can be used by federal agencies to identify peer reviewers and by majority institutions to identify possible collaborations and subcontracts. For more information visit the FEDIX home page at http://www.fie.com or call (800)875-2562.

FEDERAL AGENCY INTERNET MAILING LISTS

Several federal agencies have established Internet mailing lists to electronically disseminate news about their activities and services. You can subscribe to these listservs to help keep up to date on federal funding opportunities. The following is a list of some of the federal agencies that provide this type of service.

- National Science Foundation (NSF)—NSF has created the Custom News Service to provide you with a weekly summary of all new documents posted on the NSF Web site. It also has a personal profile component and an e-mail funding alert service. You can subscribe to the Custom News Service at http://www.nsf.gov/home/cns/start.htm.

- National Institute of Health (NIH)—National Institutes of Health will automatically send subscribers each issue of the *NIH Guide* or its table of contents. Listserv names are
  - NIHGDE-L—*NIH Guide to Grants and Contracts*
  - NIHTOC-L—Table of contents for *NIH Guide*. To subscribe, send the message *subscribe <list name> <your full name>* to listserv@list.nih.gov.
- Centers for Disease Control and Prevention (CDC)—At the Centers for Disease Control and Prevention (CDC), you can subscribe to several mailing lists, including CDC's *Morbidity and Mortality Weekly Report, Emerging Infectious Diseases, Vaccine R&D, and National Health Interview Survey.* To subscribe, complete the online form at http://www.cdc.gov/subscribe.html.
- U.S. Department of Justice (DOJ)—*JUST INFO*, sponsored by the U.S. Department of Justice National Criminal Justice Reference Service (NCJRS), is a biweekly e-mail newsletter that reports on a wide variety of criminal justice topics. To subscribe send the message *subscribe JUSTINFO <your full name>* to listproc@aspensys.com.
- U.S. Department of Education (DOE)—The Department of Education's *EDInfo* is an information service that delivers two or three e-mail messages a week featuring an education department report, initiative, or update. To subscribe send the message *subscribe EDINFO <your full name>* to listproc@inet.ed.gov.
- U.S. Agency for International Development (USAID)—The U.S. Agency for International Development will automatically send *Commerce Business Daily (CBD)* announcements via e-mail to subscribers to the USAID ListProcessor mail server. You can subscribe by sending the message *subscribe USAID-CBD-L <your full name>* to listproc@info.usaid.gov.
- National Institute for Standards and Technology (NIST)—*NIST Update* is a bimonthly report that highlights research activities, and services at the National Institute for Standards and Technology. To receive a copy of the report by e-mail send the message *subscribe nist_update <your full name>* to listproc@nist.gov.
- U.S. Department of Energy (DOE)—*ER News*, a bimonthly newsletter, covers information about research and technologies generated by the U.S. Department of Energy's Office of Energy Research. Users can receive an e-mail reminder and topic list when each new issue of *ER News* becomes available online. To subscribe send the message *subscribe ERNEWSLIST <your full name>* to listserv@listserv.pnl.gov.

- National Aeronautics and Space Administration—The National Aeronautics and Space Administration distributes its press releases and other selected documents via e-mail. To subscribe, send the message *subscribe press-release <your full name>* to domo@hq.nasa.gov.
- Administration for Children and Families (ACF)—The U.S. Department of Health and Human Services Administration for Children and Families (ACF) also maintains a press release mailing list. To subscribe, go to http://www/acf.dhhsgov/news/listmail.html and fill out the online form.

Accessing the information you need to locate available government funding is not difficult or expensive. While this chapter provides sufficient detail to satisfy the computer-literate grantseeker, such skills and equipment are not prerequisites for accessing information.

Whether you use the Internet, a commercial database, or hard copies of government publications, the key to locating federal grant funds and to commanding the respect of the funders you will interact with in your quest for grants is to do your homework and learn all you can about each program you are thinking about approaching.

CHAPTER 10

How to Contact Government Funding Sources

T he importance of pre-proposal contact with government funding sources cannot be overemphasized. In a study of 10,000 federal proposals, the only variable that was statistically significant in separating the funded and rejected proposals was pre-proposal contact with the funding source.

Chances for success increase an estimated threefold when contact with the funding source takes place before the proposal is written. Up to this point in the book, we have not discussed the writing of the proposal; instead, we have focused on efforts to get ready to seek support for your project. To write a winning proposal, you must know more about the funding source and its hidden agenda. Who will read your application? What will appeal to them? What should you avoid saying? To find the answers to these questions before you write your proposal, contact the funding source by letter, by e-mail, by phone, and, when possible and appropriate, in person.

WHEN TO MAKE PRE-PROPOSAL CONTACT

The timing of contact is critical. Each of the 1,300-plus federal programs has a unique sequence of events related to its granting cycle. Review the diagram of the federal grants clock whenever you need to determine where a particular federal agency or program is in the grants process (see figure 10.1).

The federal grants clock can be thought of as a five-step cycle or process.

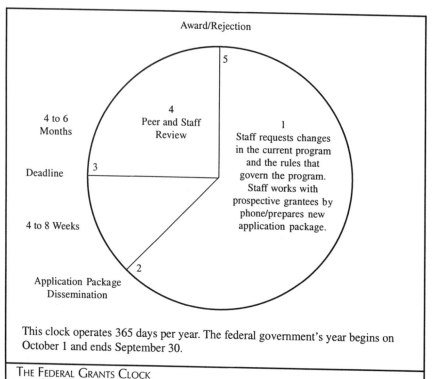

This clock operates 365 days per year. The federal government's year begins on October 1 and ends September 30.

THE FEDERAL GRANTS CLOCK

FIGURE 10.1

1. The first step involves the dissemination of and comment on the rules and regulations governing each program to be reviewed, and comments are encouraged from any interested party. The comments are published, the final rules are printed, and the announcements of deadlines are made in such publications as the *Federal Register,* the electronic *NIH Guide,* and *National Science Foundation E-Bulletin.*
2. The federal program officer then develops the actual application package and mails it to prospective grantees who have requested it. This package is referred to as the Request for Proposal (RFP) or the Request for Application (RFA).
3. The deadline for submission occurs.
4. Once proposals are submitted, they are sent to selected peer reviewers for evaluation. The reviewers must follow the agency's evaluation system and distribute points to each proposal according to the published guidelines.
5. The notices of award and rejection are made and the cycle starts again.

Establishing pre-proposal contact for the next funding cycle is most productive when initiated after the notices of award or rejection have been given (step 5) for the previous cycle and before the application packages are sent out (step 2) in the new cycle. Use the techniques outlined in this chapter to maximize the benefits of pre-proposal contact and gain the insight you will need to prepare a grant-winning proposal.

GETTING THE MOST FROM PAST GRANTEES

Use the sample letter in exhibit 10.1 to request a list of past grantees, guidelines, and an application package when it becomes available. You can either mail or e-mail the letter to the appropriate contact person. If mailing, enclose a return label or self-addressed stamped envelope with your letter for the funding source's convenience.

You may have to request the list of past grantees again by phoning the funding source. Access to this list and the valuable information it provides is your right. Let the funding source know you are aware that you are entitled to

---

Date

Name
Title
Address

Dear [Contact Person]:

I am interested in receiving information on [CFDA #, Program Title]. I am particularly interested in receiving application forms, program guidelines, and any materials you think would be helpful. Please include Web site information and Internet addresses for application forms that can be downloaded.

In order to increase my understanding of your program, I would appreciate a list of last year's grant recipients. If this list is available on the Internet, please provide the necessary instructions. If not, I have enclosed a label to assist you in forwarding the requested items. Thank you.

Sincerely,

Name/Title
Phone Number

SAMPLE LETTER TO A FEDERAL AGENCY REQUESTING INFORMATION AND GUIDELINES

EXHIBIT 10.1

this list under the Freedom of Information Act. If all else fails, you may be able to get this information from the pubic information office of the appropriate branch of government, or you can ask your congressperson to get the list for you. By law, federal bureaucrats have to respond to a congressperson's request. He or she *will* get the list. Be aware, though, that bureaucrats may react negatively to the intervention of elected officials.

Due to federal paperwork reduction guidelines, some agencies now require grantseekers who desire both information on past grantees and an application to send two separate request letters. Check with your selected grantor to determine whether you will automatically be placed on the mailing list to receive guidelines and an application or whether you need to make separate and continual requests.

With your past grantee list in hand, you are now ready to analyze your chances for success. Complete the federal funding source evaluation worksheet (exhibit 10.2) and analyze the information contained in the list of grantees.

---

1. Award Size

   • What was the largest award granted? $ _____
     For what type of project? _____

   • What was the smallest award granted? $ _____
     For what type of project? _____

   • Based on last year's grantees, what would be your project's likely award size? $ _____

2. Grantor Type

   • What characteristics or similarities can be drawn from last year's list of grant recipients?

   • What is the size or type of grantee organization?

   • What are the geographic preferences or concentrations?

3. Project Director/Principle Investigator

   • What titles or degrees appear most frequently on the list of last year's recipients?

   • Does there seem to be a relationship between award size and project director degree?

4. From the list of last year's grantees, select two to contact for more information. Select grantees that you may have a link with and/or organizations that you are familiar with.

5. Based on the information gathered in questions one through four, rate how well your proposal idea matches the prospective grantor's profile.

   ____ very well   ____ good   ____ fair   ____ not well

FEDERAL FUNDING SOURCE EVALUATION WORKSHEET

EXHIBIT 10.2

When this worksheet is completed, you will be able to approach the grantor with knowledge and insight into its granting program.

Contacting a Past Grantee

Successful grant recipients can be approached and will generally share helpful information with you. Grantees will often feel flattered that you called. They usually are not competing with you for funds because you will be seeking a first year of funding and they will be seeking a continuation grant. Select a past grantee to call. Choose one outside of your geographic area and one who is less likely to view you as a competitor. Tell the grantee how you got his or her name, congratulate him or her on the award, and then ask to speak to the person who worked on the proposal.

Select questions from the following list to ask the person who worked on the proposal, or ask any other questions that will help you learn more about the funding source.

- Did you call or go to see the funding source before writing the proposal?
- Whom did you find most helpful on the funding source's staff?
- How did you use your advocates or congressperson?
- Did the funding source review your idea or proposal before submission?
- Did you use consultants to help you on the proposal?
- Was there a hidden agenda to the program's guidelines?
- When did you begin the process of developing your application?
- When did you first contact the funding source?
- What materials did you find most helpful in developing your proposal?
- Did the funding source come to see you (site visit) before or after the proposal was awarded? Who came? What did they wear? How old were they? Would you characterize them as conservative, moderate, or liberal? Did anything surprise you during their visit?
- How close was your initial budget to the awarded amount? (You can check for honesty here by taking a look at the proposal when you visit the funding source. The Freedom of Information Act allows you to see any proposal funded by government money.)
- Who on the funding source's staff negotiated the budget?
- What would you do differently next time?

UNDERSTANDING THE PROPOSAL REVIEW PROCESS

To prepare the best possible proposal, you must know who will be reading it and how it will be reviewed. Request a list of last year's reviewers in writing, by phone, by e-mail, or in person. I suggest making a written request and then following up with the other methods if necessary. Exhibit 10.3 provides a sample letter you may use.

You want a list of last year's reviewers so you can write a proposal based on their expertise, reading level, biases, etc. Once you have the list, you can contact a reviewer to discuss the areas they look for when reviewing proposals.

Some federal programs use the same reviewers each year and may be reluctant to give you their names. If this is the case, tell the federal bureaucrat that you would like to know at least the general background and credentials of the reviewers so that you can prepare the best possible proposal by writing toward their level. You would ultimately like to know the types of organizations the reviewers come from, their titles and degrees, and, if possible, the selection criteria for choosing them. This may be a good opportunity to make your interest in becoming a reviewer known to the program officer. Whether the reviewers meet in Washington, DC, or review proposals at home, you would learn a great deal about the evaluation process and the grantor by being a member of a peer review committee.

Date

Name
Title
Address

Dear _____ :

I am presently developing a proposal under your _____ program. I would find it very helpful if you could send me a list of last year's reviewers and information on the makeup of this year's review committee.

The list of last year's reviewers and information on the composition of this year's committee will help me prepare a quality proposal based upon the level, expertise, and diversity of the reviewers.

I have enclosed a self-addressed stamped envelope for your convenience in responding to this request. I will use the materials you send, and I thank you for your consideration in providing them.

Sincerely,

Name
Title
Phone Number

SAMPLE LETTER TO A FEDERAL AGENCY FOR A LIST OF REVIEWERS

EXHIBIT 10.3

If the system that the reviewers must adhere to has been published in the *Federal Register* or an agency publication, request a copy or the date of publication. Let the funding source know that you will be using a quality circle to perform a mock review of your proposal before submission and that you would like to mirror the actual review process as closely as possible. Request a copy of their training materials or the scoring system that was used.

Contacting a Past Reviewer

As you examine the list of reviewers, look for any links you could use in contacting them. If none are apparent, select any reviewer to call. When calling a past reviewer, explain that you understand he or she was a reviewer for the program you are interested in and that you would like to ask a few questions about his or her experience as a reviewer for that program. Select a few questions to ask from the following list, or make up your own.

- How did you get to be a reviewer?
- Did you review proposals at a funding source location or at home?
- What training or instruction did the funding source give you?
- Did you follow a point system? What system? How did you follow it? What were you told to look for?
- How would you write a proposal differently now that you have been a reviewer?
- What were the most common mistakes you saw?
- Did you meet other reviewers?
- How many proposals were you given to read?
- How much time did you have to read them?
- How did the funding source handle discrepancies in point assignments?
- What did the staff members of the funding source wear, say, and do during the review process?
- Did a staff review follow your review?

TELEPHONING FEDERAL AND STATE FUNDING SOURCES

Calling public funding sources is an experience in itself. Initial research seldom yields the correct name and phone number of the best individual to handle your request, but at least it gives you a place to start. Once you have found a contact name and telephone number, call and ask who would be the best individual to help you. After several referrals, you should locate the office that administers the funds for the program you have uncovered in your research and the program officer. You could use the *United States Government Manual* or the *Federal Yellow Book* to track down the phone number of the office likely to handle the funds you are seeking.

After you have identified the program officer, the best approach is to go see him or her in person. If this is the approach you choose, use the techniques outlined in the following section on making an appointment with a public funding source official.

If you cannot visit the funding source, you should gather the same information over the phone that you would face-to-face. Since it may be difficult for the funding official to discuss your idea and approaches without seeing a written description of your project, ask whether you could mail, fax, or e-mail them a one-page concept paper. Set up a time for a return call and ask the same types of questions you would ask if you were meeting in person.

Although it may be difficult for you to "read" what the funding source is really saying through voice inflection, you must at least try to uncover any hidden agenda so that you can meet the grantor's needs and increase your chances of success. Review the list of questions in the "Questions to Ask a Program Officer" section of this chapter.

Making an Appointment with a Public Funding Source Official

The objective of seeking an appointment is to get an interview with an administrator of the program. Start by sending or e-mailing a letter requesting an appointment. Exhibit 10.4 provides a sample letter you may use. You will not get a response to this letter. Its intent is to show that you mean business. Then follow the next few steps.

1. Call and ask for the program officer or information contact.
2. Get the secretary's name and ask when his or her boss can be reached. (Some federal employees are on flextime or come in and leave at odd hours to cope with DC traffic.)
3. Call back. Try person-to-person, and, if that fails, ask the secretary whether anyone else can answer technical questions about the program. You may get an appointment with an individual whose job is to screen you from the boss, but this is still better than talking to yourself. As an alternative, try to get an advocate to help you set up an appointment, or try going in "cold" early in the week to set an appointment for later in the week. Do not be surprised if this results in an immediate appointment. Staff members may decide they would prefer to deal with you on the spot rather than later. Be careful using elected officials to make appointments for you or to accompany you on an appointment. Bureaucrats and politicians often do not get along well.
4. When you get the program person on the phone, introduce yourself and give a brief (10-word) description of your organization. Explain that

   • the need to deal with the specific problem your project addresses is extreme

- your organization is uniquely suited to deal with this problem
- you understand that the grantor's program deals with this need
- you would like to make an appointment to talk about program priorities and your approach

When you get an appointment, stop and hang up. If an appointment is not possible, tell the program representative that you have some questions and ask about the possibility of arranging a 10-minute phone call for the future. If a callback is not possible, ask whether he or she could take the time to answer your questions now. Fill in any information you get (names, phone numbers, and so on) on the federal grants research form (see chapter 9, exhibit 9.1).

VISITING PUBLIC FUNDING SOURCES

The initial meeting is vital to getting the input you need to prepare a proposal that is tailored to the funding source. A visit also will provide you with the opportunity to update any information you have gathered on the funding source through your research.

Date

Name
Title
Address

Dear [Contact Person]:

My research on your funding program indicates that a project we have developed would be appropriate for consideration by your agency for funding under _____.

I would appreciate 5 to 10 minutes of your time to discuss my project. Your insights, knowledge, and information on any grants that have been funded using a similar approach would be invaluable.

My travel plans call for me to be in your area on _____. I will phone to confirm the possibility of a brief meeting during that time to discuss this important proposal.

Sincerely,

Name
Title
Phone Number

SAMPLE LETTER TO A FEDERAL AGENCY REQUESTING AN APPOINTMENT

EXHIBIT 10.4

The objective of this pre-proposal visit is to find out as much as possible about the funding source and how it perceives its role in the awarding of grants. Then you can use the newly acquired information to produce a proposal that reflects a sensitivity to the funding source's needs and perception of its mission. According to the theory of cognitive dissonance, the more the funding source perceives a grantseeker as different from what the funding source expects, the greater the problems with communication, agreement, and acceptance. We want the funder to love us, so we need to produce as little dissonance as possible by looking and talking as the funder "thinks" we should. If you do not know the funding source's expectations on dress, play it safe and read the *New Dress for Success* by John T. Molloy (New York: Warner Books, 1988).

Plan for Your Visit

When planning for a personal visit, remember that it is better to send two people than one, and that an advocate, advisory committee member, or graduate of your program has more credibility than a paid staff member. In deciding whom to send, try to match the age, interests, and other characteristics of your people with any information you have on the funding official. Before the visit, role-play your presentation with your team members and decide who will take responsibility for various parts of the presentation.

What to Take

It may be helpful to bring the following items with you on the visit:

1. Materials that help demonstrate the need for your project.
2. Your proposal development workbook (Swiss cheese book).
3. Audiovisual aids that document the need, such as pictures or a brief (three- to five-minute) filmstrip, videotape, slide presentation, or cassette tape. Be sure you can operate all equipment with ease, and know how to replace bulbs. Bring extension cords, three-prong-to-two-prong plug adapters, and whatever other peripheral equipment you may need.
4. Information on your organization that you can leave with the funding official (but never leave a proposal).

Questions to Ask a Program Officer

Review the following list of possible questions to ask a program officer:

- Do you agree that the need addressed by our project is important?
- Your average award in this area last year to an organization like ours was $_____? Do you expect that to change?

- How will successful grantees from last year affect the chances for new or first applicants? Will last year's grantees compete with new grantees, or have their funds been set aside? If their funds have been set aside, how much is left for new awards?
- Are there any unannounced program or unsolicited proposal funds in your agency to support an important project like ours?
- The required matching portion is___percent. Would it improve our chances for funding if we provided a greater portion than this?
- If no match is required, would it help our proposal if we volunteered to cost share?
- What is the most common mistake or flaw in the proposals you receive?
- Are there any areas you would like to see addressed in a proposal that may have been overlooked by other grantees or applicants?
- We have developed several approaches to this needs area. You may know whether one of our approaches has already been tried. Could you review our concept paper and give us any guidance?
- Would you review or critique our proposal if we got it to you early?
- Would you recommend a previously funded proposal for us to read for format and style? (Remember, you are entitled to see funded proposals, but be cool.)
- What changes do you expect in type or number of awards this year (for example, fewer new awards versus continuing awards)?
- Is there a relationship between the type of project or proposal and the amount awarded? Is there a sequence or progression in the type of grant awarded? For example, do you have to get a consultant grant before you can receive a demonstration grant or an evaluation grant? Is there a hidden agenda?
- Is it okay to use tabs or dividers in my proposal?
- The guidelines call for___copies of the proposal. Could you use more? (New guidelines on paperwork reduction sometimes restrict the number of proposal copies an agency can require, but the agency may really need more copies and will be pleased if you volunteer to send extras.)

Immediately after your visit, record any information you have gathered about the funder on the funding source staff profile (exhibit 10.5). Record the results of your visit on the public funding source contact summary sheet (exhibit 10.6).

Before each visit to a funding source, review this sheet to be sure you are taking the correct materials, advocates, and staff.

Agency Director: _____ E-mail _____
Program Director: _____ E-mail _____
Contact Person: _____ E-mail _____

Profile: Birth date: _____ Birthplace: _____

Education: College: _____
                 Postgraduate: _____
Work Experience: _____
Military Service: _____
Service Clubs: _____
Religious Affiliations: _____
Interests/Hobbies: _____
Publications: _____
Comments: _____

Note: Do not ask the staff person direct questions related to these areas. Instead, record information that has been volunteered or gathered from comments or observations made in the office.

FUNDING SOURCE STAFF PROFILE

EXHIBIT 10.5

Project Title: _____

Add to this sheet each time you contact a public funding source.

Agency Name: _____
Program Officer: _____
Contacted On (Date): _____
By Whom: _____
Contacted By: Letter _____ Phone _____ Fax _____ E-mail _____
                 Personal Visit _____
Staff or Advocate Present: _____
Discussed: _____
_____
_____

Results: _____
_____
_____

PUBLIC FUNDING SOURCE CONTACT SUMMARY SHEET

EXHIBIT 10.6

MAKING YOUR DECISION TO DEVELOP A PROPOSAL

So far you have not invested a tremendous amount of time in writing your proposal. You have taken time to gather data and contact potential grantors. Now you must decide which federal grant program you will apply to.

Your best prospect is the grant program that provides the closest match between the program you want to implement, your nonprofit organization, and the profile you have developed of the grantor. Seldom is there a perfect fit between your project and the grantor's program, and some tailoring and changes in your program will likely add to your chances of success. Use the tailoring worksheet (exhibit 10.7) to analyze each grant program you are interested in and to select your first choice.

Federal Program: _____   Prospect Rating: _____
                                     Amount Requested: _____
                                     ___ Percent Match/In-kind: _____

1. How does your grant request match with the average award size to your:
    • type of organization _____
    • size of organization _____
    • location of organization _____
    • proposal focus _____
2. What was the number of applications received versus the number of grants awarded in your area of interest?
    • applications received _____
    • grants awarded _____
3. How would you rate the funding staff's interest in your concept?
    • very interested _____
    • interested _____
    • not interested _____
    • unknown _____
4. From the information you obtained on the reviewers and the review process, what should your writing strategy include? _____

5. Based on the information you obtained on the review process, how will points be distributed in the funding source's evaluation process?

         Area   *Point Value*

    _____   ____
    _____   ____
    _____   ____

TAILORING WORKSHEET

EXHIBIT 10.7

CHAPTER 11

Planning the Successful Federal Proposal

E ach federal agency has its own proposal format to which applicants must adhere. If you have been successful in obtaining a copy of a previously funded proposal, you have a quality example of what the funding source expects. After reading exemplary proposals for 30 years, I have learned that really excellent proposals do stand out. One does not have to be an expert in a proposal's particular area of interest to determine whether the proposal is good. The required components or sections of each type of proposal—a research proposal or a good proposal for a demonstration or model project—are remarkably similar. In general, federal applications include sections on

- documentation of need: to demonstrate that you have a command of the relevant literature in the field
- what you propose to study, change, or test: for a research project, the hypothesis and specific aims; for a model project, the measurable objectives
- proposed intervention: what you will do and why you have selected these methods or activities
- budget: the cost of the project broken down by category of expenditure
- evaluation: how you will establish the levels of change that constitute success and demonstrate that your intervention worked
- grantee credibility: unique qualities and capabilities that you possess and believe are relevant to support and complete the project

Most federal grantors will also require or expect a summary or abstract, a title, an agreement to comply with federal assurances, and attachment of pertinent materials that the reviewer may want to refer to while evaluating the proposal. Sections on future funding and dissemination of the research findings or model may also be included.

While the inclusion of these general components seems logical, the differences in terminology, space restrictions, and order or sequence from one federal application to another can be very perplexing. The novice grantseeker frequently asks why there is not a standard federal grant application form for all programs. It seems that this would make sense, but due to the variety of federal programs and the deep-seated conviction that each area of interest is distinct, this type of standardization will probably never happen. The point is that you must follow each agency's format exactly, make no changes and no omissions, and give each agency what it calls for, not just what you want to give.

Each federal agency has its own preferences concerning the components and the order. What is similar from agency to agency is that in one way or another, the grantseeker proposal must establish that he/she has a project that needs to be carried out in order to advance the field of research or service. Chapter 12 on conducting a quality circle or proposal improvement exercise will deal in more detail with the federal agencies' systems for evaluating and scoring proposals, including how the different sections of the proposal compare in terms of importance in the final decision. When applying to a specific agency, it is expected that you will procure a copy of the desired proposal format and develop specific insights into the agency's scoring system and an idea of what an outstanding proposal looks like.

Work through this chapter and collect the materials suggested. Then develop or rearrange your proposal in the format and order you discover is most likely to meet with success.

DOCUMENTATION OF NEED

Most grantseekers begin their proposal with *what* they propose or want to do. It is much better to begin by focusing on *why* there is a need to do anything at all, including your proposed intervention. To gain the reviewer's respect, you must show that you are knowledgeable about the need in a particular area. Your goal in this section of the proposal is to use articles, studies, and statistics to demonstrate a compelling reason or motivation to deal with the problem now.

The grantor invariably must choose which proposals to fund this year and which to reject or put on hold; therefore, you must demonstrate the urgency to close the gap between what exists now and what ought to be in your special field (see figure 11.1). Your proposed project will seek to close or reduce this gap.

THE GAP

What exists now. What is real.   What could be. The goal.
What the present situation is.   ——————   The desired state of affairs,
                                                   level of achievement.

THE GAP DIAGRAM

FIGURE 11.1

In a research proposal, need documentation involves a search of relevant literature in the field. The point of the literature search is to document that there is a gap in knowledge in a particular area. Currently in the scientific community it is necessary to enhance the motivation of the reviewer to fund your research project by suggesting the value of closing the gap, in monetary terms or in terms of increased knowledge.

In proposals for model projects and demonstration grants, this section is referred to as the needs statement or need documentation. To be successful in grantseeking, you must produce a clear, compelling picture of the current situation and the desired state. Grantors are "buying" a changed or better state of affairs.

Creating a sense of urgency depends on how well you document the need. Since not all proposals can be funded, you must make the funding source believe that movement toward the desired state cannot wait any longer. Those proposals that do not get funded did not do as good a job of

- documenting a real need (perceived as important)
- demonstrating what ought to be (for clients)
- creating the urgent need to close the gap by demonstrating that each day the need is not addressed the problem grows worse or that there is unnecessary suffering, confusion, and/or wasted efforts

Documenting What Is

Use the following steps to document a need in a model or demonstration grant:

1. Review the section on performing a needs survey (chapter 2) to assess whether any of the methods described could help document the need.
2. Use statistics from articles and research (e.g., "Approximately ___ women in the United States were murdered by their husbands or boyfriends last year.").

3. Use quotes from leaders or experts in the field (e.g., "Dr. Flockmeister said children who are raised in a family with spouse abuse have a ___ percent chance of being abused or of abusing their partners.").

4. Use case statements (e.g., "John Quek, a typical client of the Family Outreach Center, was abused as a child and witnessed his mother and aunt being abused.").

5. Describe a national need and reduce it to a local number that is more understandable (e.g., "It is estimated that ___ percent of teenagers are abused by their boyfriend or girlfriend by the time they reach age 17; this means that at the West Side High School ___ seniors in the graduating class may have already experienced abuse.").

6. State the need in terms of one person (e.g., "The abused spouse generally has . . .").

7. Use statements from community people such as police, politicians, and clergy.

When documenting what exists in a research grant, include

1. The latest studies, research articles, and presentations to demonstrate your currency in the field.

2. Studies that demonstrate the scope and sequence of work in the field and its current state, and the necessity to answer your proposed research question before the field can move ahead.

3. A thorough literature search that does not focus only on the researcher or data that reinforces your research position. Show how the diversity or conflict in the field reinforces the need to search an answer to your question.

4. A logical flow of reference to the literature. The flow may consist of a chronological and conceptual documentation that builds to the decision to fund your work. Remember, the literature search should not be a comprehensive treatise in the field that includes references to every contributor, but rather a convincing documentation of significant works.

Demonstrating What Ought to Be

To establish what ought to be, proven statistics may be difficult or impossible to find. Using experts' statements and quotes to document what ought to be is much more credible than using your opinion. Do not put your opinion in the needs statement. In this section you are demonstrating your knowledge of the field and showing that you have surveyed the literature.

Stay away from terms that point to a poorly documented needs statement. They include the words *many* and *most* and expressions like *a great number* and *everyone knows the need for.* Make sure your needs statement does not include any of these types of words or expressions.

It is relatively easy to say what ought to be in areas such as family violence or drug abuse, but more difficult when dealing with bench research. However, it is still important to demonstrate the possible uses your research could be related to even if you are working in the hard sciences. Documenting the other side of the gap is a necessity if you want to close the gap of ignorance in your field.

Creating a Sense of Urgency

The needs section should motivate the prospective funding source. One way to do this is to use the funding source's own studies, surveys, or statistics. The same basic proposal can be tailored to two different funding sources by quoting different studies that appeal to each source's own view of the need. By appealing to the views of individual sources, you will appear to be the logical choice to close the gap and move toward reducing the problem.

If the proposal format required by the funding source does not have a section that deals with your capabilities, the end of the needs statement is the best place to put your credentials. To make a smooth transition from the need to your capabilities:

- state that it is the mission of your organization to deal with this problem.
- summarize the unique qualities of your organization that make it best suited for the job. For example, your organization has the staff or facilities to make the project work.
- capitalize on the similarities you share with other organizations. For instance, "Our project will serve as a model to the other agencies that face this dilemma each day." Such statements will help the prospective grantor realize that the results of your project could affect many.
- emphasize that the needs are urgent and that each day they go unmet the problem grows. For example, "Each year that teacher education colleges put off comprehensive computer education, a new group of teachers with limited computer skills enter our schools and the problem grows."

WHAT YOU PROPOSE TO STUDY OR CHANGE

Objectives outline the steps you propose to take to narrow or close the gap created in the needs statement. Objectives follow the needs statement because they cannot be written until the need has been documented.

Since the accomplishment or attainment of each objective will help to close the gap, you must write objectives that are measurable and can be evaluated. It is critical to be able to determine the degree to which the objectives have been attained and, thus demonstrate the amount of the gap that has been closed.

Grantseekers preparing research proposals should note that the objective of a research proposal is to close the gap of ignorance.

Government grantors have been putting increasing pressure on researchers to explain how their research can be used on a very practical level. Philosophical (and the author's) arguments aside, there are conservative elements that want a component of even basic research grants to deal with such issues as dissemination of results and how findings can be applied to benefit the general public.

Objectives versus Methods

Objectives tell the grantseeker and the funding source what will be accomplished by this expenditure of funds and how the change will be measured. *Methods* state the means to the end or change. They tell how you will accomplish the desired change. Naturally, the ability to accomplish an objective depends on the methods or activities chosen.

When in doubt as to whether you have written an objective or a method, ask yourself whether there is only one way to accomplish what you have written. If your answer is yes, you have probably written a method. For example, once a participant at one of my seminars told me that his objective was to build a visitor's center for his organization's museum. When asked why he wanted to build a visitor's center, he responded, "To help visitors understand the relationship between the museum buildings so that they can more effectively use the museum." Once he stated this out loud, he realized that his objective was really the effective utilization of the museums and that building a visitors' center was just one method for accomplishing this objective. In other words, building the visitors' center was a means to an end, just one way that my seminar participant could attempt to accomplish his objective. In fact, the reason a funding source might give money to support his project would be to help people use and appreciate the museum, not to build the visitors' center. The bricks and mortar that make up the visitors' center simply do not lend themselves to the kind of measurement that the issue of effective utilization does.

The following is a technique for writing objectives:

1. Determine result areas. Result areas are the key places you will look for improvement or change in the client population. Examples include the health of people over 65 years of age in St. Louis, better educated minority students, and more efficient use of a museum.
2. Determine measurement indicators. Measurement indicators are the quantifiable parts of your result areas. By measuring your performance with these indicators, you will be able to determine how well you are doing. Examples include the number of hospital readmissions of people over 65 years old, scores on standardized tests, and the number of people

who understand the relationship between museum buildings. Brainstorm a number of measurement indicators for each of your result areas, and then select the ones that reflect your intent and are the least difficult to use.

3. Determine performance standards. Performance standards answer the question "how much (or how little) of a change do we need to consider ourselves successful?" Using our above example, we might determine the following performance standards: a 10 percent drop in hospital readmissions, scores rising from the 80th to the 90th percentile on the Flockmann reading scale, or a 50 percent reduction in direction giving by museum staff.

4. Determine the time frame. The time frame is the amount of time in which you want to reach your performance standards. It is *your* deadline. You might decide you want to see a 10 percent drop in hospital readmissions within 6 or 18 months. Usually, this time frame is determined for you by the funding source. Most grants are for 12 months. In setting your deadlines, use months 1 through 12 instead of January, February, and so on because you seldom will start the grant when you expect to.

5. Determine cost frame. This is the cost of the methods or activities you have selected to meet your objectives. (This cost estimate can be obtained retrospectively from the project planner, the document you will fill out next.)

6. Write the objective. This step combines the data you have generated in the previous five steps. The standard format for an objective is: "To [action verb and statement reflecting your measurement indicator] by [performance standard] by [deadline] at a cost of no more than [cost frame]." The example concerning reading might look like this: "To increase the reading scores of freshmen in Flockmann University's Minority Skills Program from the 80th to the 90th percentile on the Flockmann reading scale in 12 months at a cost of $50,000."

7. Evaluate the objective. Review your objective and answer the question "Does this objective reflect the amount of change we want in the result area?" If your answer is yes, you probably have a workable objective. If your answer is no, chances are that your measurement indicator is wrong or your performance standards are too low. Go back to steps two and three and repeat the process.

When writing program objectives, you should follow the same seven steps.

Again, remember to emphasize end results, not tasks or methods. Do not describe how you are going to do something; instead, emphasize what you will accomplish and the ultimate benefit of your program's work.

In a research proposal, the section on what the researcher proposes to study or change is referred to as the research question and hypothesis to be tested.

The development of research proposals follows an analogous route to model and demonstration grants. There must be a clearly defined problem, question, or gap to be addressed.

Researchers are inoculated with the same virus that all grantseekers share—the "why virus." (Why does this happen? What can be we do to change it?) The researcher asks a question and then must search the literature in the field to determine what is already known and who would care if the question was answered. (What is the value or benefit? Who would value the closing of the gap?) For example, the question of whether treatment X or Y influences the healing time of a pressure sore (bedsore) is subject to a search of the literature to see what work has already been done in this area and to determine the importance of the question. (What exists now? What is the incidence or extent of the problem, and the future impact of not addressing the question?) If there is no compelling or motivating reason to use grant monies to answer the question, the researcher is not likely to be successful.

The research question must be specific and focused. Many researchers are overly optimistic and select too broad a question or too many questions to investigate. This sets them up for failure because they cannot control the situation. In other words, they have too many forces or variables to deal with that can influence the outcome.

Researchers must develop their questions into either a null hypothesis or an alternative hypothesis The null hypothesis predicts that there is no basic difference between the two selected areas. For example, "There is no difference between pressure sores treated with X or Y." The researcher sets up the study to measure the outcome, or the *dependent* variable (increased healing of pressure sores). The researcher manipulates or changes the intervention, or the *independent* variable (use of treatment X or Y), to observe the effect of the two treatments on the depending variable. Just as behavioral objectives contain a measurement indicator for success (increasing reading scores from the 80th to the 90th percentile as measured by the Flockmann reading scale), the researcher must select a statistical evaluation mode, before data are collected, that will be used to evaluate the differences in the intervention. When there are significant differences between two treatments, the null hypothesis is disproved and the results are based on differences in treatment rather than on chance.

The alternative hypothesis predicts that there is indeed a difference between the two treatments and suggests the direction of that difference. For example, "Treatment X will result in a healing rate that is 50 percent faster than treatment Y."

PROPOSED INTERVENTION

The methods, activities, or protocol section is the detailed description of the
steps you will take to meet the objectives. Methods identify

- what will be done
- who will do it
- how long it will take
- the materials and equipment needed

The protocol of a research proposal details how each experiment or trial will
be carried out.

The methods or protocols are all a function of what you set out to accomplish. The best order to follow is to write your objectives first and then develop
your methods to meet them. In making up a realistic estimate of your project
costs, avoid inflating your budget. Instead, consider adding several more
methods to this section than absolutely necessary to ensure that your objectives
are met. When you negotiate the final award, you will gain much more
credibility with the funding source by eliminating methods instead of lowering
the price for the same amount of work.

Historically, final awards for research proposals were arrived at in a manner
much different from that for model project proposals. Notification of a research
award was frequently followed by a letter that included a dollar amount
significantly less than what was applied for, and there was little or no opportunity for negotiation. Criticism of this practice led many major grantors to
announce that the methods for both types of proposals should be cost analyzed
and negotiated. Now both demonstration and research proposals must include
an estimate of the cost of each method or activity and must show each activity's
effect of the outcome.

Your methods section should

- describe your program activities in detail and demonstrate how they
  will fulfill your objectives or research study
- describe the sequence, flow, and interrelationship of the activities
- describe the planned staffing for your program and designate who is
  responsible for which activities
- describe your client population and method for determining client
  selection
- state a specific time frame
- present a reasonable scope of activities that can be accomplished
  within the stated time frame with your organization's resources
- refer to the cost-benefit ratio of your project
- include a discussion of risk (why success is probable)
- describe the uniqueness of your methods and overall project design

The project planner (see exhibit 11.1) provides you with a format to ensure that your methods section reflects a well-conceived and well-designed plan for the accomplishment of your objectives.

The Project Planner

An outcome of my 30 years of work in grant and contract preparation, the project planner is a spreadsheet-based planning tool designed to assist you in several important ways. It will help you

- develop your budget by having you clearly define which project personnel will perform each activity for a given time frame, with the corresponding consultant services, supplies, materials, and equipment
- defend your budget on an activity-by-activity basis so that you can successfully negotiate your final award
- project a monthly and quarterly cash forecast for year one, year two, and year three of your proposed project
- identify matching or in-kind contributions

The Project Planner will also help you develop job descriptions for each individual involved in the project and a budget narrative or written explanation documenting your planned expenses. Several federal granting agencies have been criticized for not negotiating final awards with grantees. Their practice has been to provide grantees with a statement of the final award with no reference or discussion of how the award differs from the amount budgeted in the application or how the reduction will affect the methods and outcome. As more importance is placed on budget negotiation and the planning of project years, the more valuable the project planner will become.

You will find the following explanations of each project planner column helpful as you review the blank project planner in exhibit 11.1 and the sample project planner in exhibit 11.2.

1. Project objectives or outcomes (column A/B): List your objectives or outcomes as A, B, C, and so on. Use the terms the prospective grantor wants. For example, grantors may refer to the objectives as major tasks, enabling objectives, or specific aims.
2. Methods (column A/B): Also in the first column, list the methods or protocol necessary to meet the objectives or outcomes as A-1, A-2, B-1, B-2, C-1, C-2, and so on. These are the tasks you have decided upon as your approach to meeting the need.
3. Month (column C/D): Record the dates you will begin and end each activity in this column.
4. Time (column E): Designate the number of person-weeks (you can use hours or months) needed to accomplish each task.

PROJECT PLANNER

PROJECT TITLE: _____

A. List Project objectives or outcomes A. B. B. List Methods to accomplish each objective as A-1, A-2, A-3 . . . B-1, B-2 . . .	MONTH		TIME	PROJECT PERSONNEL	PERSONNEL COSTS		
	BEGIN	END			SALARIES & WAGES	FRINGE BENEFITS	TOTAL
	C / D		E	F	G	H	I

© David G. Bauer Associates, Inc.
(800) 836-0732

TOTAL DIRECT COSTS OR COSTS REQUESTED FROM FUNDER ▶

MATCHING FUNDS, IN-KIND CONTRIBUTIONS, OR DONATED COSTS ▶

TOTAL COSTS ▶

THE PROJECT PLANNER

EXHIBIT 11.1

Sheet _____ of _____

Proposal Developed for _____

PROJECT DIRECTOR: _____ Proposed starting date _____ Proposed Year _____

CONSULTANTS • CONTRACT SERVICES			NON-PERSONNEL RESOURCES NEEDED SUPPLIES • EQUIPMENT • MATERIALS				SUB-TOTAL COST FOR ACTIVITY	MILESTONES PROGRESS INDICATORS	
TIME	COST/WEEK	TOTAL	ITEM	COST/ITEM	QUANTITY	TOT. COST	TOTAL I. L. P	ITEM	DATE
J	K	L	M	N	O	P	Q	R	S
								T	◄ % OF TOTAL
									◄
								100%	◄

THE PROJECT PLANNER (continued)

EXHIBIT 11.1

PROJECT PLANNER™

SAMPLE PROJECT PLANNER

PROJECT TITLE: A Contract for Educational Cooperation – Parents Teachers & Students Charting a Course for Involvement

A. List Project objectives or outcomes A. B. B. List Methods to accomplish each objective as A-1, A-2, A-3 … B-1, B-2 …	MONTH BEGIN / END (C/O)	TIME (E)	PROJECT PERSONNEL (F)	PERSONNEL COSTS		
				SALARIES & WAGES (G)	FRINGE BENEFITS (H)	TOTAL (I)
Objective A: Increase Educational Cooperation of Teachers, Parent & Students 25% as Measured on the Educational Practices Survey in 12 Months at a Cost of $ 88,705						
A-1 Develop the Responsible Educational Practices Survey with the Advisory Committee	1/2	4	Proj. Dir.PD Smith 2 Grad students (GS)	West	State	U.
a. Write questions and develop a scale of responsibility for parents, teachers & students						
A-2 Administer the Survey to the Target Population	2/3	4	2 GS	''	''	''
a. Develop procedure		4	PD	''	''	''
b. Get human subjects approval thru West State University						
c. Graduate students to administer survey		4	2 GS	''	''	''
d. Input survey data		*4	Sec'y	800	160	*960
e. Develop results		1	PD	West	State	U.
A-3 Develop Curriculum	3/6					
a. Review results of pre-test given to parents, students & teachers		1	PD	''	''	''
b. Develop a curriculum on responsibility concepts in education for each group (includes workbook & video on each area of curriculum)		5	PD	''	''	''
		*8	Sec'y	1600	320	*1920
		8	Senior High Club–Using Video Facility	Video Jones	Corp.	
• responsible use of time						
• homework responsibility						
• communication skills						
• developing contract for change						
A-4 Promote & Carry Out Program	6/12	24	PD	West	State	U.
a. Use advisory group to announce program		24	Sec'y	4800	960	*5760
b. Public service spots on radio and television						
c. Develop and send home a program						
d. Schedule meetings with parents						
e. Develop a student video						

© David G. Bauer Associates, Inc.
(800) 836-0732

TOTAL DIRECT COSTS OR COSTS REQUESTED FROM FUNDER ▶	0
MATCHING FUNDS, IN-KIND CONTRIBUTIONS, OR DONATED COSTS ▶	8640
TOTAL COSTS ▶	8640

SAMPLE PROJECT PLANNER

EXHIBIT 11.2

Sheet 1 of 1

Proposal Developed for _____

PROJECT DIRECTOR: __D. Smith__ ___ Proposed starting date _____ Proposed Year _____

CONSULTANTS • CONTRACT SERVICES			NON-PERSONNEL RESOURCES NEEDED SUPPLIES • EQUIPMENT • MATERIALS				SUB-TOTAL COST FOR ACTIVITY	MILESTONES PROGRESS INDICATORS	
TIME	COST/WEEK	TOTAL	ITEM	COST/ITEM	QUANTITY	TOT. COST	TOTAL I. L. P	ITEM	DATE
J	K	L	M	N	O	P	Q	R	S
2	1000	2000	micro/word perfect			2500			
2	500	1000	printer/modem			175			
			phone expense			150			
4	500	2000							
4	1000	4000							
4	500	2000	travel allowance			800			
			modem/phone expense			150			
1	1000	1000	micro processor			---			
1	1000	1000							
5	1000	5000	layout & print			1250			
			workbooks	10	200	2000*			
			blank tapes	2	20	40			
			video studio	5000	5hrs	25000*			
			camera edit						
			character generation						
			video camera	1000	6	6000*			
		42000				5065	47065т	53% ◄ % OF TOTAL	
		0				33000	41640	47% ◄	
		42000				38065	88705	100% ◄	

SAMPLE PROJECT PLANNER (continued)

EXHIBIT 11.2

5. Project personnel (column F): List the key personnel who will spend measurable or significant amounts of time on this activity and the accomplishments of this objective or specific aim. The designation of key personnel is critical for developing a job description for each individual. If you list the activities for which the key personnel are responsible, and the minimum qualifications or background required, you will have a rough job description. Call a placement agency to get an estimate of the salary needed to fill the position. The number of weeks or months will determine full or part-time classification.

   This column gives you the opportunity to look at how many hours of work you are providing in a given time span. If you have your key personnel working more than 160 hours per month, it may be necessary to adjust the number of weeks in Column E to fit a more reasonable time frame. For example, you may have to reschedule activities or shift responsibility to another staff member.

6. Personnel costs (columns G, H, I): List the salaries, wages and fringe benefits for all personnel. Special care should be taken in analyzing staff donated from your organization. The donation of personnel may be a requirement for your grant or a gesture you make to show your good faith and appear as a better investment to the funding source. If you do make matching or in-kind contributions, place an asterisk by the name of each person you donate to the project. Be sure to include your donation of fringes as well as wages. As you complete the remaining columns, put an asterisk by anything else that will be donated to the project.

7. Consultants and contract services (columns J, K, L): These three columns are for the services that are most cost-efficiently supplied by individuals who are not in your normal employ. They may be experts at a skill you need that does not warrant your training a staff member or hiring an additional staff person (evaluation, computers, commercial art, etc.). There are no fringes paid to consultants or contract service providers.

8. Nonpersonnel resources needed (columns M, N, O, P): List the components that are necessary to complete each activity and achieve your objective, including supplies, equipment, and materials. Many a grantseeker has gone wrong by underestimating the nonpersonnel resources needed to successfully complete a project. Most grantseekers lose out on many donated or matching items because they do not ask themselves what they really need to complete each activity. Travel, supplies, and telephone communications are some of the more commonly donated items.

   Equipment requests can be handled in many ways. One approach is to place total equipment items as they are called for in your plan under

Column M (item) and to complete the corresponding columns appropriately—cost per item (column N), quantity (column O), and total cost (Column P). However, this approach may cause problems in the negotiation of your final award. The grantor may suggest lowering the grant amount by the elimination of an equipment item that appears as though it is related to the accomplishment of only one activity, when in actuality you plan to utilize it in several subsequent activities.

Therefore, I suggest that if you plan to list the total cost of equipment needed in your work plan next to one particular activity, designate a percentage of usage to that activity and reference the other activities that will require the equipment. This way you will show 100-percent usage and be able to defend the inclusion of the equipment in your budget request.

In some cases, you may choose to allocate the percentage of the cost of the equipment with the percentage of use for each activity. If you allocate cost of equipment to each activity, remember that if you drop an activity in negotiation you may not have all the funds you need to purchase the equipment.

9. Subtotal cost for activity (column Q): This column can be completed in two ways. Each activity can be subtotaled, or you can subtotal several activities under each objective or specific aim.
10. Milestones, progress indicators (columns R, S): Column R should be used to record what the funding source will receive as indicators that you are working toward the accomplishment of your objectives. Use Column S to list the date on which the funding source will receive the milestone or progress indicator.

Please note that you might want to develop a computer-generated spreadsheet version of the project planner so that your objectives or other information could be easily added, deleted, or changed. This would be especially useful when the grant amount awarded is less than the amount requested, because you could experiment with possible changes without too much trouble.

Indirect Costs

An aspect of federal grants that is critically important yet poorly understood by many grantseekers and other individuals connected with grants is the concept of indirect costs. Indirect costs involve repaying the recipient of a federal grant for costs that are difficult to break down individually but are indirectly attributable to performing the federal grant. These costs include such things as

- heat and lights
- building upkeep
- maintenance staff
- payroll personnel

Indirect costs are calculated by using a formula that is provided by the Federal Regional Controller's Office and are expressed as a percentage of the total amount requested from the funding source (total from Column Q of your project planner), or as a percentage of the personnel costs (total from Column I of your project planner).

Recent developments in the area of indirect costs have led the federal government to strictly enforce the definition of costs eligible for reimbursement under a grant's direct expenditures versus those eligible under its indirect expenditures. Under the Office of Management and Budget's new guidelines, costs related to the handling of increased payroll or purchase orders are already covered under indirect costs. Therefore, any added personnel that fall under the category of secretarial support are not eligible. All personnel in your grant should have a special designation, showing that their duties are not secretarial but rather extraordinary and thus eligible to be funded under the grant.

Budget

While preparing the budget may be traumatic for unorganized grantseekers, you can see that the project planner contains all the information you need to forecast your financial needs accurately. No matter what budget format you use, the information you need to construct your budget lies in your project planner. The project planner, however, is not the budget; it is the analysis of what will have to be done and the estimated costs and time frame for each activity.

In most government proposal formats, the budget section is not located near the methods section. Government funders do not understand why you want to talk about your methods when you talk about money. As you know, the budget is a result of what you plan to do. If the money you request is reduced, you know you must cut your project's methods. Draw the public funding source back into your project planner so that they too can see what will be missing as a result of a budget cut. If you must cut so many methods that you can no longer be sure of accomplishing your objectives, consider refusing the funds or reducing the amount of change (reduction of the need) outlined in your objectives when negotiating the amount of your award. The sample budget in exhibit 11.3 is provided for your review.

If you are required to provide a quarterly cash forecast, use the grants office time line in exhibit 11.4. The project activities/methods (A-1, A-2, B-1, B-2) from your project planner should be listed in the first column. The numbered columns across the top of the time line indicate the months of the duration of the project. Use a line bar to indicate when each activity/method begins and ends. Place the estimated cost per method in the far-right column. Use a triangle to indicate where milestones and progress indicators are to occur (taken from Columns R and S of your project planner). By totaling costs by

PROJECT NAME:
Nutrition Education for Disadvantaged Mothers through Teleconferencing

	Expenditure Total	Donated/ In-Kind	Requested from This Source
	$134,239	$73,113	$61,126

I. PERSONNEL

A. Salaries, Wages

	Expenditure Total	Donated/ In-Kind	Requested from This Source
Project Director @ $2,200/mo. x 12 mos. x 50% time	13,200	13,200	
Administrative Assistant @ $1,600/mo. x 12 mos. x 100% time	19,200		19,200
Secretary @ $1,200/mo. x 12 mos. x 100% time	14,400		14,400
Volunteer Time @ $5.00 x 10 mos. x 400 hours	24,000	24,000	

B. Fringe Benefits

	Expenditure Total	Donated/ In-Kind	Requested from This Source
Unemployment Insurance (3% of first $10,800 of each salary)	1,386	396	990
FICA (7.65% of first $60,600 of each employee salary)	3,580	1,010	2,570
Health Insurance ($150/mo. per employee x 12 mos.)	5,400	1,800	3,600
Workmen's Compensation (1% of salaries paid — $46,800)	468	132	336

C. Consultants/Contracted Services

	Expenditure Total	Donated/ In-Kind	Requested from This Source
Copy Editor ($200/day x 5)	1,000		1,000
PR Advisor ($200/day x 10)	2,000		2,000
Accounting Services ($250/day x 12)	3,000	3,000	
Legal Services ($500/day x 6)	3,000	3,000	
Personnel Subtotal	$90,634	$46,538	$44,096

II. NONPERSONNEL

A. Space Costs

	Expenditure Total	Donated/ In-Kind	Requested from This Source
Rent ($1.50/sq. ft. x 400 sq. ft. x 12 mos.)	7,200	7,200	
Utilities ($75/mo. x 12 mos.)	900	900	

B. Equipment

	Expenditure Total	Donated/ In-Kind	Requested from This Source
Desk ($275 x 1)	275		275
Computer, Printer, Copy Machine Rental ($300/mo. x 12 mos.)	3,600		3,600
Office Chairs (3 x $50)	150		150
File Cabinets (3 x $125)	375	375	

A SAMPLE PROJECT BUDGET

EXHIBIT 11.3

PROJECT NAME: Nutrition Education for Disadvantaged Mothers through Teleconferencing	Expenditure Total	Donated/ In-Kind	Requested from This Source
	$126,075	$60,470	$65,605
II. NONPERSONNEL (continued)			
B. Equipment (continued)			
Electronic Blackboard & Misc. Equip. for Teleconferencing	7,200		7,200
C. Supplies (Consumables)			
(3 employees x $200/yr.)	600	600	
D. Travel			
Local			
Project Director (29¢/mile x 500 miles/mo. x 12 mos.)	1,740		1,740
Administrative Assistant (29¢/mile x 750 miles/mo. x 12 mos.)	2,610		2,610
Out-of-Town			
Project Director to Nutrition Conference in St. Louis, MO			
Airfare	450		450
Per Diem ($75/day x 3)	225		225
Hotel ($100/nt. x 3)	300		300
E. Telephone			
Installation ($100/line x 3)	300	300	
Monthly Charges ($25/ line x 3 lines x 12 mos.)	900	900	
Long Distance ($40/ mo. x 12 mos.)	480		480
F. Other Nonpersonnel Costs			
Printing (30¢ x 25,000 brochures)	7,500	7,500	
Postage (34¢ x 25,000)	8,500	8,500	
Insurance ($25/mo. x 12 mos.)	300	300	
Nonpersonnel Subtotal	$43,605	$26,575	$17,030
Personnel Subtotal	$90,634	$46,538	$44,094
Project Total	$134,239	$73,113	$61,126
Percentage	100%	54%	46%

A Sample Project Budget (continued)

EXHIBIT 11.3

GRANTS OFFICE TIME LINE

ACTIV- ITY NO.	1	2	3	4	5	6	7	8	9	10	11	12	TOTAL COST FOR ACTIVITY

1st QUARTER	2nd QUARTER	3rd QUARTER	4th QUARTER	TOTAL

QUARTERLY FORECAST OF EXPENDITURES ▲

GRANTS OFFICE TIME LINE

EXHIBIT 11.4

quarter, you can develop a quarterly forecast of expenditures. Complete a separate grants office time line and project planner for each year of a continuation grant or multiyear award.

One of the more common federal budget forms for nonconstruction projects is Standard Form (SF) 424A (see exhibit 11.5). The instructions for completing SF-424A are shown in exhibit 11.6. As with other budget forms, if you have completed a project planner, you already have all the information you need to complete SF-424A.

Many grantors also require that you submit a narrative statement of your budget, explaining the basis for your inclusion of personnel, consultants, supplies, and equipment. This is known as a budget narrative. Again, your completed project planner will help you construct the budget narrative and explain the sequence of steps. The budget narrative gives you the opportunity to present the rationale for each step, piece of equipment, and key person that your proposal calls for.

EVALUATION

Federal and state funding sources generally place a much heavier emphasis on evaluation than most private sources do. While there are many books written on evaluation, the best advice is to have an expert handle it. I suggest enlisting the services of a professional at a college or university who has experience in evaluation. Professors will generally enjoy the involvement and the extra pay and can lead you to a storehouse of inexpensive labor—undergraduate and graduate students. A graduate student in statistics can help you deal with the problem of quantifying your results inexpensively, while he or she gathers valuable insight and experience.

Irrespective of who designs your evaluation, writing your objectives properly will make the process much simpler. Most grantseekers have little problem developing objectives that deal with cognitive areas or areas that provide for results that can be easily qualified. The problems start when they move into the affective domain, because values, feelings, and appreciation can be difficult to measure.

If you use the techniques presented in this chapter for writing objectives and ask yourself what your client population will do differently after the grant, you should be able to keep yourself on track and develop an evaluation design that will pass even the most critical federal and state standards. For example, a grant to increase appreciation for opera could be measured by seeing how many of the subjects attend an inexpensive performance after the free ones are completed.

BUDGET INFORMATION – Non-Construction Programs

OMB Approval No. 0348-0044

SECTION A - BUDGET SUMMARY

Grant Program Function or Activity (a)	Catalog of Federal Domestic Assistance Number (b)	Estimated Unobligated Funds		New or Revised Budget		
		Federal (c)	Non-Federal (d)	Federal (e)	Non-Federal (f)	Total (g)
1.		$	$	$	$	$
2.						
3.						
4.						
5. Totals		$	$	$	$	$

SECTION B - BUDGET CATEGORIES

6. Object Class Categories	GRANT PROGRAM, FUNCTION OR ACTIVITY				Total
	(1)	(2)	(3)	(4)	(5)
a. Personnel	$	$	$	$	$
b. Fringe Benefits					
c. Travel					
d. Equipment					
e. Supplies					
f. Contractual					
g. Construction					
h. Other					
i. Total Direct Charges (sum of 6a-6h)					
j. Indirect Charges					
k. TOTALS (sum of 6i and 6j)	$	$	$	$	$
7. Program Income	$	$	$	$	$

STANDARD FORM (SF) 424A

EXHIBIT 11.5

BUDGET INFORMATION

SECTION A -

Grant Program Function or Activity (a)	Catalog of Federal Domestic Assistance Number (b)	Estimated Unobligated	
		Federal (c)	No
1.		$	$
2.			
3.			
4.			
5. Totals		$	$

SECTION B -

6. Object Class Categories	GRA	
	(1)	(2)
a. Personnel	$	$
b. Fringe Benefits		
c. Travel		
d. Equipment		
e. Supplies		
f. Contractual		
g. Construction		
h. Other		
i. Total Direct Charges *(sum of 6a-6h)*		
j. Indirect Charges		
k. TOTALS *(sum of 6i and 6j)*	$	$
7. Program Income	$	$

STANDARD FORM (SF) 424A *(detail)*

EXHIBIT 11.5

I - Non-Construction Programs

OMB Approval No. 0348-0044

BUDGET SUMMARY

Funds	New or Revised Budget		
n-Federal (d)	Federal (e)	Non-Federal (f)	Total (g)
	$	$	$
	$	$	$

BUDGET CATEGORIES

NT PROGRAM, FUNCTION OR ACTIVITY		Total
(3)	(4)	(5)
$	$	$
$	$	$
$	$	$

STANDARD FORM (SF) 424A *(detail)*

EXHIBIT 11.5

SECTION C - NON-FEDERAL RESOURCES				
(a) Grant Program	(b) Applicant	(c) State	(d) Other Sources	(e) TOTALS
8.	$	$	$	$
9.				
10.				
11.				
12. TOTAL (sum of lines 8-11)	$	$	$	$

SECTION D - FORECASTED CASH NEEDS

	Total for 1st Year	1st Quarter	2nd Quarter	3rd Quarter	4th Quarter
13. Federal	$	$	$	$	$
14. Non-Federal					
15. TOTAL (sum of lines 13 and 14)	$	$	$	$	$

SECTION E - BUDGET ESTIMATES OF FEDERAL FUNDS NEEDED FOR BALANCE OF THE PROJECT

(a) Grant Program	FUTURE FUNDING PERIODS (Years)			
	(b) First	(c) Second	(d) Third	(e) Fourth
16.	$	$	$	$
17.				
18.				
19.				
20. TOTAL (sum of lines 16-19)	$	$	$	$

SECTION F - OTHER BUDGET INFORMATION

21. Direct Charges:	22. Indirect Charges:

23. Remarks:

Authorized for Local Reproduction   Standard Form 424A (Rev. 7-97) Page 2

STANDARD FORM (SF) 424A (continued)

EXHIBIT 11.5

SECTION C - NON-FEDER		
(a) Grant Program		(b) Applican
8.		$
9.		
10.		
11.		
12. TOTAL *(sum of lines 8-11)*		$

SECTION D - FORECAST		
	Total for 1st Year	1st Quarte
13. Federal	$	$
14. Non-Federal		
15. TOTAL *(sum of lines 13 and 14)*	$	$

SECTION E - BUDGET ESTIMATES OF FEDERAL FUN	
(a) Grant Program	
	(b) First
16.	$
17.	
18.	
19.	
20. TOTAL *(sum of lines 16-19)*	$

SECTION F - OTHER BUDG	
21. Direct Charges:	22. Ir
23. Remarks:	

Authorized for Local I

STANDARD FORM (SF) 424A *(detail)*

EXHIBIT 11.5

RAL RESOURCES

nt	(c) State	(d) Other Sources	(e) TOTALS
	$	$	$
	$	$	$

ED CASH NEEDS

er	2nd Quarter	3rd Quarter	4th Quarter
	$	$	$
	$	$	$

DS NEEDED FOR BALANCE OF THE PROJECT

	FUTURE FUNDING PERIODS (Years)		
	(c) Second	(d) Third	(e) Fourth
	$	$	$
	$	$	$

ET INFORMATION

ndirect Charges:

Reproduction   Standard Form 424A (Rev. 7-97) Page 2

STANDARD FORM (SF) 424A *(detail)*

EXHIBIT 11.5

INSTRUCTIONS FOR THE SF-424A

Public reporting burden for this collection of information is estimated to average 180 minutes per response, including time for reviewing instructions, searching existing data sources, gathering and maintaining the data needed, and completing and reviewing the collection of information. Send comments regarding the burden estimate or any other aspect of this collection of information, including suggestions for reducing this burden, to the Office of Management and Budget, Paperwork Reduction Project (0348-0044), Washington, DC 20503.

PLEASE DO NOT RETURN YOUR COMPLETED FORM TO THE OFFICE OF MANAGEMENT AND BUDGET. SEND IT TO THE ADDRESS PROVIDED BY THE SPONSORING AGENCY.

General Instructions

This form is designed so that application can be made for funds from one or more grant programs. In preparing the budget, adhere to any existing Federal grantor agency guidelines which prescribe how and whether budgeted amounts should be separately shown for different functions or activities within the program. For some programs, grantor agencies may require budgets to be separately shown by function or activity. For other programs, grantor agencies may require a breakdown by function or activity. Sections A, B, C, and D should include budget estimates for the whole project except when applying for assistance which requires Federal authorization in annual or other funding period increments. In the latter case, Sections A, B, C, and D should provide the budget for the first budget period (usually a year) and Section E should present the need for Federal assistance in the subsequent budget periods. All applications should contain a breakdown by the object class categories shown in Lines a-k of Section B.

Section A. Budget Summary Lines 1-4 Columns (a) and (b)

For applications pertaining to a *single* Federal grant program (Federal Domestic Assistance Catalog number) and *not requiring* a functional or activity breakdown, enter on Line 1 under Column (a) the Catalog program title and the Catalog number in Column (b).

For applications pertaining to a *single* program *requiring* budget amounts by multiple functions or activities, enter the name of each activity or function on each line in Column (a), and enter the Catalog number in Column (b). For applications pertaining to multiple programs where none of the programs require a breakdown by function or activity, enter the Catalog program title on each line in *Column* (a) and the respective Catalog number on each line in Column (b).

For applications pertaining to *multiple* programs where one or more programs *require* a breakdown by function or activity, prepare a separate sheet for each program requiring breakdown. Additional sheets should be used when one form does not provide adequate space for all breakdown of data required. However, when more than one sheet is used, the first page should provide the summary totals by programs.

Lines 1-4, Columns (c) through (g)

For new applications, leave Column (c) and (d) blank. For each line entry in Columns (a) and (b), enter in Columns (e), (f), and (g) the appropriate amounts of funds needed to support the project for the first funding period (usually a year).

For continuing grant program applications, submit these forms before the end of each funding period as required by the grantor agency. Enter in Columns (c) and (d) the estimated amounts of funds which will remain unobligated at the end of the grant funding period only if the Federal grantor agency instructions provide for this. Otherwise, leave these columns blank. Enter in columns (e) and (f) the amounts of funds needed for the upcoming period. The amount(s) in Column (g) should be the sum of amounts in Columns (e) and (f).

For supplemental grants and changes to existing grants, do not use Columns (c) and (d). Enter in Column (e) the amount of the increase or decrease of Federal funds and enter in Column (f) the amount of the increase or decrease of non-Federal funds. In Column (g) enter the new total budgeted amount (Federal and non-Federal) which includes the total previous authorized budgeted amounts plus or minus, as appropriate, the amounts shown in Columns (e) and (f). The amount(s) in Column (g) should not equal the sum of amounts in Columns (e) and (f).

Line 5 - Show the totals for all columns used.

Section B Budget Categories

In the column headings (1) through (4), enter the titles of the same programs, functions, and activities shown on Lines 1-4, Column (a), Section A. When additional sheets are prepared for Section A, provide similar column headings on each sheet. For each program, function or activity, fill in the total requirements for funds (both Federal and non-Federal) by object class categories.

Line 6a-i - Show the totals of Lines 6a to 6h in each column.

Line 6j - Show the amount of indirect cost.

Line 6k - Enter the total of amounts on Lines 6i and 6j. For all applications for new grants and continuation grants the total amount in column (5), Line 6k, should be the same as the total amount shown in Section A, Column (g), Line 5. For supplemental grants and changes to grants, the total amount of the increase or decrease as shown in Columns (1)-(4), Line 6k should be the same as the sum of the amounts in Section A, Columns (e) and (f) on Line 5.

Line 7 - Enter the estimated amount of income, if any, expected to be generated from this project. Do not add or subtract this amount from the total project amount. Show under the program

SF-424A (Rev. 7-97) Page 3

INSTRUCTIONS FOR COMPLETING STANDARD FORM (SF) 424A

EXHIBIT 11.6

narrative statement the nature and source of income. The estimated amount of program income may be considered by the Federal grantor agency in determining the total amount of the grant.

Section C. Non-Federal Resources

Lines 8-11 Enter amounts of non-Federal resources that will be used on the grant. If in-kind contributions are included, provide a brief explanation on a separate sheet.

> **Column (a)** - Enter the program titles identical to Column (a), Section A. A breakdown by function or activity is not necessary.
>
> **Column (b)** - Enter the contribution to be made by the applicant.
>
> **Column (c)** - Enter the amount of the State's cash and in-kind contribution if the applicant is not a State or State agency. Applicants which are a State or State agencies should leave this column blank.
>
> **Column (d)** - Enter the amount of cash and in-kind contributions to be made from all other sources.
>
> **Column (e)** - Enter totals of Columns (b), (c), and (d).

Line 12 - Enter the total for each of Columns (b)-(e). The amount in Column (e) should be equal to the amount on Line 5, Column (f), Section A.

Section D. Forecasted Cash Needs

Line 13 - Enter the amount of cash needed by quarter from the grantor agency during the first year.

Line 14 - Enter the amount of cash from all other sources needed by quarter during the first year.

Line 15 - Enter the totals of amounts on Lines 13 and 14.

Section E. Budget Estimates of Federal Funds Needed for Balance of the Project

Lines 16-19 - Enter in Column (a) the same grant program titles shown in Column (a), Section A. A breakdown by function or activity is not necessary. For new applications and continuation grant applications, enter in the proper columns amounts of Federal funds which will be needed to complete the program or project over the succeeding funding periods (usually in years). This section need not be completed for revisions (amendments, changes, or supplements) to funds for the current year of existing grants.

If more than four lines are needed to list the program titles, submit additional schedules as necessary.

Line 20 - Enter the total for each of the Columns (b)-(e). When additional schedules are prepared for this Section, annotate accordingly and show the overall totals on this line.

Section F. Other Budget Information

Line 21 - Use this space to explain amounts for individual direct object class cost categories that may appear to be out of the ordinary or to explain the details as required by the Federal grantor agency.

Line 22 - Enter the type of indirect rate (provisional, predetermined, final or fixed) that will be in effect during the funding period, the estimated amount of the base to which the rate is applied, and the total indirect expense.

Line 23 - Provide any other explanations or comments deemed necessary.

INSTRUCTIONS FOR COMPLETING STANDARD FORM (SF) 424A *(continued)*

EXHIBIT 11.6

THE SUMMARY OR ABSTRACT

The summary or abstract is written after the proposal is completed. After the title, the summary is the second most often read part of a proposal. The summary must be succinct and motivating so the reader (reviewer) does not lose interest.

The summary is a much-abbreviated version of your proposal and should contain a concise description of the need for your project, your project's goals or hypothesis, objectives or specific aims, approach or protocol, and evaluation design. You can determine which of these components to emphasize in your summary or abstract by reviewing the point or evaluation system the funding source will apply. Use your summary or abstract to show readers that they will find what they want in your proposal.

Many funding sources have explicit requirements concerning the summary or abstract. Some designate the space and number of words or characters that can be used, while others require potential grantees to underline a certain number of key words or phrases. Be sure to verify the rules before constructing this critical part of your proposal.

TITLE PAGE

Federal granting programs have a required face sheet or title page that must be attached to federal grant applications or proposals. The most common is Standard Form (SF) 424 (exhibit 11.7; instructions for completing the form are included in exhibit 11.8). Remember, you are dealing with a bureaucracy and, therefore, should double-check all requirements and make sure all necessary forms are completed per instructions.

The title of a proposal is very important. It is the first part of your proposal to be read by reviewers, and, if it's not good, it may be the only part read! Take the time to develop a title that ensures your proposal will get attention.

The title of your proposal should

- describe your project
- express your project's end results, not methods
- describe your project's benefits to clients
- be short and easy to remember

The best titles are like newspaper titles, descriptive and to the point. Titles that try to entice the reader by giving only part of the story seldom work.

Do not use biblical characters or Greek gods in your proposal title since you cannot be sure that the funding source will be familiar with your reference. For example, calling your solar energy project "Apollo's Flame" could work to your disadvantage if the reviewer does not know who Apollo is or fails to make the connection.

Acronyms should be used only if the funding source has a preference for them. Trying to develop a title that describes the benefits of your project is difficult enough without trying to use specific words that will result in a catchy acronym.

Since you have written the proposal, it is easy for you to develop tunnel vision and attribute more meaning to the words in the title than a person reading it for the first time would. To make sure this does not happen, read your title to other people who know little or nothing about your proposal and then ask them what they think the proposal is about based on the title. You may find that you are not the best person to write the title. Have friends read the proposal and ask them for title suggestions.

Titles can vary in length and can be up to 10–13 words. Some federal programs have rules on the number of characters or spaces used in a title. Check the rules.

APPLICATION FOR FEDERAL ASSISTANCE

OMB Approval No. 0348-0043

2. DATE SUBMITTED	Applicant Identifier

1. TYPE OF SUBMISSION:

Application
- [ ] Construction
- [ ] Non-Construction

Preapplication
- [ ] Construction
- [ ] Non-Construction

3. DATE RECEIVED BY STATE	State Application Identifier
4. DATE RECEIVED BY FEDERAL AGENCY	Federal Identifier

5. APPLICANT INFORMATION

Legal Name:

Organizational Unit:

Address (give city, county, State, and zip code):

Name and telephone number of person to be contacted on matters involving this application (give area code)

6. EMPLOYER IDENTIFICATION NUMBER (EIN):

☐☐ - ☐☐☐☐☐☐☐

7. TYPE OF APPLICANT: (enter appropriate letter in box) ☐

A. State
B. County
C. Municipal
D. Township
E. Interstate
F. Intermunicipal
G. Special District

H. Independent School Dist.
I. State Controlled Institution of Higher Learning
J. Private University
K. Indian Tribe
L. Individual
M. Profit Organization
N. Other (Specify) _____

8. TYPE OF APPLICATION:

- [ ] New [ ] Continuation [ ] Revision

If Revision, enter appropriate letter(s) in box(es) ☐ ☐

A. Increase Award   B. Decrease Award   C. Increase Duration
D. Decrease Duration   Other(specify):

_____

9. NAME OF FEDERAL AGENCY:

10. CATALOG OF FEDERAL DOMESTIC ASSISTANCE NUMBER:

☐☐ - ☐☐☐

TITLE:

11. DESCRIPTIVE TITLE OF APPLICANT'S PROJECT:

12. AREAS AFFECTED BY PROJECT (Cities, Counties, States, etc.):

13. PROPOSED PROJECT | **14. CONGRESSIONAL DISTRICTS OF:**

Start Date	Ending Date	a. Applicant	b. Project

15. ESTIMATED FUNDING:

a. Federal	$	.00
b. Applicant	$	.00
c. State	$	.00
d. Local	$	.00
e. Other	$	.00
f. Program Income	$	.00
g. TOTAL	$	.00

16. IS APPLICATION SUBJECT TO REVIEW BY STATE EXECUTIVE ORDER 12372 PROCESS?

a. YES. THIS PREAPPLICATION/APPLICATION WAS MADE AVAILABLE TO THE STATE EXECUTIVE ORDER 12372 PROCESS FOR REVIEW ON:

DATE _____

b. No. ☐ PROGRAM IS NOT COVERED BY E. O. 12372
☐ OR PROGRAM HAS NOT BEEN SELECTED BY STATE FOR REVIEW

17. IS THE APPLICANT DELINQUENT ON ANY FEDERAL DEBT?

☐ Yes   If "Yes," attach an explanation.   ☐ No

18. TO THE BEST OF MY KNOWLEDGE AND BELIEF, ALL DATA IN THIS APPLICATION/PREAPPLICATION ARE TRUE AND CORRECT, THE DOCUMENT HAS BEEN DULY AUTHORIZED BY THE GOVERNING BODY OF THE APPLICANT AND THE APPLICANT WILL COMPLY WITH THE ATTACHED ASSURANCES IF THE ASSISTANCE IS AWARDED.

a. Type Name of Authorized Representative	b. Title	c. Telephone Number
d. Signature of Authorized Representative		e. Date Signed

Previous Edition Usable
Authorized for Local Reproduction

Standard Form 424 (Rev. 7-97)
Prescribed by OMB Circular A-102

STANDARD FORM (SF) 424

EXHIBIT 11.7

INSTRUCTIONS FOR THE SF-424

Public reporting burden for this collection of information is estimated to average 45 minutes per response, including time for reviewing instructions, searching existing data sources, gathering and maintaining the data needed, and completing and reviewing the collection of information. Send comments regarding the burden estimate or any other aspect of this collection of information, including suggestions for reducing this burden, to the Office of Management and Budget, Paperwork Reduction Project (0348-0043), Washington, DC 20503.

PLEASE DO NOT RETURN YOUR COMPLETED FORM TO THE OFFICE OF MANAGEMENT AND BUDGET. SEND IT TO THE ADDRESS PROVIDED BY THE SPONSORING AGENCY.

This is a standard form used by applicants as a required facesheet for preapplications and applications submitted for Federal assistance. It will be used by Federal agencies to obtain applicant certification that States which have established a review and comment procedure in response to Executive Order 12372 and have selected the program to be included in their process, have been given an opportunity to review the applicant's submission.

Item:	Entry:
1.	Self-explanatory.
2.	Date application submitted to Federal agency (or State if applicable) and applicant's control number (if applicable).
3.	State use only (if applicable).
4.	If this application is to continue or revise an existing award, enter present Federal identifier number. If for a new project, leave blank.
5.	Legal name of applicant, name of primary organizational unit which will undertake the assistance activity, complete address of the applicant, and name and telephone number of the person to contact on matters related to this application.
6.	Enter Employer Identification Number (EIN) as assigned by the Internal Revenue Service.
7.	Enter the appropriate letter in the space provided.
8.	Check appropriate box and enter appropriate letter(s) in the space(s) provided:

  -- "New" means a new assistance award.

  -- "Continuation" means an extension for an additional funding/budget period for a project with a projected completion date.

  -- "Revision" means any change in the Federal Government's financial obligation or contingent liability from an existing obligation.

9.	Name of Federal agency from which assistance is being requested with this application.
10.	Use the Catalog of Federal Domestic Assistance number and title of the program under which assistance is requested.
11.	Enter a brief descriptive title of the project. If more than one program is involved, you should append an explanation on a separate sheet. If appropriate (e.g., construction or real property projects), attach a map showing project location. For preapplications, use a separate sheet to provide a summary description of this project.

Item:	Entry:
12.	List only the largest political entities affected (e.g., State, counties, cities).
13.	Self-explanatory.
14.	List the applicant's Congressional District and any District(s) affected by the program or project.
15.	Amount requested or to be contributed during the first funding/budget period by each contributor. Value of in-kind contributions should be included on appropriate lines as applicable. If the action will result in a dollar change to an existing award, indicate *only* the amount of the change. For decreases, enclose the amounts in parentheses. If both basic and supplemental amounts are included, show breakdown on an attached sheet. For multiple program funding, use totals and show breakdown using same categories as item 15.
16.	Applicants should contact the State Single Point of Contact (SPOC) for Federal Executive Order 12372 to determine whether the application is subject to the State intergovernmental review process.
17.	This question applies to the applicant organization, not the person who signs as the authorized representative. Categories of debt include delinquent audit disallowances, loans and taxes.
18.	To be signed by the authorized representative of the applicant. A copy of the governing body's authorization for you to sign this application as official representative must be on file in the applicant's office. (Certain Federal agencies may require that this authorization be submitted as part of the application.)

SF-424 (Rev. 7-97) Back

INSTRUCTIONS FOR COMPLETING STANDARD FORM (SF) 424

EXHIBIT 11.8

The key to writing a good title is to ask funding officials what they prefer and to examine a list of titles used by past grantees. This will give you a more accurate idea of what the funding source really likes.

FUTURE FUNDING

Most funding sources are buying a piece of the future. It is in their best interest to see any project they fund continue. This way, they are able to take credit for the project and its benefits over a greater length of time. Unfortunately, many grantseekers ignore the funding sources' need to keep their investment alive and neglect to mention a future financing plan in their proposal. If you cannot think of ways to finance your project after your federal grant funds run out, think again. Perhaps you could continue your project through

- service fees
- membership fees
- support from agencies like the United Way
- big gift campaigns aimed at wealthy individuals
- an endowment program
- foundation and corporate grants
- a direct-mail campaign
- other fund-raising mechanisms

Include the cost of one or more of these activities in your expenses, and budget them in the grant. You are not automatically considered an ingrate for doing this; rather, you may come across as a good executor of the funding source's estate. You are planning for continuation.

DISSEMINATION

In addition to the good that will come from meeting the objectives and closing the gap established in your needs statement, much good can come from letting others know what you and the funding source have accomplished. Others in your field will come to know your name and ask you to enter into consortia with them. In addition, other funding sources will solicit your application.

You can disseminate the results of your grant by

- mailing a final report, quarterly journal, or a newsletter to others in your field
- sponsoring a seminar or conference on the topic
- attending a national or international conference to deliver the results of the project (many government funding officials cannot travel to conferences, but they can fund you to go and disseminate the results)
- producing a film or slide/tape presentation of the project

Activities aimed at disseminating project results are viewed positively by most funding sources. In general, they want their name up in lights and are willing to pay for it. So, build the costs related to dissemination into your budget.

ATTACHMENTS (APPENDIX)

The attachments can provide the "winning edge" when your proposal is compared to a competitor's. Throughout the proposal development process, you should be gathering materials that could be used in the attachment section of your proposal. Your final task is to select which materials to include. Naturally, you want to choose those that will best support your proposal and build credibility. Whether the funding source skims over them or examines them in detail, attachments may include

- studies or research, tables, and graphs
- vitae of key personnel
- minutes of advisory committee meetings
- list of board members
- auditor's report or statement
- letters of recommendation or endorsement
- copy of your IRS tax-exempt designation
- pictures or architect's drawings
- copies of your agency's publications
- list of other funding sources you will approach for support

Check funding source rules to determine how long your attachments section can be. Guidelines may state that the attachments can be up to twice as long as the proposal. Also check funding source rules for the appropriate appendix format. Provide a separate table of contents for your appendix, and number the pages for easy reference.

WRITING YOUR FEDERAL OR STATE PROPOSAL

Your proposal must reflect what the funding source wants and what the reviewers will be looking for. In general

- follow the guidelines exactly (even when they seem senseless)
- fill in all the blanks
- double-check all computations
- include anything the funding source asks for, even if you think you already provided the information under another section of your proposal

When writing your proposal, keep in mind that it must be readable and easy to skim. Place special emphasis on vocabulary, style, and visual attractiveness.

Vocabulary

Your contact with a past reviewer will have given you an idea of the reviewers' level of expertise and their depth of knowledge in your subject area. Be sure your proposal uses language appropriate to the reviewers. Shorter words are generally better than long, complex words, and avoid buzzwords unless you are sure the reviewer expects them. Define all acronyms.

Writing Style

By now you should know the background of the typical reviewer selected by the grantor agency and how much time the reviewers spend reading each proposal. These peer reviewers are under pressure to use their time efficiently, so you must produce a proposal that is poignant, yet organized and easy to read.

- Use simple sentences (no more than two commas) and short paragraphs (five to seven lines).
- Begin each section with a strong motivating "lead" sentence.
- Make sure your writing style cannot be construed as cute or offensive to the reader. Avoid stating the obvious and talking down to the reviewer.
- Develop a "user-friendly" proposal. One of the peer reviewers may be chosen to defend your proposal to the rest of the review panel. In this case, you want to be certain to make the reviewer your friend by organizing and referencing attachments in such a way that they can be used to mount a good defense and to answer the other panelists' questions.

Visual Attractiveness

Even scientific research need not look boring to the reviewer. To enhance the "readability" of your proposal and make your points stand out use

- underlining
- bullets
- different type faces
- various margins and spacing
- bold headings
- pictures
- charts and graphs
- handwriting

While you must follow the grantor's rules regarding type font, number of characters per inch, line spacing, and so on, your computer and laser printer can provide you with a wealth of creative ways to make your proposal more readable.

You will understand how important readability, writing style, and visual attractiveness are after your read several samples of funded proposals followed by your own. Tired reviewers need all the help you can give them to locate and score the important sections of your proposal. Avoid creativity for its own sake, but think of the reader and your goal as you write, type, and print your proposal.

Keep foremost in your mind that these federal funds are the result of taxes paid by individuals like you, as well as corporations. It is your responsibility to make the plan for how your propose to spend these monies as precise and as clearly related to the project outcome as possible. The tendency to "round up" numbers and pad budgets is a threat to your credibility and could affect your ability to gain the peer reviewers' and federal staff's confidence.

Remember, do not leave anything to chance. All required forms must be completed precisely.

CHAPTER 12

Improving Your Federal Proposal
The Grants Quality Circle

Proactive grantseekers initiate proposal development early in the federal grant cycle and therefore have sufficient time to have their proposals reviewed by their peers before submission. You will improve your proposal and significantly increase your chances for success by asking several colleagues or members of your grants advisory committee to voluntarily role-play the review team that will ultimately pass judgement on your proposal. This pre-submission review process is really a test run or mock review, and the group conducting it is, in essence, your quality circle, as described in Walter Edward Deming's work in total quality management (TQM).[1] If you follow the TQM model, you will not pay your mock reviewers to take part in the activity. They should be motivated by their desire to help you improve your proposal, increase its probability of acceptance, and, thus, enhance the image of your organization.

The most significant factor in the success of this improvement exercise is how closely each aspect of the mock review resembles the actual federal or state review. The benefits you can derive from this technique are directly related to your ability to create the scenario in which the actual reviewers will find themselves.

To arrange a mock review that is similar to what the actual review will be like, procure a list of last year's reviewers, a copy of the scoring system that will be used, and a sample of an exemplary proposal. You should also gather information about the setting in which your proposal will be reviewed.

To make this exercise as valuable as possible, provide your mock review group or grants quality circle with data on the following:

- the training each reviewer receives
- the setting in which proposals are reviewed (the federal agency, the reviewer's home, both sites, and so on)
- the review process: (Does one reviewer defend the proposal while others try to locate flaws or weaknesses?)
- the scoring system: (Are scores averaged? Are the highest and lowest scores eliminated and the remainder averaged?)
- the amount of time spent reviewing each proposal

It is essential that you instruct the members of your grants quality circle to spend only the same amount of time reviewing your proposal as the actual reviewers will. Some of your mock reviewers may mistakenly think they will be helping you by taking an inordinate amount of time to read your proposal carefully. You must inform them right away that this would be counterproductive to the end results. If actual reviewers will skim parts of the proposal, then your mock reviewers should do the same. Remind your quality circle participants that they should be trying to *mirror* the actual reviewers, not to do a better job than they do! If the actual reviewers will invest over 90 minutes reviewing and scoring each proposal, consider distributing your draft proposal to the members of your grants quality circle before they come together. If a corporate or foundation official is likely to spend 10 minutes reviewing it, then disseminate the proposal at your quality circle meeting.

The sample letter inviting an individual to participate in a grants quality circle (exhibit 12.1) and the grants quality circle worksheet (exhibit 12.2) will help you carry out this valuable exercise. After the suggestions from your mock review have been incorporated into your final proposal, you are ready to move on to submission.

In some cases it is not feasible to assemble a group of volunteers for a quality circle. There may be too few colleagues in your organization to conduct a role-playing activity such as this, or confidentiality may be an issue if personality problems exist or if competition in the field is fierce. One option in these instances is to ask one or two individuals you trust to review your proposal. Provide them with the same data and worksheets discussed above, and, if necessary, offer them an honorarium for their efforts. ($100 or $200 is common). You could request that they sign a nondisclosure agreement. Most university grant offices have these agreement forms and will be happy to share a copy with you. This way you can tailor the agreement to your organization with minimal effort. Seldom are these extraordinary security measures necessary.

Date

Name
Address

Dear _____:

I would like to take this opportunity to request your input in helping our organization submit
the very best grant proposal possible. We are asking that you review the enclosed proposal
from the point of view of the federal reviewer. The attached materials will help you role-play
the actual manner in which this proposal will be evaluated.

Please read the information on the reviewers' backgrounds and the scoring system and limit
the time you spend reading the proposal to the time constraints that the real reviewers will
observe. A grants quality circle worksheet has been provided to assist you in recording your
scores and comments.

A meeting of all mock reviewers comprising our quality circle has been scheduled for
[date _____]. Please bring your grants quality circle worksheet with you to this meeting. The
meeting will last less than one hour. Its purpose is to analyze the scores and brainstorm
suggestions to improve this proposal.

Sincerely,

Name
Phone Number

SAMPLE LETTER INVITING AN INDIVIDUAL TO PARTICIPATE IN A GRANTS QUALITY CIRCLE

EXHIBIT 12.1

The following information is designed to help you develop the proper focus for the review of
the attached proposal.

1.   The Review Panelists

Proposals are read by review panelists with the following degrees and backgrounds:

Degrees: _____
_____
_____

Backgrounds (Age, Viewpoints, Biases, and So On): _____
_____
_____
_____

GRANTS QUALITY CIRCLE WORKSHEET

EXHIBIT 12.2

2. The Time Element and Setting

Number of proposals read by each reviewer: _____

Average length of time spent reading each proposal _____

Proposals are read at the: _____ reviewer's home
_____ reviewer's work
_____ funder's location
_____ other site

3. The Scoring System
    a. The scoring system that will be employed is based on a scale of _____
       _____

    b. The areas to be scored are (list or include attachment):

Area	Total Possible Points	Your Score

    c. According to the total points per area, how many points represent an outstanding, superior, adequate, weak, or poor score? For example, if the total points possible for one area are 25, 0-8 = poor, 9-12 = weak, 13-19 = adequate, 20-23 = superior, and 24-25 = outstanding.
       _____
       _____
       _____

    d. After recording your scores, list the positive points of the proposal that may appeal to the actual reviewer. Also list those areas that seem weak and may cost valuable points. List suggestions for improvement.
       _____
       _____
       _____
       _____

GRANTS QUALITY CIRCLE WORKSHEET *(continued)*

EXHIBIT 12.2

A look at a few selected scoring systems points out the importance of knowing how your proposal will be reviewed and sharing this information with your mock reviewers. The first example from the Office of Educational Research and Improvement is characterized by a specific point system, heavily weighed toward national significance and project design.

Example 1

- National significance   35 points
- Quality of project design   35 points

- Quality of potential contribution of personnel   15 points
- Adequacy of resources   5 points
- Quality of management plan   <u>10 points</u>
  Total   100 points

In examples 2 and 3 the National Institute on Aging (example 2) and the National Science Foundation (example 3) do not use evaluation systems based on points and weights. In situations like these, the grantseeker must ask more questions of the grantor so that he or she can ascertain what looks "good" under each criterion. After all, to play the game you need to know *all* the rules!

Example 2

- Scientific, technical, or medical significance
- Appropriateness and adequacy of approach
- Qualifications of principal investigator/staff
- Availability of resource
- Appropriateness of budget
- Adequacy of plans to include both genders and minorities
- Protection of human subjects

Example 3

- Criterion 1:   What is the intellectual merit of the proposed activity?
- Criterion 2:   What are the broader impacts of the proposed activity?

Few techniques suggested in this book will have a more dramatic effect on the quality of your proposals than the grants quality circle. Support for this activity will be rewarded through the promotion of a better image with reviewers and federal staff, as well as an increase in quality proposals from staff members participating in the activity.

REFERENCE

1. Gary Fellers, *The Deming Vision: SPC/TQM for Administrators* (Milwaukee: ASQC Quality Press, 1992).

CHAPTER 13

Submission

What To Do and What Not To Do

Although this chapter addresses the federal grants arena, much of the information it contains can also be applied to other government funding sources such as state, county, and city. Irrespective of which type of public funding source you are submitting your proposal to, you do not want to do anything at this late stage that may have a negative impact on your proposal's outcome.

WHAT TO DO

Submit your proposal early. Do not position yourself as a "last-minute applicant." Follow all instructions and every rule. Do not wait until your proposal has been written, has undergone a mock review, and is ready to be sent out before you read the submission rules. Review the submittal requirements early to make sure you have enough time to comply with them. After all of your hard work, it would be ridiculous to jeopardize your chances for success by failing to show funders that you have read and complied with their rules for submission.

Since each government agency and even some of the grant programs within agencies have different submittal procedures, they cannot all be listed here. Several federal programs require you to initial a special sign-on section and provide signatures next to each of the requirements that are most often overlooked. Others call for the inclusion of notarized copies of the board minutes and resolutions that authorized your organization's approval to submit the proposal (especially when matching or in-kind contributions are required). Many agencies require letters of commitment from consortia members.

Unfortunately, many grantseekers read the requirements too late and find that their board will not meet again before the grantor's deadlines. They then include a note with their proposal saying that they will forward the necessary documents at a later date. This is a red flag to grantors and alerts them that an applicant may be a problem.

Even with extensive instructions, grantseekers make mistakes in signing, page length, number of copies, assurances, and so on. In fact, it would be too time-consuming to list all of the problems federal grantors have in gaining compliance with their rules. Review and follow the submittal procedures contained in your application package carefully.

Keep the cover clear and simple. If the grantor requires a special cover sheet, use it. If the grantor does not require a special cover sheet, make sure the cover you place on the application does not interfere with the handling of your proposal. Your cover should act as a luggage tag, allowing for the easy identification of where your proposal is going. The cover should clearly designate the office, division, mail stop, and so on; the program title and CFDA number, the name and phone number of the program officer; your organization's name and return address; and your name.

WHAT NOT TO DO

It is recommended that you limit the use of elected representatives in the grants process, especially at submittal time. Federal bureaucrats view the use of congresspeople and their aides as potentially unethical and possibly illegal. Elected officials want to be viewed by you, the voter, as ready to help in any way, but their assistance should be limited to pre-proposal contact and gathering information about past grantees and reviewers when you are unable to get the information on your own.

Do not ask for extra time or a later submittal date, and do not ask to send in any parts of the proposal after the deadline. Do not contact federal bureaucrats after submission. This is viewed as an attempt to influence their review process and decision.

OTHER SUBMISSION TECHNIQUES

Several optional techniques may be helpful.

1. You could hand deliver your proposal (and all the copies the agency could use) to the designated grants logging center for that agency. While doing so, stop by the program office to thank staff members for their assistance.

2. You could submit your proposal electronically. It is becoming more common for federal programs to have their application forms available online and to encourage and accept (and even require) proposals submitted electronically over the Internet. For example, the National Science Foundation (NSF) uses an electronic submittal system known as *Fast Lane* to redesign and streamline the way it does business. The purpose of the program is to use the World Wide Web to facilitate business transactions and the exchange of information between NSF and its client community. (To obtain instructions on how to use *FastLane* visit http://www.fastlane.nsf.gov/).

   Internet transmittal is becoming so common that now it is even the preferred method for peer reviewers to submit their proposal critiques. Because the use of the Internet is growing in this field, it is a good idea to check to see what your proposal looks like when received by electronic submission. What happens to graphics and to the layout and design? A little care may pay off dramatically.

3. You could send (or deliver) a copy of your proposal abstract or summary to your congressperson's office. Advise the congressperson that you do not want or expect any intervention at this point, but let him or her know the approximate or anticipated date of the notice of award (usually several months away). Many times, federal granting officials will inform the congressperson of awards before they notify the grantee. Therefore, it is important to alert your congressperson that you have submitted a proposal and that you will contact him or her again closer to the notification date.

   Check with your program officer or contact person to confirm the preferred method of submission.

Submission is the final step in demonstrating your ability and desire to comply with the federal granting source's rules and regulations. Hopefully your attention to detail will lead the grantor to believe that you will be equally precise in executing your funded grant. One thing is certain, however; if you fail to comply with all submission rules you will lose your credibility and drastically diminish your chances of being funded.

CHAPTER 14

Federal Grant Requirements

M any nonprofit agencies exhibit great fear and trepidation over the rules regarding federal grant monies. These fears are basically unwarranted and should be of concern only to nonprofit organizations that do not have adequate fiscal rules and regulations. The restrictions governing usage of federal funds are understandable and in most cases reasonable. Yes, there are instances of disallowed expenditures two or three years after a grant has been completed, but they are avoidable. Most people remember the exception rather than the rule. Over $90 billion in federal grant funds are awarded each year, and only a small fraction of grantees have their expenditures disallowed or experience a problem with an audit. Most likely, your existing personnel, accounting, and purchasing procedures will be adequate. If you must make changes in your system to ensure the adequate handling of federal funds, however, do so. Such changes will increase the credibility of your system.

The federal grants requirement worksheet (see exhibit 14.1) will help you comply with most federal grant requirements. If your organizations has a grants administration office, this worksheet may not be necessary, but you, the project director, still need to know the facts so that you can help in the overall administration of your grant.

Project Title: _____

Project Director: _____

Federal Account Identification Number: _____

Agency Staff: _____

Agency Phone No.: _____ Agency Fax No.: _____

Notification of Award Received On (Date): _____

Start Date of Project: _____

End Date of Project: _____

Dates Reports Are Due: _____

Final Report Due On (Date): _____

Number of Years Funding Can Be Applied For: _____

Matching or In-Kind Requirements: _____% $ _____

Where Matching or In-Kind Records Will Be Kept: _____

Who Will Be Responsible for Keeping Them: _____

Federal Rules Governing This Grant

- OMB Circulars/Guidelines Governing Grant Expenditures:

  _____

  _____

  _____

  _____

- Location of OMB Circulars/Guidelines Governing Grant Expenditures: _____

  _____

  _____

  _____

  _____

- Special Rules and Federal Management Circulars (List from Assurances Section of Proposal): _____

  _____

  _____

  _____

  _____

- Location of Special Rules and Federal Management Circulars:

  _____

  _____

  _____

  _____

- Federal Rules and Your Organization's Policy On

  Copyrights:

  Patents:

FEDERAL GRANTS REQUIREMENT WORKSHEET

EXHIBIT 14.1

Human Subjects Review (Include Person Responsible for Compliance and Approval):

Drug Usage and Counseling:

Ownership and Use:

Fair and Equal Employment:

Other:

FEDERAL GRANTS REQUIREMENT WORKSHEET *(continued)*

EXHIBIT 14.1

FEDERAL GRANTS REQUIREMENT WORKSHEET

The federal grants requirement worksheet will help you familiarize yourself with and keep abreast of the basic obligations your nonprofit organization agrees to fulfill by accepting federal grant funds.

1. Complete the first section of the worksheet when you receive notice of funding. Include the federal account identification number and all other information you can supply. It is critical that you record the actual start date or date funded so that you do not change any part of the grant before its official award date. Review your project planner and record the dates on which you must supply progress indicators.
2. List the Office of Management and Budget (OMB) circulars that will govern your grant expenditures and where the circulars are located.
3. Record any information about the number of years of funding that can be applied for.
4. Indicate the percentage and dollar total of the cost-sharing require-ments, where the records will be kept, and who will be responsible for keeping them.
5. List the office or person responsible for approval of projects that involve the use of human and animal subjects and for ensuring compliance with federal regulations. If you work for an organization that already has a human subjects review committee, be sure to check with that commit-tee. If your organization does not have a human subjects review commit-tee, do not initiate one. Instead, involve a university- or college-related

individual on your grants advisory committee. Even though your proposal may not call for the performance of hard-core research, the federal government is very broad in its interpretation of what activities pose a potential danger to humans. In fact, federal officials even require human subjects approval for some needs assessment surveys, model projects, and demonstration grants.

6. Acceptance of federal funds require that your organization have a policy regarding drug use and counseling of employees.
7. If your grant calls for the creation of unique materials, make note of the rules regarding ownership and use. Noting these in advance reduces problems later.
8. The fair and equal employment rules are reasonable and should pose no problems for most nonprofit organizations.

RAISING AND DOCUMENTING MATCHING FUNDS

One of the most common characteristics of federal grants is the requirement of matching funds or in-kind contributions (also known as cost sharing). An organization can be asked to supply either cash, services, or facilities to match a percentage of the grant. This requirement may change over the years that federal funds support the project. For example, year one may require a 20 percent match, year two a 40 percent match, and year three a 50 percent match.

The worksheet on sources of matching funds (see exhibit 14.2) can help you plan a successful matching funds campaign before you approach federal agencies. The worksheet contains several standard methods for cost sharing and provides an evaluation system for each method. (This worksheet can also be

---

Project Title: _____

Total Project Cost: _____

Match Required: _____% $ _____

Review each of the following sources of matching funds. Check with federal officials to ensure that your match is in compliance with their rules and will be accepted. Make sure that nothing listed under your match has been provided from federal funds.

1. Personnel—List the percentage of time and effort of each individual who will be contributing to the match. Include salaries, wages, and fringe benefits.

WORKSHEET ON SOURCES OF MATCHING FUNDS

EXHIBIT 14.2

Options:

- Include the time and effort of volunteers, consultants, and/or corporate sponsors if allowable by the grantor.

- If the project calls for staff training or development, will your organization be required to increase salaries? If so, check with the grantor to see whether this can be listed as a match.

2. Equipment—List any equipment that will be purchased primarily to carry out this project. Include the cost of each piece and the total equipment cost.

3. Facilities—List the location, square footage, and cost per foot for each facility and the total facilities (space) cost.

4. Foundation/Corporate Grantors—What other grantors could you approach for a grant to match this grant?

   - Foundations:

   - Corporations:

5. Fund-Raising Activities—In some cases you may have to resort to fund-raising activities to develop your matching portion. List the activities and the net return expected from each.

   - Special Events (Dance, Raffle, etc.):

   - Sales of Products:

   - Other:

WORKSHEET ON SOURCES OF MATCHING FUNDS (continued)

EXHIBIT 14.2

useful when working with foundations and corporations that request matching support.)

FEDERAL GRANTS MANAGEMENT CIRCULARS

The highly regulated, detailed rules about grant management are probably the most imposing characteristic of federal grants. These rules may specify allowable costs, indirect cost rates, accounting requirements, and the like. Before getting involved in government grants, you and/or your accounting department should review the appropriate grants management circulars. Such a review usually diminishes fears about your organization's ability to comply with federal grant requirements. In most cases you will find that your organization has safeguards in effect that meet the requirements.

The Office of Management and Budget (OMB) produces circulars outlining uniform standards for financial dealings with government granting agencies. These circulars can be ordered from the Superintendent of Documents, Government Printing Office, Washington, DC 20402-9238, (202)512-1800. They can also be obtained from the Internet at http://www.doleta.gov/regs/omb/index.htm.

The following section is a broad description of OMB Circular A-110.

OMB Circular A-110

OMB Circular A-110 is entitled "Uniform Administrative Requirements for Grants and Other Agreements with Institutions of Higher Education, Hospitals and Other Non-Profit Organizations." This circular, along with its updates and attachments, budget forms, and cash request instructions, is a guide to the rules regarding federal grants. Attachments to the circular cover the following areas:

- cash depositories
- bonding and insurance
- retention and custodial requirements for records
- program income
- cost sharing and matching
- standards for financial management systems
- financial reporting requirements
- monitoring and reporting program performance
- payment requirements
- revision of financial plans
- close-out procedures
- suspension and termination
- standards for applying

- property management standards
- procurement standards

Colleges and universities will also be interested in OMB Circular A-21, which defines cost principles for federal research and development grants to educational institutions. All nonprofit organizations should familiarize themselves with OMB Circular A-122, "Cost Principles for Non-Profit Organizations," and state and local governments must also review OMB Circular A-87,"Cost Principles for State, Local, and Indian Tribal Governments" and OMB Circular A-102, "Grants and Cooperative Agreements with State and Local Governments." Please be advised that you should always refer to the most current circular for the specific rules and regulations in your area.

Exhibit 14.3 lists all available OMB Circulars in numerical sequence. Fears concerning the expenditure of federal grant funds are reduced when you request the appropriate OMB circulars for your type of organization and review the rules with your fiscal staff. From purchasing to personnel, your organization will most likely already have the necessary safeguards in place. Those areas that look as if they will pose a problem can be addressed in a general manner, for all federal grants, or handled separately, case by case, to avoid any difficulties.

OMB Circular A-1
    System of Circulars and Bulletins to Executive Departments and Establishments

OMB Circular A-11
    Preparation and Submission of Budget Estimates (Part 1), Preparation and Submission of Strategic Plans and Annual Performance Plans (Part 2), Planning, Budgeting, and Acquisition of Capital Assets (Part 3), Supplement to Part 3, Capital Programming Guide

OMB Circular A-16
    Coordination of Surveying, Mapping, and Related Spatial Data Activities

OMB Circular A-19
    Legislative Coordination and Clearance

OMB Circular A-21
    Cost Principles for Educational Institutions

OMB Circular A-25
    User Charges

OMB Circular A-34
    Instructions on Budget Execution

OMB CIRCULARS

EXHIBIT 14.3

OMB Circular A-45
   Rental and Construction of Government Quarters

OMB Circular A-50
   Audit Followup

OMB Circular A-76
   Supplemental Handbook in HTML or PDF, Performance of Commercial
   Activities

OMB Circular A-87
   Cost Principles for State, Local, and Indian Tribal Governments

OMB Circular A-89
   Catalog of Federal Domestic Assistance

OMB Circular A-94
   Discount Rates to be Used in Evaluating Time-Distributed Costs and Benefits

OMB Circular A-97
   Specialized or Technical Services for State and Local Governments

OMB Circular A-102
   Grants and Cooperative Agreements with State and Local Governments

OMB Circular A-109
   Major Systems Acquisitions

OMB Circular A-110
   Uniform Administrative Requirements for Grants and Other Agreements with
   Institutions of Higher Education, Hospitals and Other Non-Profit Organizations

OMB Circular A-122
   Cost Principles for Non-Profit Organizations

OMB Circular A-123
   Management Accountability and Control

OMB Circular A-125
   Prompt Payment

OMB Circular A-126
   Improving the Management and Use of Government Aircraft, Attachment A,
   Attachment B

OMB Circular A-127
   Financial Management Systems

OMB Circular A-129
   Managing Federal Credit Programs

OMB Circulars (continued)

EXHIBIT 14.3

OMB Circular A-130
  Management of Federal Information Resources

OMB Circular A-131
  Value Engineering

OMB Circular A-133
  Audits of States, Local Governments, and Nonprofit Organizations, Appendix
  A: Data Collection Form (Form SF-SAC) (PDF file, 56kb), Appendix B: May
  1998 Compliance Supplement

OMB Circular A-134
  Financial Accounting Principles and Standards

OMB Circular A-135
  Management of Federal Advisory Committees

OMB Circulars *(continued)*

EXHIBIT 14.3

CHAPTER 15

Dealing with the Decision of Public Funding Sources

The federal government is attempting to streamline the grants process. This includes making award determinations that are understandable and the same across all granting programs. Instead of making confusing determinations (such as "supportable but not fundable"), the federal government is now using these determinations:

- accepted (as written)
- accepted with modifications (usually budget modifications, which will affect some activities)
- rejected (the proposal did not reach the level or score required for funding)

ACCEPTED

If your proposal is accepted, consider taking the following steps:

1. Thank the grantor. Whether you are notified by phone, letter, or electronically, send the program or project officer a thank-you letter expressing your appreciation for the time and effort staff and reviewers expended on your proposal.
2. Request the reviewers' comments and include a self-addressed label for the funding source's convenience.
3. Ask the federal official for insight into what you could have done better.
4. Invite the program or project officer for a site visit.

5. Ask the official what mistakes successful grantees often make in carrying out their funded grant so you can be sure to avoid these errors.
6. Review the reporting structure. What does the grantor require and when? Will your dates for milestones and progress indicators be helpful?

ACCEPTED WITH BUDGET MODIFICATIONS

Should your proposal receive this response, do the following:

1. Send the funding source a thank-you letter.
2. Call the funding source and suggest that the program officer refer to your project planner to negotiate the budget terms.
3. Discuss the option of eliminating some of the project's methods or activities.
4. If several activities must be eliminated, consider dropping the accomplishment of an objective or reducing the expected degree of change.
5. If you are forced to negotiate away the supporting structure necessary to achieve your objectives, be prepared to turn down the funds. After all, you do not want to enter into an agreement that will cause you to lose credibility later.

REJECTED

If your proposal is rejected, take the following actions aimed at developing insight into the changes you need to make in your proposal for the next submission cycle:

1. Send the funding official a thank-you letter in appreciation for his or her time and effort as well as that of the reviewers and staff. Let the funding official know that although you were aware of the risk of failure before you invested your time in applying, you would appreciate assistance in reapplying.
2. Request the reviewers' comments. Enclose a self-addressed stamped envelope for their convenience.
3. Ask the funding official for his or her suggestions.
4. Find out whether your proposal could possibly be funded as a pilot project, as a needs assessment, or in some other way.
5. Ask whether there are any ways the funding source could assist you in getting ready for the next submission cycle, such as conducting a preliminary review.
6. Ask whether it would be wise for you to reapply. What are your chances and what would you have to change?

7. Ask whether you could become a reviewer to learn more about the review process.

By examining the reviewers' comments you may find that some reviewers scored a section of your proposal as outstanding, while others gave the same section a low score. This situation can create a dilemma. Changing your proposal to reflect one reviewer's comments may negate another reviewer's comments, and your changes could result in resubmission scores that are just average. Ask the grantor what you can do about this situation. Also, ask an outside expert to review your proposal; even if you must pay someone to review the proposal, you need insight into what is causing this discrepancy.

Some federal agencies inform grantseekers at the time of rejection whether they should change their proposal and reapply or avoid resubmittal and change their approach entirely.

Your response to your grant application's outcome must be positive. Whether you are jubilant or depressed, thank the grantor and seek to learn as much as possible from the experience. Demonstrate your willingness to learn from the funding source's feedback. You will find reinforcement for your positive behavior and become aware of how to avoid making the same mistakes.

CHAPTER 16

Follow-Up with Government Funding Sources

The object of following up is to position yourself as an asset to funding sources and not as a pest. You want to develop professional relationships and maintain contact with funding sources throughout the grants process, not just at award time. In addition to advising funders of your willingness to serve as a reviewer, consider

- forwarding notes on special articles or books in your area to them
- inviting them to visit your organization
- asking whether they would like to speak at your professional group or association's conference or at a special grants conference
- asking them what meetings or conferences they will be attending so that you can look them up
- requesting information about what you can do to have an impact on legislation affecting their funding levels or allocations

By remaining on grantors' mailing lists and reviewing the *Federal Register*, you will gain advance knowledge of the next funding opportunity. Do not wait until next year's deadline to begin thinking about your ensuing application. Start to plan for next year right after funding decisions are made for the current year.

The best way to learn what is going on is to visit the funding source personally. Keep in touch. Watch for meeting announcements in the *Federal Register*. Testify at committee hearings that will affect the agency and its funding level. Send the agency blind copies of your efforts to have an impact on legislation for them (and yourself). Use your association memberships and legislative committees to push for changes that benefit the particular agency, and write to Senate and House appropriations committees.

DEVELOPING CONTINUED GRANT SUPPORT

The key to continued success is to repeat the steps that have brought you to this point. If you have used the concepts presented in this manual to develop a proactive grants process, you have a system that alerts you to changes in program rules, deadlines, and the like through the *Federal Register*, mailing lists, personal contacts, and established links.

Although federal officials may change jobs and positions, they seem to reappear again and again. A systematic approach to recording research on funding sources and officials will prove useful as you come across old friends and make new ones. By maintaining your relationships, whether you have received funding or not, you demonstrate to funding sources that you plan to be around for awhile and that you will not forget them as soon as you receive their check.

Unfortunately, changes in staffing at government agencies make maintaining contacts more difficult. Just when things are going great, the program officers you have been working with will move on. But take heart, they may appear again somewhere down the grants road, so keep on their good side!

PART THREE

• • • • • • • • • • • • •

Pivate Funding Sources

CHAPTER 17

The Differences between Private and Public Funding

The private marketplace consists of two major segments—5 million corporations and 41,588 foundations. Estimates are that only 35 per cent of corporations are contributors in this marketplace; therefore the *total* number of potential private grantors is approximately 1,750,000 corporations and 41,588 foundations.

The foundation marketplace can be divided into several categories:

- national general purpose
- special purpose
- community
- family
- corporate

Foundations in each of these categories not only fund different types of proposals, they also look for different characteristics in those organizations they select as grantees.

Another important, but sometimes overlooked, private funding type is nonprofit organizations. This group includes professional associations, like Hellenic groups, business groups, service clubs, and membership groups. Like foundations, corporations, and government grantors, nonprofit organizations have specific funding preferences and needs.

In 1997 foundations and corporations awarded over $21.6 billion in grants while the government awarded approximately $90 billion. Total amount awarded is one of the major differences between the two marketplaces. When asked about the grants marketplace, most grantseekers believe that foundation and corporate giving is about equal to the federal government's. They are surprised, even shocked, to learn the truth. The amount of federal money awarded is more than four times the amount of private money awarded, which is one of the reasons why it is always good practice to check out federal funds first.

The private grants marketplace is very different from the public marketplace in many other ways too. For example, the federal government has many bureaucrats involved in awarding and monitoring its $90 billion. The private sector, on the other hand, is characterized by having little to no staff to assist them in their grantmaking. Even some of the largest foundations have only small, part-time, or shared staff. In fact, there are approximately only 1,000 foundations with an office, and only 1,500 professionals and 1,700 support staff members in all 41,588 plus foundations.

GRANTSEEKERS' DECISION MATRIX

The grantseekers' decision matrix (see table 17.1) will help you develop your knowledge of the principal types of funding sources and their differences and similarities. The matrix summarizes the major funding characteristics and preferences of federal funding programs, state funding programs, foundations, corporations, and nonprofit organizations.

Column 1 of the matrix lists the major funding source types. Columns 2 through 10 provide information on variables such as geographic area/need, type of project, and award size. This information will help you select the best type of funding source for your project. Please note that the matrix is meant to point you in the right direction only. Follow-up research will allow the proactive grantseeker to determine the funder's interest, the appropriateness of the project, and the proper request amount before proposal preparation and submission.

To achieve grants success you must be vigilant in attempting to consider your proposal, including the amount of your request, from the grantor's point of view. It should be increasingly evident that the "one proposal fits all" method of grantseeking will not meet with a positive response from such a diverse group of private grantors.

TABLE 17.1

GRANTSEEKERS' DECISION MATRIX

Type Funder	Geographic/Need	Type of Project	Grant Award Size for Field of Interest	Image	Credentials of P.I. or P.D.	Pre-proposal Contact	Application	Review System	Grants Administration (Rules)
Government									
1. Federal	Varies—but mostly national/inter-national perspective	Model Innovative Research	Large	Very national image +	National image	Write, phone, go and see	Extensive—many forms	Staff and peer review Human subjects and animals	Many / complies with OMB cir/audits + match $
2. State	State / local need	Model Innovative Replication	Medium Small	Statewide images+	Statewide image	Write, phone, go and see	Extensive—many forms	Staff and some peer review	Many / complex/ audits + match $
Foundation									
3. National General Purpose	National need—local regional population	Model Innovative	Large Medium	National image+	National+	Write, phone	Short—concept paper—longer form if interested	Staff and some peer review	Few audits and rules
4. Special Purpose	Need in area of interest	Model Innovative Research	Large to Small	Image not as critical as solution	Image in field of interest+	Write, phone	Short—concept paper—longer form if interested	Board review (some staff)	Few audits and rules
5. Community	Local need	Operation Replication Building/Equipment	Small	Local image+	Respected locally	Write, phone, go and see	Short—letter proposal	Board review	Few audits and rules
6. Family	Varies—but geographic concern for need	Innovative Replication Building/Equipment Some Research	Medium Small	Regional image+	Local/regional	Write, phone	Short—letter proposal	Board review	Very few audits and rules
Corporate									
7. Corporate —Large	Near plants or offices	Product Development, Replication Building/ Equipment	Medium Small	Local image+ Employee involvement	Local, national	Write, phone, go and see	Short—letter proposal	Contributions committee	Very few audits and rules
8. Corporate —Small	Very near to company	Same	Medium Small	Local image critical	Local	Write, phone, go and see	Short—letter proposal	Owner/Family	Very few audits and rules
Other									
9. Nonprofit Organizations and Service Clubs	Local	Replication Building/ Equipment Scholarship	Small	Local image and member involvement	Local	Write, phone, present to committee or to members	Short—letter proposal	Committee review and/or member vote	Few rules and audit

CHAPTER 18

How to Record Research and Information

A key to successful grantseeking with foundations and corporations is to gather the most complete and accurate information possible on funding sources before you approach them. The corporate and foundation research form (see exhibit 18.1) will help you do this. Complete one worksheet for each granting agency you research. Try to provide as much information on the form as possible, but remember that even a partially completed worksheet will help you make a more intelligent decision on whether you should solicit grant support from a particular funding source. Enlist volunteers to ferret out the information you need. Let your research guide your solicitation strategy and proposal development process.

Bauer Associates' *Winning Links* software program has been designed to assist you in recording and accessing data in an efficient manner. (For ordering information, see the list of resources available from Bauer Associates at the end of the book.)

In addition to the research you conduct on grantmaking organizations, you should also uncover and record as much information as possible on the decision makers in those organizations. The funding executive research worksheet (see exhibit 18.2) is designed to help you do this.

The following form outlines the data you need to collect in order to make a decision to seek fund from this grant source. Your attempts to collect as much of this information as possible will prove rewarding. (When feasible, record the source of the information and the date it was recorded.)

1. Name of Corporation/Foundation: _____
    Address: _____
    Phone: _____ Fax: _____ E-mail: _____

2. Contact Person: _____
    Title: _____
    Links from Our Organization to Contact Person: _____
    _____
    _____
    _____

3. Grantor's Areas of Interest: _____
    _____
    _____
    _____

4. Eligibility Requirements/Restrictions:
    a.   Activities Funded: _____
    _____
    _____

    b.   Organizations Funded: _____
    _____
    _____

    c.   Geographic Funding Preferences: _____
    _____
    _____

    d.   Other Requirements/Restrictions: _____
    _____
    _____
    _____

CORPORATE AND FOUNDATION RESEARCH FORM

EXHIBIT 18.1

5.   Information Available

	Sent For	Received
Guidelines	_____	_____
Newsletters	_____	_____
Annual Report	_____	_____
_____	_____	_____
_____	_____	_____

6.   a. Contributions Committee Members/Board of Directors/Officers:

_____

_____

_____

b. Staff   Full Time   Part Time

_____   _____   _____

_____   _____   _____

_____   _____   _____

7.   Deadline: _____
      Application Process/Requirements: _____

      _____

8.   Financial Information: Fiscal Year _____
      Corporation (Not Corporate Foundation): _____
      Sales: $_____ Parent Company: _____
      Corp. Sites: _____

      # of Employees: _____
      Credit Rating: _____ Source: _____
      Private or Publicly Held: _____
      If Publicly Held: Stock Price: $_____
                             Dividend: ___$_____
      Products Produced/Distributed: _____

      _____

CORPORATE AND FOUNDATION RESEARCH FORM *(continued)*

EXHIBIT 18.1

Foundation: Corporate_____ Private _____

Asset Base: $_____

Are there current gifts to build the asset base?

yes _____   no _____

If yes, how much in the most recent year? $_____

Total No. of Grants Awarded in 19___: _____

Total Amt. Awarded in Grants in 19__: $_____

High Grant: $ _____

Low Grant: $ _____

Average Grant: $ _____

In our interest area there were _____ grants, totaling $_____

High Grant in Our Interest Area: $ _____

Low Grant in Our Interest Area: $ _____

Average Grant in Our Interest Area: $ _____

9.   Number of Proposals Received in 19___: _____

       Number of Proposals Awarded in 19___: _____

Sample Grants in Our Area of Interest:

Recipient Organization	Amount
_____	$_____
_____	$_____
_____	$_____

CORPORATE AND FOUNDATION RESEARCH FORM (continued)

EXHIBIT 18.1

Do not ask funding executives for the information on the worksheet. Instead, use books such as *Trustees of Wealth, Dun & Bradstreet's Directory of Corporate Management,* and *Who's Who* publications to find information on funding officials (see chapter 20). Also check periodical indexes, newspapers, and funding source publications such as newsletters and annual reports. Ask your advisory committee members whether they know the funding executives, know of them, or know a person who has firsthand knowledge of them. You can also pick up useful information from telephone conversations and personal visits. If you visit a grantor in person, be sure to use your observation skills. Look for favorite pictures, memorabilia, college diplomas, certificates, notices of appreciation, and so on.

1.   Funding Source Name: _____

2.   Name of Contact Person/Director/Contributions Officer: _____

3.   Title:_____ Birth Date: _____

4.   Business Address:_____
       _____

5.   Home Address: _____
       _____

6.   Education:
       Secondary:_____
       College: _____
       Postgraduate: _____

7.   Military Service: _____

8.   Clubs/Affiliations:_____
       _____

9.   Corporate Board Memberships: _____
       _____

10.   Business History (Promotions, Other Firms, etc.):_____
       _____
       _____
       _____

11.   Religious Affiliation:

12.   Other Philanthropic Activities:
       _____

13.   Newspaper/Magazine Clipping(s) Attached: yes   no

14.   Contacts in Our Organization: _____
       _____

15.   Recent Articles/Publications: _____
       _____
       _____

16.   Awards/Honors: _____
       _____
       _____

FUNDING EXECUTIVE RESEARCH WORKSHEET

EXHIBIT 18.2

Naturally, you do not have to have funding executive information in order to consider submitting a proposal, but it will increase your chances of success. The information you collect and record on your funding executive research worksheet will help you in two major ways.

1. It will allow you to determine, in advance, likely preferences and biases you will encounter at an in-person interview.
2. It will make it easier to locate links between your organization and a funding source.

Recording accurate research on foundation and corporate decision makers will raise your chances of success. In addition, your ability to attract future funding will increase as you develop a history and file on each of the grantors you are interested in.

CHAPTER 19

Foundation Funding Source Research Tools

B asic research tools for developing your list of potential foundation grantors can be accessed at little or no charge and usually within a short distance from your workplace. The foundations themselves have developed a network of libraries where foundation grantseekers can access foundation grant information. A list of this network can be found at the end of this chapter.

Before you begin searching for your best possible grantor, review the following resources. Although you may purchase resources or access them through electronic transmission, first explore the hard-copy version to determine your level of usage and the cost-effectiveness of purchasing versus traveling to a cooperating collection of the public library.

The whole point of your research effort is to focus on the sources most likely to fund your proposal. Even if you are a novice grantseeker, do not be tempted to send letters to any and all foundations that are even remotely related to your project area. If pre-proposal contact is allowed or a proposal format is provided or suggested, take every opportunity to develop an individualized, tailored proposal for each of your best prospects.

THE FOUNDATION DIRECTORY

The Foundation Directory is the major source of information on larger foundations. The 1999 edition provides information on approximately 10,000 foundations. These 10,000 foundations hold assets in excess of $304 billion. The foundations described in *The Foundation Directory* make grants totaling over $14 billion. To be included in *The Foundation Directory* a foundation must

- hold assets of at least $2 million, or
- distribute $200,000 or more in grants each year.

The directory contains information on independent, community, and company-sponsored foundations. (Company-sponsored foundations are foundations that corporations have initiated as part of their philanthropy program. Only those company-sponsored foundations that meet the criteria outlined above appear in the directory.) Foundations included in the directory appear in numerical order, and each has its own entry number.

The directory contains seven indexes to assist in your search for appropriate funding sources:

1. Index to donors, officers, and trustees
2. Geographic index
3. International giving index
4. Types of support index
4. Subject index
5. Foundations new to edition index
6. Foundation name index

One technique that will add a whole new dimension to your foundation grants effort is to become adept at using the index to donors, officers, and trustees. When your organization's "friends" provide you with their links, pay special attention to those people who list board memberships or friends on foundation boards. In most cases, your "friend" will be willing to discuss your project with fellow board members or with friends who serve on other boards.

The Foundation Directory Part 2 is also available for your use. The 1999 edition of this supplemental directory includes over 5,700 midsize foundations with annual grant programs from $50,000 to $200,000. Both directories are published by the Foundation Center, 79 Fifth Avenue, Dept. FJ, New York, NY 10003-3076, (800) 424-9836.

Using *The Foundation Directory*

The most productive approach to using the directory is to first review chapter 5 on redefining your project idea. After identifying key words and fields of interest (e.g., environment, health education curriculum development, folk arts for children), you can use the directory's subject index to determine which foundations have an active interest in the area for which you are seeking grant support. Another approach is to use the types of support index to identify foundations interested in your type of project (e.g., conferences/seminars, building/renovation, equipment, program development, matching or challenge grants).

Before you rush into reviewing the actual foundation entries, remember that a significant portion of foundations possess a geographic homing device. In other words, they give only where they live. The directory's geographic index will point you in the direction of those foundations that may be interested in your project because of its location.

The best match will be a foundation that funds your subject area, type of project, and geographic area. Do not despair if the use of the geographic index produces limited prospects. Many foundations have a national and even international interest in certain areas. While these foundations may not have granted funds in your state or community before, they may do so if approached properly.

As you do your research, be sure to record the name of the foundation, the state, and the directory entry number for each foundation you are interested in. Recording this information will help you refer to the foundation quickly.

The contents of the entries in *The Foundation Directory* vary but in general, the entries consist of

- entry number
- name, address, and telephone number
- former name when applicable
- contact person
- additional address such as separate application address
- donors
- foundation type
- financial data—including year-end date of foundation's accounting period, asset type, gifts received, expenditures, qualifying distributions, total number of grant dollars paid, number of grants made, high and low grant awards, total value of set asides, grants made directly to or on behalf of individuals, employee matching gifts, dollars expended for programs administered by the foundation, dollar amount and number of loans, number and amount of loans to individuals, and in-kind gifts. (One important variable that is not covered in this section is which areas of interest received the high and low grants. You will need to do more in-depth research to uncover this information.)
- purpose and activities—what areas the foundation prefers to support. (This information does not include how much of the foundation's grant money is attributed to each area.)
- fields of interest—the stated interests of the funding source. (Use this information to narrow down your funding source choices by comparing your proposal to the foundation's stated interests.)
- international giving interests

- types of support—the funding mechanisms used by the grantor to support its stated fields of interest. (Use this information to match your proposal with the type of grant the foundation supports. For example, if the foundation prefers research over model or demonstration grants, you could consider adding a research component to your proposal.)
- limitations—including geographic preferences, restrictions by subject or type of recipient, and specific types of support the foundation does not provide.
- publications or other printed materials distributed by the foundation.
- application information—including the preferred form of application, the number of copies of proposals requested, application deadlines, frequency and dates of board meetings, and the general amount of time the foundation takes to notify applicants of the board's decision. Some foundations will indicate that they contribute to preselected organizations only, that applications are not being accepted, or that their funds are currently committed to ongoing projects. When this occurs, your only chance for a grant is to review the list of officers and trustees with your grants advisory group to see whether you have a link to the foundation. In other instances, foundations will state that they do not allow pre-proposal contact and that the desired contact is by letter only. The letter they are referring to and its development are the focus of chapter 22.
- officers, principal administrators, trustees, or directors—names and titles of members of the foundation's governing body
- number of staff—number of professional and support staff employed by the foundation and the part-time or full-time status of these employees
- EIN—Employer Identification Number assigned by the Internal Revenue Service
- list of selected grants

A fictitious *Foundation Directory* entry is provided in exhibit 19.1. For the purpose of explanation, assume that the grantseeker is interested in securing grants for projects related to substance abuse services. Entry number 5215, The Jon Foundation, is a good choice for the prospective grantee to examine further because the grantseeker's project falls within the foundation's stated fields of interest and will take place in the foundation's preferred geographic funding area—New York State. The prospective grantee will have to conduct more in-depth research to discover how much money the Jon Foundation has actually awarded to projects related to substance abuse services and the high and low grants in that particular area.

5218
The Jon Foundation
108 9th Ave., 18th Fl.
New York, NY 10019
Contact: Larry T. Jon, Pres.

Established in 1990 in NY.
Donor(s): Larry T. Jon, Sally M. Lyon.
Foundation type: Independent
Financial data (yr. ended 12/31/97): Assets, $25,240, 036 (M); gifts received $200,000; expenditures $1,253,373; qualifying distributions, $856,460; giving activities include $846,320 for 75 grants (high: $240,000; low: $700; average: $25,000-$30,000).
Fields of interest: Human services; children & youth, substance abuse services, arts/cultural programs, women, economically disadvantaged.
Types of support: General/operating support; capital campaigns; building/renovation; program development; continuing support; equipment; emergency funds.
Limitation: Giving primarily in the city of New York and the northeastern U.S. No grants to individuals.
Publications: Annual report (including application guidelines), application guidelines.
Application information: Application form required.
Initial approach: Letter requesting application form
Copies of proposal: 1
Deadline(s): None
Board meeting date(s): Quarterly
Officers and Trustees: *Larry T. Jon, Pres.; *Sally M. Lyon, Exec. Dir.; Stephen Mardner, Marsha Raydeck, John Sloan.
Number of staff: 1 full-time professional; 1 part-time support.
EIN: 258000113
Selected grants: The following grants were reported in 1997:
$240,000 to Blake Hall for Women, NYC, NY. For renovation of substance abuse recovery center.
$100,000 to New York City Children's Collaborative, NYC, NY. For continued support
$50,000 to the Northeast June Arts Festival, Boston, MA. For general support.

FOUNDATION DIRECTORY ENTRY (FICTITIOUS DATA)

EXIBIT 19.1

$35,000 to the Family Preservation Center, NYC, NY. For program development.
$20,000 to the Kowl Children and Youth Learning Assessment Center, Hartford, CT. For equipment.
$25,000 to the Addiction Prevention Program, NYC, NY. For expansion of services.
$10,000 to the Harlem Community of Churches, NYC, NY. To start-up neighborhood credit union.
$5,000 to Start Fresh Clinic, Portland, ME. To maintain outreach program.

FOUNDATION DIRECTORY ENTRY (continued)

EXHIBIT 19.1

THE FOUNDATION GRANTS INDEX

The Foundation Grants Index contains over 86,000 descriptions of grants of $10,000 or more, and each grant description has an identification number. You can use this reference book to search for the right grantor before consulting *The Foundation Directory* or after you have located a prospective grantor to see exactly what grant awards it has made in your field of interest. In either case, the goal is to find accurate information on the size, number, and recipients of grants awarded by each foundation you anticipate approaching.

The Foundation Grants Index is divided into seven sections:

1. Grants: Contains the main listing of grants and is arranged by major subject fields. The grants are listed alphabetically by state, foundation name, and recipient organization name within the foundation. Grant descriptions are arranged in numerical order for easy reference.
2. Recipient name index: An alphabetical index of domestic and foreign recipients.
3. Subject index: Will be particularly helpful if you begin your search for prospective grantors with *The Foundation Grants Index.* By using the subject index in conjunction with the key words you have developed, you can discover what grants have been awarded in your area of interest and by what foundations. The more varied your key words are, the greater the likelihood of locating an interested grantor.
4. Type of support/geographic index: Useful in locating those foundations whose geographic preferences coincide with your location.
5. Recipient category index: Provides insight into what foundations fund your competitors and other organizations with similar interests. This index is useful in educating your administration about the role that foundation grants play in organizations similar to yours.

6. Index to grants by foundation: Lists all the grants found in section 1 alphabetically by foundation state, then by foundation name.

7. Foundations (addresses and limitations): Alphabetically lists the foundations included in the book, along with their addresses, telephone numbers, and limitations, including geographic, program, and type of support restrictions.

In our example, we can use a variety of key terms to uncover foundations that have funded substance abuse projects in the past or have given to a related field. For instance, we could look in section 3, the subject index, under *substance abuse services, drug/alcohol abusers, alcoholism,* or *abuse prevention.* Let's assume we look under *substance abuse services* and find several grants, including entry number 53061, 53062, 53063, and 53064. By looking for these identification numbers in section 1, "Grants," we can find the funding sources that awarded these grants.

Unfortunately, the entries under these identification numbers will not provide you with the same information you will find in *The Foundation Directory.* In fact, in section 1 of *The Foundation Grants Index* you will not even be able to ascertain the complete address of a funding source; however, you can locate this information in Section 7, "Foundations." Once you have done so, you should go to *The Foundation Directory* to gather more information on the potential grantor.

If you locate a prospective funding source in *The Foundation Directory* first, then you can use *The Foundation Grants Index* to find out how many of the foundation's grants in excess of $10,000 went to each area of interest. For example, using the subject index in *The Foundation Grants Index,* you could look up relatively quickly the grants awarded by the fictitious Jon Foundation. In the subject index, the entry "substance abuse" has 45 subentries for different areas of substance abuse. The subentry "services" would lead us to the Jon Foundation.

In general, entries in *The Foundation Grants Index* include the subject category, foundation location (state), foundation name, grants identification number, recipient, recipient location, grant amount, year authorized, description of grant, and source of data.

As you can see from the hypothetical *Foundation Grants Index* entry in exhibit 19.2, you can find the grants for over $10,000 awarded by the Jon Foundation first under the subject field ("Health—Mental Health and Substance Abuse"), then by the state in which the foundation is located ("New York"), and then by the foundation name ("Jon"). A review of the list of grants and the information already gathered from *The Foundation Directory* indicates that the Jon Foundation does indeed value the area of substance abuse because its high grant of $240,000 (taken from the financial data provided in *The Foundation Directory*) was awarded in this area.

Health—Mental Health and Substance Abuse

NEW YORK

Jon Foundation, The

53061. The Institute on Addiction and Substance Abuse, Baltimore, MD. $30,000, 1997. For adolescent study program. 1997 990.

53062. Blake Hall for Women, NYC, NY. $240,000, 1997. For renovation of substance abuse recovery center. 1997 990.

53063. Addiction Prevention Program, NYC, NY. $25,000, 1997. For expansion of services. 1997 990.

53064. KTUROD Outreach, New Haven, CT. $25,000, 1997. For temporary housing and employment training for individuals enrolled in substance abuse programs.

FOUNDATION GRANTS INDEX ENTRY (FICTITIOUS DATA)

EXHIBIT 19.2

INTERNAL REVENUE SERVICE TAX RETURNS

Federal law requires that all foundations provide their tax returns for public information purposes. A foundation's 990-PF return gives fiscal details on receipts and expenditures, compensation of officers, capital gains or losses, and other financial matters. Form 990-AR includes information on foundation managers, assets, and grants paid or committed for future payments.

Exhibit 19.3 is a sample of the form that all private foundations must return to the Internal Revenue Service. While *The Foundation Directory* and *Foundation Grants Index* are useful reference tools, they are basically compilations of information from many sources, and there is no guarantee as to the accuracy of the information provided. In fact, *The Foundation Grants Index* is based on only 60 percent of the actual total foundation grants.

The Internal Revenue Service, however, deals in specifics. By reviewing the returns of the private foundations you believe to be your best funding prospects, you can find valuable information such as the actual amount of assets, new gifts received, total grants paid out, and so on. Most important, you can view a list of all the grants they have paid, including grants for less than $10,000.

Copies of tax returns for the past three years for all 41,588 foundations can be viewed for free at the Foundation Center's reference collections in New

Form **990-PF**

Return of Private Foundation
or Section 4947(a)(1) Nonexempt Charitable Trust
Treated as a Private Foundation

Department of the Treasury
Internal Revenue Service

Note: *The organization may be able to use a copy of this return to satisfy state reporting requirements.*

OMB No. 1545-0052

19

For calendar year 1995, or tax year beginning   , 19   and ending   , 19

Use the IRS label. Otherwise, please print or type. See Specific Instructions.	Name of organization **NAME**		A Employer identification number
	Number and street (or P.O. box number if mail is not delivered to street address) Room/suite **ADDRESS**		B State registration number (see instruction F)
	City or town, state		C If exemption application is pending, check here ▶ ☐
			D 1. Foreign organizations, check here ▶ ☐

H Check type of organization: ☐ Section 501(c)(3) exempt private foundation
☐ Section 4947(a)(1) nonexempt charitable trust ☐ Other taxable private foundation

2. Organizations meeting the 85% test, check here and attach computation ▶ ☐
E If private foundation status was terminated under section 507(b)(1)(A), check here . ▶ ☐

I Fair market value of all assets at end of year **ASSETS*** line 16)

J Accounting method: ☐ Cash ☐ Accrual
☐ Other (specify) ....
(Part I, column (d) must be on cash basis.)

F If the foundation is in a 60-month termination under section 507(b)(1)(B), check here . ▶ ☐
G If address changed, check here . . ▶ ☐

Part I Analysis of Revenue and Expenses *(The total of amounts in columns (b), (c), and (d) may not necessarily equal the amounts in column (a) (see page 8 of the instructions).)*

		(a) Revenue and expenses per books	**(b)** Net investment income	**(c)** Adjusted net income	**(d)** Disbursements for charitable purposes (cash basis only)
Revenue	1 Contributions, gifts, grants, etc., received (attach schedule)				
	2 Contributions from split-interest trusts . . .				
	3 Interest on savings and temporary cash investments				
	4 Dividends and interest from securities				
	5a Gross rents				
	b (Net rental income or (loss) _____)				
	6 Net gain or (loss) from sale of assets not on line 10				
	7 Capital gain net income (from Part IV, line 2) .				
	8 Net short-term capital gain				
	9 Income modifications				
	10a Gross sales less returns and allowances				
	b Less: Cost of goods sold . .				
	c Gross profit or (loss) (attach schedule)				
	11 Other income (attach schedule)				
	12 **Total** (add lines 1 through 11)				
Operating and Administrative Expenses	13 Compensation of officers, directors, trustees, etc.				
	14 Other employee salaries and wages				
	15 Pension plans, employee benefits				
	16a Legal fees (attach schedule)				
	b Accounting fees (attach schedule)				
	c Other professional fees (attach schedule) . . .				
	17 Interest				
	18 Taxes (attach schedule) (see page 11 of the instructions)				
	19 Depreciation (attach schedule) and depletion .				
	20 Occupancy				
	21 Travel, conferences, and meetings				
	22 Printing and publications				
	23 Other expenses (attach schedule)				
	24 **Total** operating and administrative expenses (add lines 13 through 23)				
	25 Contributions, gifts, grants paid . . . **GRANTS PAID**				
	26 **Total** expenses and disbursements (add lines 24 and 25)				
	27a Excess of revenue over expenses and disbursements (line 12 minus line 26)				
	b Net investment income (if negative, enter -0-) .				
	c Adjusted net income (if negative, enter -0-) . .				

For Paperwork Reduction Act Notice, see page 1 of the instructions.   Cat. No. 11289X   Form **990-PF** (1995)

***If blank, see page 2, line 16, column (c)**

IRS FOUNDATION ANNUAL RETURN (ONLY PAGE 1 OF 4 IS SHOWN HERE)

EXHIBIT 19.3

York City and Washington, DC. The Atlanta, Cleveland, and San Francisco offices contain IRS Form 990-PF returns for the Southeastern, Midwestern, and Western states respectively.

THE FOUNDATION CENTER

Incorporated as a nonprofit organization in 1953, the Foundation Center was formed by foundations as an independent national service center. Part of the Foundation Center's mission is to provide accurate information on philanthropy with special emphasis on foundation grantmaking. The center covers its operating expenses through grants from foundations and corporations, the sale of publications, and fee-based subscriber services. The center operates five reference collections, one in New York, one in Washington, DC, one in Cleveland, one in San Francisco, and one in Atlanta. Each of these is staffed by Foundation Center employees. As previously mentioned, the New York and Washington, DC, collections have the Internal Revenue Service records for all foundations. The Cleveland, San Francisco, and Atlanta collections have Internal Service records for foundations located in their respective geographic regions.

Exhibit 19.4 shows the locations of the reference collections operated by the Foundation Center, as well as the 211 cooperating collections operated by libraries, community foundations, and other nonprofit agencies. Those cooperating collections marked with a bullet have Internal Revenue Service returns on microfiche for their state or region.

Locate the collection nearest you and make a visit. In addition to having the most current editions of *The Foundation Directory, The Foundation Grants Index,* and IRS tax returns, the collection probably will have several other valuable grants resource materials including

- computer-generated printouts or guides that list grants by subject area
- state foundation directories
- other publications from the Foundation Center and other sources (see the list of resources for more detail).

FOUNDATION CENTER COOPERATING COLLECTIONS   FREE FUNDING INFORMATION CENTERS

The Foundation Center is an independent national service organization established by foundations to provide an authoritative source of information on foundation and corporate giving. The New York, Washington, D.C., Atlanta, Cleveland, and San Francisco reference collections operated by the Foundation Center offer a wide variety of services and comprehensive collections of information on foundations and grants. Cooperating Collections are libraries, community foundations, and other nonprofit agencies that provide a core collection of Foundation Center publications and a variety of supplementary materials and services in areas useful to grantseekers. The core collection consists of:

THE FOUNDATION DIRECTORY 1 AND 2, AND SUPPLEMENT
THE FOUNDATION 1000
FOUNDATION FUNDAMENTALS
FOUNDATION GIVING
THE FOUNDATION GRANTS INDEX

THE FOUNDATION GRANTS INDEX QUARTERLY
FOUNDATION GRANTS TO INDIVIDUALS
GUIDE TO U.S. FOUNDATIONS, THEIR TRUSTEES, OFFICERS, AND DONORS
THE FOUNDATION CENTER'S GUIDE TO PROPOSAL WRITING

NATIONAL DIRECTORY OF CORPORATE GIVING
NATIONAL DIRECTORY OF GRANTMAKING PUBLIC CHARITIES
NATIONAL GUIDE TO FUNDING IN. . . . (SERIES)
USER-FRIENDLY GUIDE

All five Center libraries have *FC Search: The Foundation Center's Database on CD-ROM* available for patron use, and most Cooperating Collections have it as well, as noted by the symbol (✦). Also, many of the network members make available for public use sets of private foundation information returns (IRS Form 990-PF) for their state and/or neighboring states noted by the symbol (✱). A complete set of U.S. foundation returns can be found at the New York and Washington, D.C., offices of the Foundation Center. The Atlanta, Cleveland, and San Francisco offices contain IRS Form 990-PF returns for the southeastern, midwestern, and western states, respectively. Because the collections vary in their hours, materials, and services, *it is recommended that you call the collection in advance.* To check on new locations or current holdings, call toll-free 1-800-424-9836, or visit our Web site at http://fdncenter.org/library/library.html.

REFERENCE COLLECTIONS OPERATED BY THE FOUNDATION CENTER

THE FOUNDATION CENTER
8th Floor
79 Fifth Ave.
New York, NY 10003
(212) 620-4230

THE FOUNDATION CENTER
312 Sutter St., Rm. 312
San Francisco, CA 94108
(415) 397-0902

THE FOUNDATION CENTER
1001 Connecticut Ave., NW
Washington, DC 20036
(202) 331-1400

THE FOUNDATION CENTER
Kent H. Smith Library
1422 Euclid, Suite 1356
Cleveland, OH 44115
(216) 861-1933

THE FOUNDATION CENTER
Suite 150, Grand Lobby
Hurt Bldg., 50 Hurt Plaza
Atlanta, GA 30303
(404) 880-0094

ALABAMA

BIRMINGHAM PUBLIC LIBRARY ✱ ✦
Government Documents
2100 Park Place
Birmingham 35203
(205) 226-3600

HUNTSVILLE PUBLIC LIBRARY ✦
915 Monroe St.
Huntsville 35801
(205) 532-5940

UNIVERSITY OF SOUTH ALABAMA ✱
Library Building
Mobile 36688
(334) 460-7025

AUBURN UNIVERSITY AT MONTGOMERY ✱ ✦
7300 University Dr.
Montgomery 36117-3596
(334) 244-3653

ALASKA

UNIVERSITY OF ALASKA AT ANCHORAGE ✱ ✦
Library
3211 Providence Dr.
Anchorage 99508
(907) 786-1847

JUNEAU PUBLIC LIBRARY ✦
Reference
292 Marine Way
Juneau 99801
(907) 586-5267

ARIZONA

PHOENIX PUBLIC LIBRARY ✱ ✦
Information Services Department
1221 N. Central
Phoenix 85004
(602) 262-4636

TUCSON PIMA LIBRARY ✱ ✦
101 N. Stone Ave.
Tucson 87501
(520) 791-4010

ARKANSAS

WESTARK COMMUNITY COLLEGE—BORHAM LIBRARY ✱ ✦
5210 Grand Ave.
Ft. Smith 72913
(501) 788-7200

CENTRAL ARKANSAS LIBRARY SYSTEM ✱ ✦
700 Louisiana
Little Rock 72201
(501) 370-5952

PINE BLUFF-JEFFERSON COUNTY LIBRARY SYSTEM
200 E. Eighth
Pine Bluff 71601
(870) 534-2159

CALIFORNIA

HUMBOLDT AREA FOUNDATION ✱ ✦
P.O. Box 99
Bayside 95524
(707) 442-2993

VENTURA COUNTY COMMUNITY FOUNDATION ✱ ✦
Funding and Information Resource Center
1317 Del Norte Rd., Suite 150
Camarillo 93010
(805) 988-0196

FRESNO REGIONAL FOUNDATION ✦
Nonprofit Advancement Center
1999 Tuolumne St., Suite 650
Fresno 93721
(209) 498-3929

EAST BAY RESOURCE CENTER FOR NONPROFIT SUPPORT ✦
1203 Preservation Pkwy., Suite 100
Oakland 94612
(510) 834-1010

FLINTRIDGE FOUNDATION
Philanthropy Resource Library
1040 Lincoln Ave., Suite 100
Pasadena 91103
(626) 449-0839

GRANT & RESOURCE CENTER OF NORTHERN CALIFORNIA ✱ ✦
Building C, Suite A
2280 Benton Dr.
Redding 96003
(916) 244-1219

LOS ANGELES PUBLIC LIBRARY
West Valley Regional Branch Library
19036 Van Owen St.
Reseda 91335
(818) 345-4393

RIVERSIDE PUBLIC LIBRARY
3581 Mission Inn Ave.
Riverside 92501
(919) 782-5202

NONPROFIT RESOURCE CENTER ✦
Sacramento Public Library
828 I St., 2nd Floor
Sacramento 95814
(916) 264-2772

SAN DIEGO FOUNDATION ✱ ✦
Funding Information Center
1420 Kettner Blvd., Suite 500
San Diego 92101
(619) 239-8815

NONPROFIT DEVELOPMENT CENTER ✦
Library
1922 The Alameda, Suite 212
San Jose 95126
(408) 248-9505

PENINSULA COMMUNITY FOUNDATION ✱ ✦
Peninsula Nonprofit Center
1700 S. El Camino Real, R201
San Mateo 94402-3049
(650) 358-9392

LOS ANGELES PUBLIC LIBRARY ✦
San Pedro Regional Branch
9131 S. Gaffey St.
San Pedro 90731
(310) 548-7779

VOLUNTEER CENTER OF GREATER ORANGE COUNTY ✦
Nonprofit Management Assistance Center
1901 E. 4th St., Suite 100
Santa Ana 92705
(714) 953-5757

SANTA BARBARA PUBLIC LIBRARY ✦
40 E. Anapamu St.
Santa Barbara 93101
(805) 962-7653

SANTA MONICA PUBLIC LIBRARY ✦
1343 Sixth St.
Santa Monica 90401-1603
(310) 458-8600

SONOMA COUNTY LIBRARY ✦
3rd & E Sts.
Santa Rosa 95404
(707) 545-0831

SEASIDE BRANCH LIBRARY ✦
550 Harcourt St.
Seaside 93955
(408) 899-8131

SONORA AREA FOUNDATION ✦
20100 Cedar Rd., N.
Sonora 95370
(209) 533-2596

COLORADO

EL POMAR NONPROFIT RESOURCE CENTER ✦
1661 Mesa Ave.
Colorado Springs 80906
(800) 554-7711

DENVER PUBLIC LIBRARY ✱ ✦
General Reference
10 West 14th Ave. Pkwy.
Denver 80204
(303) 640-6200

CONNECTICUT

DANBURY PUBLIC LIBRARY ✦
170 Main St.
Danbury 06810
(203) 797-4527

GREENWICH LIBRARY ✱ ✦
101 West Putnam Ave.
Greenwich 06830
(203) 622-7910

HARTFORD PUBLIC LIBRARY ✱ ✦
500 Main St.
Hartford 06103
(860) 543-8656

NEW HAVEN FREE PUBLIC LIBRARY ✦
Reference Dept.
133 Elm St.
New Haven 06510-2057
(203) 946-8130

DELAWARE

UNIVERSITY OF DELAWARE ✱ ✦
Hugh Morris Library
Newark 19717-5267
(302) 831-2432

FLORIDA

VOLUSIA COUNTY LIBRARY CENTER ✦
City Island
Daytona Beach 32014-4484
(904) 257-6036

FOUNDATION CENTER COOPERATING COLLECTIONS

EXHIBIT 19.4

NOVA SOUTHEASTERN UNIVERSITY ✳ ✦
Einstein Library
3301 College Ave.
Fort Lauderdale 33314
(954) 262-4601

INDIAN RIVER COMMUNITY COLLEGE ✦
Charles S. Miley Learning Resource
Center
3209 Virginia Ave.
Fort Pierce 34981-5599
(561) 462-4757

JACKSONVILLE PUBLIC LIBRARIES ✳ ✦
Grants Resource Center
122 N. Ocean St.
Jacksonville 32202
(904) 630-2665

MIAMI-DADE PUBLIC LIBRARY ✳ ✦
Humanities/Social Science
101 W. Flagler St.
Miami 33130
(305) 375-5575

ORLANDO PUBLIC LIBRARY ✳
Social Sciences Department
101 E. Central Blvd.
Orlando 32801
(407) 425-4694

SELBY PUBLIC LIBRARY
Reference
1001 Blvd. of the Arts
Sarasota 34236
(941) 316-1181

TAMPA-HILLSBOROUGH COUNTY
PUBLIC LIBRARY ✳ ✦
900 N. Ashley Dr.
Tampa 33602
(813) 273-3628

COMMUNITY FOUNDATION OF PALM
BEACH & MARTIN COUNTIES ✳ ✦
324 Datura St., Suite 340
West Palm Beach 33401
(407) 659-6800

GEORGIA

ATLANTA-FULTON PUBLIC LIBRARY ✳ ✦
Foundation Collection—Ivan Allen
Department
1 Margaret Mitchell Square
Atlanta 30303-1089
(404) 730-1900

UNITED WAY OF GEORGIA ✳ ✦
Community Resource Center
277 Martin Luther King Jr. Blvd.,
Suite 301
Macon 31201
(912) 745-4732

SAVANNAH STATE UNIVERSITY ✦
Asa Gordon Library
Savannah 31404
(912) 356-2185

THOMAS COUNTY PUBLIC
LIBRARY ✳ ✦
201 N. Madison St.
Thomasville 31792
(912) 225-5252

HAWAII

UNIVERSITY OF HAWAII ✳ ✦
Hamilton Library
2550 The Mall
Honolulu 96822
(808) 956-7214

HAWAII COMMUNITY FOUNDATION
RESOURCE LIBRARY ✦
900 Fort St., Suite 1300
Honolulu 96813
(808) 537-6333

IDAHO

BOISE PUBLIC LIBRARY ✳ ✦
715 S. Capitol Blvd.
Boise 83702
(208) 384-4024

CALDWELL PUBLIC LIBRARY ✳ ✦
1010 Dearborn St.
Caldwell 83605
(208) 459-3242

ILLINOIS

DONORS FORUM OF CHICAGO ✳ ✦
208 South LaSalle, Suite 735
Chicago 60604
(312) 578-0175

EVANSTON PUBLIC LIBRARY ✳ ✦
1703 Orrington Ave.
Evanston 60201
(847) 866-0305

ROCK ISLAND PUBLIC LIBRARY ✦
401 - 19th St.
Rock Island 61201
(309) 788-7627

UNIVERSITY OF ILLINOIS AT
SPRINGFIELD ✳ ✦
Brookens Library
Shepherd Rd.
Springfield 62794-9243
(217) 206-6633

INDIANA

EVANSVILLE-VANDERBURGH COUNTY
PUBLIC LIBRARY ✦
22 Southeast Fifth St.
Evansville 47708
(812) 428-8200

ALLEN COUNTY PUBLIC LIBRARY ✳ ✦
900 Webster St.
Ft. Wayne 46802
(219) 424-0544

INDIANA UNIVERSITY NORTHWEST
LIBRARY ✦
3400 Broadway
Gary 46408
(219) 980-6582

INDIANAPOLIS-MARION COUNTY
PUBLIC LIBRARY ✳ ✦
Social Sciences
40 E. St. Clair
Indianapolis 46206
(317) 269-1733

VIGO COUNTY PUBLIC LIBRARY ✦
1 Library Sq.
Terre Haute 47807
(812) 232-1113

IOWA

CEDAR RAPIDS PUBLIC LIBRARY ✳
Foundation Center Collection
500 First St., SE
Cedar Rapids 52401
(319) 398-5123

SOUTHWESTERN COMMUNITY
COLLEGE ✦
Learning Resource Center
1501 W. Townline Rd.
Creston 50801
(515) 782-7081

PUBLIC LIBRARY OF DES MOINES ✳ ✦
100 Locust
Des Moines 50309-1791
(515) 283-4152

SIOUX CITY PUBLIC LIBRARY ✳ ✦
529 Pierce St.
Sioux City 51101-1202
(712) 252-5669

KANSAS

DODGE CITY PUBLIC LIBRARY ✳
1001 2nd Ave.
Dodge City 67801
(316) 225-0248

TOPEKA AND SHAWNEE COUNTY
PUBLIC LIBRARY ✳ ✦
1515 SW 10th Ave.
Topeka 66604-1374
(913) 233-2040

WICHITA PUBLIC LIBRARY ✳ ✦
223 S. Main St.
Wichita 67202
(316) 262-0611

KENTUCKY

WESTERN KENTUCKY UNIVERSITY ✦
Helm-Cravens Library
Bowling Green 42101-3576
(502) 745-6125

LEXINGTON PUBLIC LIBRARY ✳
140 E. Main St.
Lexington 40507-1376
(606) 231-5520

LOUISVILLE FREE PUBLIC LIBRARY ✳ ✦
301 York St.
Louisville 40203
(502) 574-1611

LOUISIANA

EAST BATON ROUGE PARISH LIBRARY ✳ ✦
Centroplex Branch Grants Collection
120 St. Louis
Baton Rouge 70802
(504) 389-4960

BEAUREGARD PARISH LIBRARY ✳ ✦
205 S. Washington Ave.
De Ridder 70634
(318) 463-6217

NEW ORLEANS PUBLIC LIBRARY ✳ ✦
Business & Science Division
219 Loyola Ave.
New Orleans 70140
(504) 596-2580

SHREVE MEMORIAL LIBRARY ✳
424 Texas St.
Shreveport 71120-1523
(318) 226-5894

MAINE

MAINE GRANTS INFORMATION
CENTER ✳ ✦
University of Southern Maine Library
314 Forrest Ave.
Portland 04104-9301
(207) 780-5029

MARYLAND

ENOCH PRATT FREE LIBRARY ✳ ✦
Social Science & History
400 Cathedral St.
Baltimore 21201
(410) 396-5430

MASSACHUSETTS

ASSOCIATED GRANTMAKERS OF
MASSACHUSETTS ✳ ✦
294 Washington St., Suite 840
Boston 02108
(617) 426-2606

BOSTON PUBLIC LIBRARY ✳ ✦
Soc. Sci. Reference
700 Boylston St.
Boston 02117
(617) 536-5400

WESTERN MASSACHUSETTS FUNDING
RESOURCE CENTER ✳
65 Elliot St.
Springfield 01101-1730
(413) 732-3175

WORCESTER PUBLIC LIBRARY ✳ ✦
Grants Resource Center
Salem Square
Worcester 01608
(508) 799-1655

MICHIGAN

ALPENA COUNTY LIBRARY ✳ ✦
211 N. First St.
Alpena 49707
(517) 356-6188

UNIVERSITY OF MICHIGAN–ANN
ARBOR ✳ ✦
Graduate Library
Reference & Research Services
Department
Ann Arbor 48109-1205
(313) 764-9373

WILLARD PUBLIC LIBRARY ✳ ✦
7 W. Van Buren St.
Battle Creek 49017
(616) 968-8166

HENRY FORD CENTENNIAL
LIBRARY ✳ ✦
Adult Services
16301 Michigan Ave.
Dearborn 48126
(313) 943-2330

WAYNE STATE UNIVERSITY ✳ ✦
Purdy/Kresge Library
5265 Cass Ave.
Detroit 48202
(313) 577-6424

MICHIGAN STATE UNIVERSITY ✳ ✦
Social Sciences/Humanities
Main Library
East Lansing 48824-1048
(517) 353-8818

FARMINGTON COMMUNITY LIBRARY ✳ ✦
32737 West 12 Mile Rd.
Farmington Hills 48018
(810) 553-0300

UNIVERSITY OF MICHIGAN—FLINT ✳
Library
Flint 48502-2186
(810) 762-3408

GRAND RAPIDS PUBLIC LIBRARY ✳ ✦
Business Dept.—3rd Floor
60 Library Plaza NE
Grand Rapids 49503-3093
(616) 456-3600

MICHIGAN TECHNOLOGICAL
UNIVERSITY ✳
Van Pelt Library
1400 Townsend Dr.
Houghton 49931
(906) 487-2507

MAUD PRESTON PALENSKE MEMORIAL
LIBRARY ✦
500 Market St.
Saint Joseph 49085
(616) 983-7167

NORTHWESTERN MICHIGAN
COLLEGE ✳ ✦
Mark & Helen Osterin Library
1701 E. Front St.
Traverse City 49684
(616) 922-1060

MINNESOTA

DULUTH PUBLIC LIBRARY ✳ ✦
520 W. Superior St.
Duluth 55802
(218) 723-3802

SOUTHWEST STATE UNIVERSITY ✳ ✦
University Library
Marshall 56258
(507) 537-6176

MINNEAPOLIS PUBLIC LIBRARY ✳ ✦
Sociology Department
300 Nicollet Mall
Minneapolis 55401
(612) 630-6300

ROCHESTER PUBLIC LIBRARY
101 2nd St.
Rochester 55904-3776
(507) 285-8002

ST. PAUL PUBLIC LIBRARY ✦
90 W. Fourth St.
St. Paul 55102
(612) 266-7000

FOUNDATION CENTER COOPERATING COLLECTIONS (continued)

EXHIBIT 19.4

MISSISSIPPI

JACKSON/HINDS LIBRARY SYSTEM ✳ ✦
300 N. State St.
Jackson 39201
(601) 968-5803

MISSOURI

CLEARINGHOUSE FOR
MIDCONTINENT FOUNDATIONS ✳ ✦
University of Missouri
5110 Cherry, Suite 310
Kansas City 64110
(816) 235-1176

KANSAS CITY PUBLIC LIBRARY ✳ ✦
311 E. 12th St.
Kansas City 64106
(816) 221-9650

METROPOLITAN ASSOCIATION FOR
PHILANTHROPY, INC. ✳ ✦
One Metropolitan Square, Suite 1295
211 North Broadway
St. Louis 63102
(314) 621-6220

SPRINGFIELD-GREENE COUNTY
LIBRARY ✳ ✦
397 E. Central
Springfield 65802
(417) 837-5000

MONTANA

MONTANA STATE UNIVERSITY—
BILLINGS ✳ ✦
Library—Special Collections
1500 North 30th St.
Billings 59101-0298
(406) 657-1662

BOZEMAN PUBLIC LIBRARY ✳ ✦
220 E. Lamme
Bozeman 59715
(406) 582-2402

MONTANA STATE LIBRARY ✳ ✦
Library Services
1515 E. 6th Ave.
Helena 59620
(406) 444-3004

UNIVERSITY OF MONTANA ✳ ✦
Maureen & Mike Mansfield Library
Missoula 59812-1195
(406) 243-6800

NEBRASKA

UNIVERSITY OF NEBRASKA—
LINCOLN ✳ ✦
Love Library
14th & R Sts.
Lincoln 68588-0410
(402) 472-2848

W. DALE CLARK LIBRARY ✳ ✦
Social Sciences Department
215 S. 15th St.
Omaha 68102
(402) 444-4826

NEVADA

LAS VEGAS-CLARK COUNTY LIBRARY
DISTRICT ✳ ✦
1401 E. Flamingo
Las Vegas 89119
(702) 733-3642

WASHOE COUNTY LIBRARY ✳ ✦
301 S. Center St.
Reno 89501
(702) 785-4010

NEW HAMPSHIRE

PLYMOUTH STATE COLLEGE ✳ ✦
Herbert H. Lamson Library
Plymouth 03264
(603) 535-2258

CONCORD COUNTY LIBRARY
45 Green St.
Concord 03301
(603) 225-8670

NEW JERSEY

CUMBERLAND COUNTY LIBRARY ✦
800 E. Commerce St.
Bridgeton 08302
(609) 453-2210

FREE PUBLIC LIBRARY OF ELIZABETH ✳ ✦
11 S. Broad St.
Elizabeth 07202
(908) 354-6060

COUNTY COLLEGE OF MORRIS ✳ ✦
Learning Resource Center
214 Center Grove Rd.
Randolph 07869
(201) 328-5296

NEW JERSEY STATE LIBRARY ✳ ✦
Governmental Reference Services
185 W. State St.
Trenton 08625-0520
(609) 292-6220

NEW MEXICO

ALBUQUERQUE COMMUNITY
FOUNDATION ✳
3301 Menual NE, Suite 30
Albuquerque 87176-6960
(505) 883-6240

NEW MEXICO STATE LIBRARY ✳ ✦
Information Services
1209 Camino Carlos Rey
Santa Fe 87505-9860
(505) 476-9714

NEW YORK

NEW YORK STATE LIBRARY ✳ ✦
Humanities Reference
Cultural Education Center
Empire State Plaza
Albany 12230
(518) 474-5355

SUFFOLK COOPERATIVE LIBRARY
SYSTEM ✦
627 N. Sunrise Service Rd.
Bellport 11713
(516) 286-1600

NEW YORK PUBLIC LIBRARY ✦
Bronx Reference Center
2556 Bainbridge Ave.
Bronx 10458-4698
(718) 579-4257

THE NONPROFIT CONNECTION, INC. ✦
One Hanson Place—Room 2504
Brooklyn 11243
(718) 230-3200

BROOKLYN PUBLIC LIBRARY ✦
Social Sciences Division
Grand Army Plaza
Brooklyn 11238
(718) 780-7700

BUFFALO & ERIE COUNTY PUBLIC
LIBRARY ✳ ✦
Business & Labor Dept.
Lafayette Square
Buffalo 14203
(716) 858-7097

HUNTINGTON PUBLIC LIBRARY ✦
338 Main St.
Huntington 11743
(516) 427-5165

QUEENS BOROUGH PUBLIC LIBRARY ✦
Social Sciences Division
89-11 Merrick Blvd.
Jamaica 11432
(718) 990-8671

LEVITTOWN PUBLIC LIBRARY ✦
1 Bluegrass Lane
Levittown 11756
(516) 731-5728

NEW YORK PUBLIC LIBRARY ✦
Countee Cullen Branch Library
104 W. 136th St.
New York 10030
(212) 491-2070

NORTH CAROLINA

ADRIANCE MEMORIAL LIBRARY ✦
Special Services Department
93 Market St.
Poughkeepsie 12601
(914) 485-3445

ROCHESTER PUBLIC LIBRARY ✳ ✦
Social Sciences
115 South Ave.
Rochester 14604
(716) 428-7328

ONONDAGA COUNTY PUBLIC
LIBRARY ✦
447 S. Salina St.
Syracuse 13202-2494
(315) 435-1800

UTICA PUBLIC LIBRARY
303 Genesee St.
Utica 13501
(315) 735-2279

WHITE PLAINS PUBLIC LIBRARY ✦
100 Martine Ave.
White Plains 10601
(914) 422-1480

COMMUNITY FDN. OF WESTERN
NORTH CAROLINA ✳ ✦
Learning Resources Center
16 Biltmore Ave., Suite 201
P.O. Box 1888
Asheville 28802
(704) 254-4960

THE DUKE ENDOWMENT ✳ ✦
100 N. Tryon St., Suite 3500
Charlotte 28202
(704) 376-0291

DURHAM COUNTY PUBLIC LIBRARY ✦
301 North Roxboro
Durham 27702
(919) 560-0110

STATE LIBRARY OF NORTH
CAROLINA ✳ ✦
Government and Business Services
Archives Bldg., 109 E. Jones St.
Raleigh 27601
(919) 733-3270

FORSYTH COUNTY PUBLIC
LIBRARY ✳ ✦
660 W. 5th St.
Winston-Salem 27101
(336) 727-2680

NORTH DAKOTA

BISMARCK PUBLIC LIBRARY
515 N. Fifth St.
Bismarck 58501
(701) 222-6410

FARGO PUBLIC LIBRARY ✳ ✦
102 N. 3rd St.
Fargo 58102
(701) 241-1491

OHIO

STARK COUNTY DISTRICT LIBRARY ✳ ✦
Humanities
715 Market Ave. N.
Canton 44702
(330) 452-0665

PUBLIC LIBRARY OF CINCINNATI &
HAMILTON COUNTY ✳ ✦
Grants Resource Center
800 Vine St.—Library Square
Cincinnati 45202-2071
(513) 369-6940

COLUMBUS METROPOLITAN
LIBRARY ✦
Business and Technology
96 S. Grant Ave.
Columbus 43215
(614) 645-2590

DAYTON & MONTGOMERY COUNTY
PUBLIC LIBRARY ✳ ✦
Grants Resource Center
215 E. Third St.
Dayton 45402
(937) 227-9500 x211

MANSFIELD/RICHLAND COUNTY
PUBLIC LIBRARY ✳ ✦
42 W. 3rd St.
Mansfield 44902
(419) 521-3110

TOLEDO-LUCAS COUNTY PUBLIC
LIBRARY ✳ ✦
Social Sciences Department
325 Michigan St.
Toledo 43624-1614
(419) 259-5245

PUBLIC LIBRARY OF YOUNGSTOWN &
MAHONING COUNTY ✳ ✦
305 Wick Ave.
Youngstown 44503
(330) 744-8636

MUSKINGUM COUNTY LIBRARY ✦
220 N. 5th St.
Zanesville 43701
(614) 453-0391

OKLAHOMA

OKLAHOMA CITY UNIVERSITY ✳ ✦
Dulaney Browne Library
2501 N. Blackwelder
Oklahoma City 73106
(405) 521-5822

TULSA CITY-COUNTY LIBRARY ✳ ✦
400 Civic Center
Tulsa 74103
(918) 596-7944

OREGON

OREGON INSTITUTE OF
TECHNOLOGY ✦
Library
3201 Campus Dr.
Klamath Falls 97601-8801
(503) 885-1773

PACIFIC NON-PROFIT NETWORK ✳ ✦
Grantsmanship Resource Library
33 N. Central, Suite 211
Medford 97501
(503) 779-6044

MULTNOMAH COUNTY LIBRARY ✦
Government Documents
801 SW Tenth Ave.
Portland 97205
(503) 248-5123

OREGON STATE LIBRARY ✳ ✦
State Library Building
Salem 97310
(503) 378-4277

PENNSYLVANIA

NORTHAMPTON COMMUNITY
COLLEGE ✦
Learning Resources Center
3835 Green Pond Rd.
Bethlehem 18017
(610) 861-5360

ERIE COUNTY LIBRARY SYSTEM ✦
160 East Front St.
Erie 16507
(814) 451-6927

DAUPHIN COUNTY LIBRARY SYSTEM ✦
Central Library
101 Walnut St.
Harrisburg 17101
(717) 234-4976

LANCASTER COUNTY PUBLIC
LIBRARY ✦
125 N. Duke St.
Lancaster 17602
(717) 394-2651

FOUNDATION CENTER COOPERATING COLLECTIONS *(continued)*

EXHIBIT 19.4

FREE LIBRARY OF PHILADELPHIA ✱ ✚
Regional Foundation Center
Logan Square
Philadelphia 19103
(215) 686-5423

CARNEGIE LIBRARY OF PITTSBURGH ✱ ✚
Foundation Collection
4400 Forbes Ave.
Pittsburgh 15213-4080
(412) 622-1917

POCONO NORTHEAST
DEVELOPMENT FUND ✚
James Pettinger Memorial Library
1151 Oak St.
Pittston 18640-3795
(717) 655-5381

READING PUBLIC LIBRARY ✚
100 South Fifth St.
Reading 19602
(610) 655-6355

MARTIN LIBRARY ✱ ✚
159 Market St.
York 17401
(717) 846-5300

RHODE ISLAND

PROVIDENCE PUBLIC
LIBRARY ✱ ✚
225 Washington St.
Providence 02906
(401) 455-8088

SOUTH CAROLINA

ANDERSON COUNTY LIBRARY ✱ ✚
202 East Greenville St.
Anderson 29621
(864) 260-4500

CHARLESTON COUNTY LIBRARY ✱ ✚
68 Calhoun St.
Charleston 29401
(843) 805-6950

SOUTH CAROLINA STATE LIBRARY ✱ ✚
1500 Senate St.
Columbia 29211
(803) 734-8666

SOUTH DAKOTA

SOUTH DAKOTA STATE LIBRARY ✱ ✚
800 Governors Dr.
Pierre 57501-2294
(605) 773-5070
(800) 592-1841 (SD residents)

NONPROFIT MANAGEMENT
INSTITUTE ✚
132 S. Dakota Rd.
Sioux Falls 57102
(605) 367-5380

SIOUXLAND LIBRARIES ✱ ✚
201 N. Main Ave.
Sioux Falls 57102-1132
(605) 367-7081

TENNESSEE

KNOX COUNTY PUBLIC LIBRARY ✱ ✚
500 W. Church Ave.
Knoxville 37902
(423) 544-5700

MEMPHIS & SHELBY COUNTY PUBLIC
LIBRARY ✱ ✚
1850 Peabody Ave.
Memphis 38104
(901) 725-8877

NASHVILLE PUBLIC LIBRARY ✱ ✚
Business Information Division
225 Polk Ave.
Nashville 37203
(615) 862-5843

TEXAS

NONPROFIT RESOURCE CENTER ✚
Funding Information Library
500 N. Chestnut. Suite 1511
Abilene 79604
(915) 677-8166

AMARILLO AREA FOUNDATION ✱ ✚
700 First National Place
801 S. Fillmore
Amarillo 79101
(806) 376-4521

HOGG FOUNDATION FOR
MENTAL HEALTH ✱ ✚
3001 Lake Austin Blvd.
Austin 78703
(512) 471-5041

BEAUMONT PUBLIC LIBRARY ✚
801 Pearl St.
Beaumont 77704
(409) 838-6606

CORPUS CHRISTI PUBLIC LIBRARY ✱ ✚
805 Comanche St.
Reference Dept.
Corpus Christi 78401
(512) 880-7000

DALLAS PUBLIC LIBRARY ✱ ✚
Urban Information
1515 Young St.
Dallas 75201
(214) 670-1487

CENTER FOR VOLUNTEERISM &
NONPROFIT MANAGEMENT ✚
1918 Texas Ave.
El Paso 79901
(915) 532-5377

SOUTHWEST BORDER NONPROFIT
RESOURCE CENTER ✚
Nonprofit Resource Center
1201 W. University Dr.
Edinburgh 78539
(956) 316-2610

FUNDING INFORMATION CENTER OF
FORT WORTH ✱ ✚
329 S. Henderson
Ft. Worth 76104
(817) 334-0228

HOUSTON PUBLIC LIBRARY ✱ ✚
Bibliographic Information Center
500 McKinney
Houston 77002
(713) 236-1313

LONGVIEW PUBLIC LIBRARY ✱
222 W. Cotton St.
Longview 75601
(903) 237-1352

LUBBOCK AREA FOUNDATION, INC. ✚
1655 Main St., Suite 209
Lubbock 79401
(806) 762-8061

NONPROFIT RESOURCE CENTER
OF TEXAS ✱ ✚
111 Soledad, Suite 200
San Antonio 78205
(210) 227-4333

WACO-MCLENNAN COUNTY
LIBRARY ✱ ✚
1717 Austin Ave.
Waco 76701
(254) 750-5975

NORTH TEXAS CENTER FOR
NONPROFIT MANAGEMENT ✱ ✚
624 Indiana, Suite 307
Wichita Falls 76301
(940) 322-4961

UTAH

SALT LAKE CITY PUBLIC LIBRARY ✱
209 East 500 South
Salt Lake City 84111
(801) 524-8200

VERMONT

VERMONT DEPT. OF LIBRARIES ✱ ✚
Reference & Law Info. Services
109 State St.
Montpelier 05609
(802) 828-3268

VIRGINIA

HAMPTON PUBLIC LIBRARY ✚
4207 Victoria Blvd.
Hampton 23669
(757) 727-1312

RICHMOND PUBLIC LIBRARY ✱ ✚
Business, Science & Technology
101 East Franklin St.
Richmond 23219
(804) 780-8223

ROANOKE CITY PUBLIC LIBRARY
SYSTEM ✱
706 S. Jefferson
Roanoke 24016
(540) 853-2477

WASHINGTON

MID-COLUMBIA LIBRARY ✱
405 South Dayton
Kennewick 99336
(509)586-3156

SEATTLE PUBLIC LIBRARY ✱ ✚
Science, Social Science
1000 Fourth Ave.
Seattle 98104
(206) 386-4620

SPOKANE PUBLIC LIBRARY ✱
Funding Information Center
West 811 Main Ave.
Spokane 99201
(509) 626-5347

UNITED WAY OF PIERCE COUNTY ✱ ✚
Center for Nonprofit Development
1501 Pacific Ave., Suite 400
P.O. Box 2215
Tacoma 98401
(206) 272-4263

GREATER WENATCHEE COMMUNITY
FOUNDATION AT THE WENATCHEE
PUBLIC LIBRARY
310 Douglas St.
Wenatchee 98807
(509) 662-5021

WEST VIRGINIA

KANAWHA COUNTY PUBLIC
LIBRARY ✱ ✚
123 Capitol St.
Charleston 25301
(304) 343-4646

WISCONSIN

UNIVERSITY OF WISCONSIN–
MADISON ✱ ✚
Memorial Library
728 State St.
Madison 53706
(608) 262-3242

MARQUETTE UNIVERSITY MEMORIAL
LIBRARY ✱ ✚
Funding Information Center
1415 W. Wisconsin Ave.
Milwaukee 53201-3141
(414) 288-1515

UNIVERSITY OF WISCONSIN–
STEVENS POINT ✱
Library—Foundation Collection
99 Reserve St.
Stevens Point 54481-3897
(715) 346-4204

WYOMING

NATRONA COUNTY PUBLIC
LIBRARY ✱ ✚
307 E. 2nd St.
Casper 82601-2598
(307) 237-4935

LARAMIE COUNTY COMMUNITY
COLLEGE ✱ ✚
Instructional Resource Center
1400 E. College Dr.
Cheyenne 82007-3299
(307) 778-1206

CAMPBELL COUNTY PUBLIC
LIBRARY ✱ ✚
2101 4-J Rd.
Gillette 82716
(307) 682-3223

TETON COUNTY LIBRARY ✱ ✚
125 Virginia Lane
Jackson 83001
(307) 733-2164

ROCK SPRINGS LIBRARY ✚
400 C St.
Rock Springs 82901
(307) 352-6667

PUERTO RICO

UNIVERSIDAD DEL SAGRADO
CORAZON ✚
M.M.T. Guevara Library
Santurce 00914
(809) 728-1515 x 4357

Participants in the Foundation Center's Cooperating Collections network are libraries or nonprofit information centers that provide fundraising information and other funding-related technical assistance in their communities. Cooperating Collections agree to provide free public access to a basic collection of Foundation Center publications during a regular schedule of hours, offering free funding research guidance to all visitors. Many also provide a variety of services for local nonprofit organizations, using staff or volunteers to prepare special materials, organize workshops, or conduct orientations.

The Foundation Center welcomes inquiries from libraries or information centers in the U.S. interested in providing this type of public information service. If you are interested in establishing a funding information library for the use of nonprofit organizations in your area or in learning more about the program, please write to: Rich Romeo, Coordinator of Cooperating Collections, The Foundation Center, 79 Fifth Avenue, New York, NY 10003-3076 or e-mail rromeo@fdncenter.org.   8/98

FOUNDATION CENTER COOPERATING COLLECTIONS (continued)

EXHIBIT 19.4

ELECTRONIC RETRIEVAL AND DATABASE SEARCHES

Many public libraries, university libraries, and higher education grants offices are able to perform electronic searches of *The Foundation Directory*, *Foundation Grants Index*, and other resources containing foundation grants information. Explore the possibility of computer search and retrieval by contacting an established grants office near you.

The Foundation Center offers *FC Search: The Foundation Center's Database on CD-ROM*. It covers over 47,000 foundations and corporate givers, describes almost 200,000 associated grants, and lists approximately 200,000 trustees, officers, and donors. Other electronic resources that can be found at the Foundation center include *Oryx GRANTS Database*, *The Chronicle Guide to Grants*, *Taft's Prospector's Choice*, and *Tax Analysts' Infotax*.

Dialog Inc. is a commercial organization that provides access to hundreds of databases in a range of subject areas. The Foundation Center offers *The Foundation Directory* file and *The Foundation Grants Index* file online through Dialog. In addition, Dialog has several comprehensive grants databases, including the *GRANTS Database*, available online or through *Dialog OnDisc*, which contains information on foundation grants as well as government and corporate grants (see the list of resources for more information).

Foundation Web Sites and the Internet

The use of the Internet to research private grantors is expanding. More and more of the 41,588 foundations have a Web site. In fact, according to the Foundation Center, the number has grown from a handful in 1996 to over 700 in 1999. (However, only 12 foundations allow for electronic submissions at this time.) Many of the Web sites list contact people plus phone numbers and e-mail addresses. In addition, several nonprofit organizations have developed Web sites with grantor information. The information provided on Web sites is often more current than what is in the print directories since Web sites are usually updated daily or weekly as opposed to annually or semiannually. Also, new programs or interests of foundation may be announced on Web sites long before they are printed in directories. Just remember that information obtained from the Web should be double-checked, especially if you suspect a Web page has not been updated in some time (most sites have "last updated" dates).

There are also bulletin boards, listservs, and chat rooms that focus on foundation and corporate grantors. E-mail listservs can provide grantseekers with much information, contacts, and opportunities for networking. One example of this kind of listserv is CharityChannel (http://charitychannel.com/forums/), which hosts a number of listservs on many different aspects of private funding. Check with your membership groups and your peers to see what is available, or perform your own Internet search. In addition, the Foundation

Center publishes a book entitled *Guide to Grantseeking on the Web*, which includes abstracts of hundreds of grantmaker Web sites and a variety of related nonprofit sites of interest. This publication may be a good starting point for your search of online resources available to grantseekers (see List of Resources for ordering information).

Research to locate your most likely foundation grantor need not be labor intensive or costly. Using electronic databases and Web sites in your search will save you time and in many instances the information you find will complement the information found in print form. The key is to locate the data that will enable you to estimate your chances for success before you invest any more time in seeking a foundation grant.

CHAPTER 20

Researching Corporate Grant Opportunities

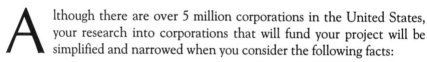lthough there are over 5 million corporations in the United States, your research into corporations that will fund your project will be simplified and narrowed when you consider the following facts:

- Of the 5 million corporations in the United States, only 35 percent make any philanthropic contributions at all.
- Of those that make contributions, only a small percent contribute over $500 a year.
- Of the $143.46 billion contributed to nonprofit organizations through private philanthropy in 1997, corporate giving accounted for approximately 5.7 percent, or $8.2 billion.
- Corporate *foundation* giving accounted for only 20 percent of the $8.2 billion reported in 1997.

The Foundation Center is a good resource for information on corporate foundation grants. Its publication *National Directory of Corporate Giving* provides information on 1,905 foundations and 990 direct giving programs. *Corporate Foundation Profiles,* also published by the Foundation Center, contains grants information on 195 of the largest corporate foundations in the United States. The *Corporate Giving Directory*, published by the Taft Group, is another good resource. It provides profiles on 1,000 of the largest corporate foundations and corporate charitable giving programs. (See List of Resources for ordering information.)

You will find much less information available on corporate grants awarded by companies that do not use a foundation to make their grants, and the information you do find will be much less reliable. The reason for the lack of sound data on corporate giving is that there are no laws allowing public review of corporate contributions programs. Companies must record their corporate charitable contributions on their Internal Revenue Service tax return, but no one, not even a stockholder, has the right to see the return.

The data on corporate giving are derived from self-reported, voluntary responses to surveys and questionnaires. Even the corporate contributions data reported in *Giving USA* (published by the AAFRC Trust for Philanthropy) are based on a voluntary survey conducted by the Conference Board, a nonprofit organization with a reputation for keeping corporate responses confidential.

Armed with the knowledge that corporate giving is based on a "quid-pro-quo," or "this-for-that," approach, your foremost strategy should be to look at your proposal idea and redefine it, if necessary, in a way that could attract corporate support. Do not start by purchasing an expensive national reference book on corporate giving unless you plan to move your organization to another city. Corporations usually give where they live. Corporate plants, workers, product development, and other vested interests such as geographic proximity all play a role in motivating corporate contributions. Your best bet is to draw a circle with a 25-mile radius around your organization, identify the larger employers in the circle (companies employing 100 or more), and determine which of these corporations your project could most easily be related to.

While it still makes sense to check out the corporate grant resource books available in your local public library and Foundation Center regional collection, a more important source for data is your local chamber of commerce. The chamber of commerce can provide you with a list of local corporations and information on number of employees, total value of payroll, and products and services provided.

Those local companies whose products, employees, communities, or families would be affected by your proposal are your best choices for pre-proposal contact. Since corporate contributions depend on a company's profitability, your corporate research should include information on revenue. One way to obtain accurate data on profitability is to ask a corporate member of your grants advisory committee who subscribes to Dun and Bradstreet's financial services to request a Dun and Bradstreet report on the prospective corporate grantor. This report will rate the fiscal stability of the company and give you a sense of the company's ability to support your proposal.

Another technique for keeping abreast of local corporations is to purchase one share of stock in each publicly held company in your area. If you receive a dividend check, you will know the company made money! Using this technique, you will also get information on top corporate administrators and board member changes.

If your corporate proposal involves research, product development, or product positioning with your clients, you can move beyond local boundaries and corporate locations. To do so, refer to the *North American Industry Classification System(NAICS) Manual*, which should be available at your local public college library. It can also be purchased through the National Technical Information Service (see the list of resources at the back of this book). The *NAICS Manual* is based on the United States' new industry classification system which has recently replaced the Standard Industrial Classification (SIC) system. The publication references companies by the types of goods they produce. The *NAICS Manual* can be a valuable resource if you have a project that can either position a company's products or provide a model that others could follow to increase sales and profits. For example, if your project uses innovative ways to educate people with vision impairments, you might use the *NAICS Manual* to locate companies that manufacture state-of-the-art telecommunications equipment that could be used in your solution.

Your public library or local college library will have information about the companies you identify. Any one of the Dun and Bradstreet research tools or Standard and Poor's publications will provide the basic information you will need to determine your best prospects for funding.

Exhibit 20.1 is an example of what an entry in *Dun and Bradstreet's Million Dollar Directory* looks like. As you can see, entries in the directory include the following information on corporations:

- D&B D-U-N-S number
- company name, address, and phone number
- state of incorporation
- primary and secondary SIC codes
- sales volume
- number of employees
- parent company and location
- year started/ownership date
- key executives' names and titles
- primary bank and accounting firm
- import/export designation
- stock exchange symbol and indicator for publicly owned companies
- line of business description
- trade name
- directors other than officers

All entries in the directory are indexed alphabetically and cross referenced geographically and by industry classification.

Volume 1 of *Standard and Poor's Register of Corporations, Directors, and Executives* provides similar information (see exhibit 20.2). Entries include:

D-U-N-S 00-656-4690
HENTLEY & CO (DE)
10 SE Main St, Washville, IL
Zip 81829   *Tel* (309)545-2000
Sales 11100MM   *Emp* 49900

Tkr sym BTL   *Exch* BSE CIN MSE NYS PBS
                                       PCS
SIC 7361 7363 Employment agencies; temporary help service
BK Congressional Bk NA, Chicago, IL
Accts Proven Way
  *Mark V. Franz   Ch Bd CEO
  *James C. Luch   Pr
   Ken A Ruchan   Sec
   Thomas Glianno   Ex VP, Finance
   Stefan Ziegler   Sr VP
   Karl Boggle   VP, Sales

Entry From *Dun & Bradstreet's Million Dollar Directory* (Ficititious Data)

EXHIBIT 20.1

- corporate name, address, and phone number
- an extensive list of officers
- sales volume
- number of employees
- a description of products

Because a corporation's executives often make up its contributions committee, I have chosen to show a list of officers for volume 1 of *Standard and Poor's
Register of Corporation, Directors, and Executives* sample entry in exhibit 20.2.

In both *Dun and Bradstreet's Million Dollar Directory* and volume 1 of
Standard and Poor's Register of Corporations, Directors, and Executives, the
names designated with an asterisk appear in each publication's companion
book (or volume) on directors and executives. For example, after searching in
volume 1 of *Standard and Poor's Register of Corporations, Directors, and Executives*, you may decide you want to locate more information on William S.
Chasel Jr., vice chairman and chief financial officer of American Communications Company. There is an asterisk next to his name in volume 1 of the
Register, so you can look for further information in volume 2. Exhibit 20.3 is a
sample of what you might find.

AMERICAN COMMUNICATIONS CO.
99 Brady Ave., New York, NY 10007
Tel. 212-897-8888

* Chrm & Chief Exec Officer—Charles L. Brown
* Pres & Chief Oper Officer—William M. Ellinghouse
* Vice-Chrm & Chief Fin Officer—William S. Chasel, Jr.
  Exec V-P (Business)—Thomas E. Bolger
  Exec V-P (Network)—Richard R. Hough
  Exec V-P—Charles E. Hugel
  Exec V-P—Morris Tanebaum
  Exec V-P (Residence)—Kenneth J. Whaling
  Exec V-P—S.R. Wilcox
  V-P & Asst to Chrm—Alvin von Auw
  V-P (Bus Services)—Robert E. Allen
  V-P (Network Plan & Design)—Jack A. Baird
  V-P (Fed Reg Matters)—James R. Billings
  V-P (Pub Rel & Empl Inf)—Edward M. Block
  V-P (Residence Mktg Sales & Serv)—John L. Clendenin
  V-P & Treas—Virginia A. Dwyer
  V-P (Pub Affairs)—John G. Fox
  V-P (Pres—Long Lines Dept)—Robert W. Kleinert
  V-P (Tariffs & Costs)—Walter B. Kelly
  V-P (Bus Mktg)—Archie J. McGill
  V-P (State Reg Matters)—Alfred G. Hartoll
  V-P (Labor Rel Cor Per & Policy Seminar)—Rex V. Reed
  V-P (Fin Mgt)—John L. Segally
  V-P (Plan & Admin D)—William G. Sharell
  Secy—Frank A. Hutson, Jr.
  Accts—Coopers & Lybrand
  Revenue: $45.41 Bil Employees 984,000
  Stock Exchange(s): NYS, BST, PAC, MID, CIN, PSE
* ALSO DIRECTORS—Other Directors Are:
  Edward W. Carter   Catherine M. Bleary
  Archie W. Davis   John D. de Butts
  BUSINESS: Communications
  S.I.C. 4844; 4833

Entry from Volume 1 of Standard and Poor's Register of Corporations,
Directors, and Executives (Fictitious Data)

EXHIBIT 20.2

As you can see from the sample, the information provided in volume 2 of *Standard and Poor's Register of Corporations, Directors, and Executives* includes the age, educational background, and residence of the corporate executive, as well as his or her other corporate affiliations and activities. This biographical information is very valuable in that it can be used with your grants advisory committee to uncover links and expand corporate relationships. For example, in the sample entry we can see that William S. Chasel Jr. graduated from Dartmouth College. Therefore, if you have an advocate or grants advisory committee member who is a graduate of Dartmouth, you will be wise to take that individual with you when you make pre-proposal contact.

CHASEL, WILLIAM S., JR. (b. 1944 Brooklyn—Dartmouth Coll. Amos Tuck Sch. of Bus. Admin., 1966)—Vice-Chrm, Chief Fin Officer & Dir., American Communications Co., 99 Brady Ave., New York, NY 10007
      Campbell Soup Co., Dir
      Southside Telephone Company, Dir
      Manufacturers Hanner Corp. & Trust Co., Dir
      Philadelphia Fund Savings Group, Trustee

CHASHELL, GEORGE R. (b. 1939 Mansfield, OH—BPOE)—Secy, Bopping Paines, Inc., 664 S. West St., Mannington, OH 44902—Res: 355 Oak St., Mannington 44904
      Bopping Paines Inc. (California), Secy
      Bopping Paines Inc. (Delaware), Secy
      Bopping Disc Inc., Asst Secy
      Smith Water System Co., Secy
      National Construction Sacky Credit Group, Mem

CHASIN, EDWARD A. (b. 1941 Duluth, MN—Univ of Chicago, 1961)—Exec. V-P & Dir (Mktg Sales), Complete Controls Inc., 6777 Washington St., Minneapolis 56654—Res: 555 Shoreside Ave., Wayzata, MN 55392
      Fireside Country Club, 1st V-P & Dir

ENTRY FROM *STANDARD AND POOR'S REGISTER OF CORPORATIONS, DIRECTORS, AND EXECUTIVES, VOLUME 2—DIRECTORS AND EXECUTIVES* (FICTITIOUS DATA)

EXHIBIT 20.3

CHASMAN, EDMUND JOSEPH (b. 1942 Rockville Square, NY—St. Patrick's Coll, 1964)—Exec V-P & Dir Hoggens Mason Wood Walker, Inc., 6 Maple Ave., Baltimore, MD 32241—Res: 7878 A Frame Rd., Huxton, MD 32256
  Peacon Picture Services, Inc., Dir
  RFS Financial Services (subs Hoggens Mason), Dir
  Garden Capital (subs Hoggens Mason), Dir

CHASMANN, GEORGE D. (b. 1939 NYC)—V-P (Intl), Gordon Guaranty Trust Co. of New York, 23 Hall St., New York 10008—Res: 23 Midwood Dr., Kendall Park, NJ 08824
  U.S. Chamber of Comm. on Import Trade Policy, Chrm
  Import Expansion Comm. of the Bankers Assn. for Foreign Trade, Mem
  National Overseas Trade Council, Inc., Dir

ENTRY FROM *STANDARD AND POOR'S REGISTER OF CORPORATIONS, DIRECTORS, AND EXECUTIVES, VOLUME 2--DIRECTORS AND EXECUTIVES* (FICTITIOUS DATA) *(continued)*

EXHIBIT 20.3

In addition to these national reference books, your library should also have *Who's Who in America* and other books on outstanding individuals in your geographic area. The more you know about the people you will be approaching for a grant, the more prepared you will be to create a powerful appeal that motivates the grantor to award you funds. Corporate leaders have much more written about them than federal bureaucrats, and your local librarian can show you how to use free resource tools to learn more about corporate grant prospects. Check the list of resources for commercially available materials that you will find helpful in your search for corporate funding sources.

Doing your homework on corporate grantors can be more frustrating than researching federal or foundation sources. Except for the portion of corporate grants that are awarded through corporate foundations, corporate data are not subject to validation and hence the reporting is not always accurate.

CHAPTER 21

Contacting a Private Funding Source Before Submission

Contacting the funding source before you write your proposal will help you validate your research and gather additional information about the grantor's priorities and interests. More importantly, pre-proposal contact will allow you to tailor your proposal according to the particular approach or method that each funding source will find interesting. The purpose of this contact is not to convince the grantor to fund your proposal but to ensure that your approach will meet the grantor's needs. By contacting the funding source you increase your chances of success over five times.

HOW TO CONTACT GRANTORS

Since most private funding sources are understaffed, making contact with them can be difficult. Many foundation and corporate grantor application instructions state "no contact except by letter," and your research will show that many addresses for private funding sources are actually addresses for trust departments of banks.

Naturally, you do not want to talk to a trust officer at a bank, but speaking with a foundation or corporate board member would be a big help. With only 1,000 foundations occupying their own offices, the chances of talking to a foundation's director or staff are limited to the largest foundations. What is significant, however, is that each foundation and corporate contributions committee has 8 to 10 members. This means that the 41,588 foundations have over 332,000 board members plus hundreds of thousands of corporate officials.

These are the actual decision makers, and they can be contacted effectively through your webbing system.

One foundation director underscored the importance of using links to board members when she told me that

- one-third of her foundation's grants will be awarded to her board members' favorite nonprofit organizations
- one-third will go to her board members' friends' favorite nonprofits
- one-third will be "up-for-grabs" to those who write creative, persuasive proposals that match the interests and values of her foundation

At this point your research should already include the names of your best prospects' decision makers (board members, corporate contribution committee members, and so on). Ask the leaders of your organization whether they know any of these people and, if so, whether they would help you by using this informal means of contact. Perhaps, your link can set up lunch or a conference call. If you do not uncover a link, your plan should be to follow the grantor's guidelines as outlined in the various resource publications (see chapter 7 for more information on webbing and links).

If there is an office and contact is not ruled out or discouraged, you should

- write an inquiry letter
- telephone to set up a visit or a phone interview
- make a personal visit to the grantor

Contact by Letter

Be very selective when sending a letter requesting an appointment and information on a grantor's program. Since very few private grantors have the staff resources necessary to respond to written requests, do not be surprised if you receive a rejection notice even though you only asked for application guidelines.

Exhibit 21.1 provides a sample inquiry letter. Please note that this is not a letter proposal or a letter of intent. The letter proposal will be described in chapter 22.

Date

Name
Title
Address

Dear _____ :

I am developing a project which deals with _____ and provides
benefits to [or in] _____. My research indicates that this
area is an important concern of the [name of foundation/funding source].

Please use the enclosed label to send me your current priority statement and
information on your desired format for proposals or other guidelines. I would also
appreciate it if you could add us to your mailing list so that we could receive your
annual reports, newsletters, and any other materials you think might be useful to us
as we work on this and related projects.

Thank you for your cooperation.

Sincerely,

Name/Title
Organization
Address

SAMPLE INQUIRY LETTER

EXHIBIT 21.1

Contact by Telephone

Telephone contact with a private grantor may take the place of face-to-face
contact or may be used to set up a visit. When you are successful at telephoning
a private grantor, you can be sure you have contacted one that falls within the
small percentage of private funding sources that have an office and a paid staff.
Even if you are telephoning the grantor in hopes of setting up a visit, be ready to
discuss your project. Many grantors use the telephone very effectively for
assessing projects and their interest in them before agreeing to discuss the
project face-to-face. After all, it is much easier to tell a grantseeker that they
are not really interested in a project over the telephone than it is in person.

If the grantor wants to discuss your project before giving you an appointment, ask whether you could fax, e-mail, or mail a one- or two-page concept
paper and call back when he or she has your outline in hand.

If they agree to a visit, set the date. Do not offer any more information at this
time, but do ask them what they recommend that you bring. Also ask about

- the use of audiovisual equipment in your presentation (restrictions, availability of electrical outlets, etc.)
- the number of staff to be present so that you can bring the appropriate number of copies of information about your organization
- the possibility of their making a visit to your location
- their travel plans, whether they will be near your organization, or whether they will be attending any conferences or meetings you will attending or where you will be presenting

If personal visits are not allowed, you will be forced to discuss your project over the telephone. Again, request that you be allowed to forward a concept paper and set up a telephone appointment to discuss your project and their interest in it. Your questions will actually be the same as those you would ask if you were to make a personal visit. Therefore, review the following section on the visit and questions to ask a funding source.

The Visit

Visiting in person is the best way to get to know the funding source, but visits can be difficult to arrange, because foundations are not heavily staffed and corporate people are occupied in important profit-making jobs. If you are fortunate enough to get a visit, use your time wisely.

Who Should Go? Your credibility will be higher if you take a non-staff representative with you. An articulate, impressive volunteer, advocate, or advisory committee member is an excellent choice. Use the information you collected from your webbing and links to choose a close match to the funding source. Use age, education, club affiliation, and other personal characteristics as the basis for your choice. Dress according to the information you have about the funding source. Dress in the foundation and corporate world is generally conservative, and usually it is better to be overdressed than underdressed. Dress codes differ in the East, West, South, and Midwest, so be aware of geographic influences. The best person to ask about the appropriate dress for a particular funding source is a link who knows the grantor or a past grantee.

Materials to Bring. The materials you will need to bring are those you have already gathered and organized in your proposal development workbook (Swiss cheese book). You may also want to bring simple audiovisual aids that document the need in a more interesting or vivid manner and help show the funding source how important it is the meet the need *now*. If you do use audiovisual aids, make sure they are in balance with your request. A three-to five-minute video would be appropriate if you are making a large request ($250,000), but inappropriate for a smaller ($5,000) request. At this point it is still proper to have several possible approaches to meeting the need. Therefore, you should have the cost and benefits and pros and cons of each approach outlined and ready for presentation. You want to learn which approach the prospective funding source likes best; you are not trying to convince the grantor that you have "the one and only way to solve the problem." Your cost-benefit analysis worksheet from chapter 4 will usually elicit more than enough response to begin a conversation.

Be ready to use the various parts of your Swiss cheese book for answers to questions like "Why should we give the money to you instead of some other organization?" Refer to your section on the uniquenesses of your organization (personnel, mission, and so on).

Questions to Ask a Funding Source. Review these questions to determine which would be the most appropriate to ask based on your current knowledge of the funding source. You may want to assign specific questions to each of the two individuals going to the meeting and prepare for the visit by role-playing various answers.

1. We have developed several feasible approaches. Would you please look at them and comment on which one looks the most interesting to you (or would look the most interesting to the board)?
2. Last year, your foundation/corporation awarded $_____ to our kind of project and the average size was $_____. Will this remain consistent?
3. Our research indicates that your deadlines last year were _____ and _____. Will they be the same this year?
4. Does it help you if proposals are submitted early? Do proposals that are submitted early receive more favorable treatment?
5. How are proposals reviewed by your foundation/corporation? Who performs the review? Outside experts? Board members? Staff? Is there a scoring system or checklist that they use?
6. Are there current granting priorities? (Give them a copy of your research sheet to determine whether your research accurately reflects their priorities.)
7. What do you think of submitting more than one proposal in a funding cycle?
8. Is the amount we are requesting realistic in light of your current goals?
9. Have you ever provided grant support jointly with another funding source and, if so, is that approach appropriate here?

The following two questions should be asked only when the grantor seems very encouraging.

10. Would you look over our proposal before our formal submission if we finished it early?
11. May I see a proposal you have funded that you think is well written? This would provide us with a model for style and format.

Ask question 12 only if the grantor is not very encouraging.

12. Can you suggest any other funders who may be appropriate for this project?

Private Funding Source Report Form

Each time a member of your staff contacts a funder in person, over the phone, or through e-mail, he or she should complete and file a private funding source report form (see exhibit 21.2). This simple procedure has a number of important benefits. It will keep you from damaging your credibility by repeating the same questions or having the funder say, "I gave that information to _____ from your organization. Don't you people ever talk to each other?" Also, it will allow another person from your organization to pick up where you leave off.

Successful grantees will recognize the importance of contacting the funding source before writing the proposal. The purpose of the contact is not to make small talk, but to validate research and gather data needed to address the grantor's hidden agenda. Using the techniques in this chapter to contact and record contact with private grantors will be an essential part of your grantseeking strategy.

Complete one of these forms after each contact with a private funding source.

Funding Source: _____

_____

Funding Source Address: _____

_____

_____

Funding Source Contact Person: _____
Telephone Number: _____

Contacted On (Date): _____
Contacted By (Name): _____
Type of Contact: Phone_____   Visit _____

Objective of Contact: _____

_____

_____

_____

Results of Contact: _____

_____

_____

_____

_____

Follow-Up: _____

_____

_____

_____

_____

PRIVATE FUNDING SOURCE REPORT FORM

EXHIBIT 21.2

CHAPTER 22

Applying for Private Funds
Creating a Winning Letter Proposal

Historically, private sources have used the letter proposal format as the primary component of their application process. Now federal and state granting programs are showing a shift in this direction, and many have instituted a pre-application process that is similar to creating a letter proposal or concept paper. Public funding sources may call the letter proposal a pre-proposal concept paper or a letter of intent. In some cases they will not send a prospective grantee an application package unless they like the approach outlined in this paper or letter. Although this pre-proposal screening may sound negative at first, it really is not such a bad idea because it prevents grantseekers from completing a more lengthy application for a project that the prospective grantor has little interest in funding or reviewing.

Foundations and corporations use the letter proposal format simply because they do not have the time or staff to read long, tedious proposals. They *want* short, concise letters and grant billions of dollars each year based on two to three pages of contents.

Letter proposals are often read by board members during relatively brief meetings. A survey of foundations revealed that most foundations meet one to three times a year for an average of one to three hours each time. Within this short time frame, they must read an overwhelming number of letter proposals; therefore, it is imperative that your proposal attract and retain their interest.

If your research provides you with an application format to follow, use it exactly as outlined. However, review the components presented here to be sure that the suggested areas are included in the required format. Some foundations that have Web sites provide an application form that can be printed, but the majority still request a letter proposal.

CONSTRUCTING A LETTER PROPOSAL

The main components of a letter proposal are

- an introductory paragraph stating the reason for writing
- a paragraph explaining why this grantor was selected
- a needs paragraph
- a solution paragraph
- a uniqueness paragraph
- a request for funds paragraph
- a closing paragraph
- signatures
- attachments, if allowed

Introductory Paragraph

Begin by stating your reason for writing to the funding source, and mention your link to the grantor when possible. In some cases your link may prefer to remain anonymous and endorse your proposal at a board meeting. In other instances your link may actually instruct you to refer to him or her in your proposal. If so, you could say something like

> Kate Macrae [your link, a past board member, trustee, or staff member of the foundation or corporation] and I have discussed the mutual concerns of the Kleineste Foundation [funding source] and my organization in meeting the nutritional needs of the elderly [subject area or problem].

If your prospective funding source is a corporation, you can use a link or demonstrate a volunteer connection to the company. Many corporations will not invest in a local nonprofit organization unless their employees are voluntarily involved with it. Therefore, your opening paragraph could refer to the commitment of their employees to your cause. For example:

> Will Olsen, your Region Four supervisor, and I have discussed Oak Computer's role in increasing the performance of our students through the use of applied technology. As chairperson of our school advisory committee, Mr. Olsen has donated over 100 hours of time and has been instrumental in making our computer lab a reality.

If you cannot mention a link or the commitment of the funding source's employees in your introductory paragraph, begin your letter proposal with the next most important factor—why the grantor was selected for solicitation or how you knew it would be interested in your proposal.

Why the Grantor Was Selected

Foremost in the reader's mind is why he or she should be reading your proposal. This is your opportunity to position yourself and your organization as winners that do their homework. You want the prospective funding source to know you are not operating a hit-or-miss grantseeking operation, or blanketing the foundation and corporate world with a "one proposal fits all" approach. What you need to make clear in this paragraph is that, based on what you have discovered through your research, you believe the funding source is likely to find your proposal interesting. This does not mean merely saying something like "We know you will find our proposal of interest," but rather: "Our research indicates that your foundation is committed to the support of health care for the indigent. In the last three years you have dedicated over $400,000 to this area." In this example you could also refer to the percentage of the funding source's total grant dollars that went to supporting health care for the indigent or mention a major or significant accomplishment made in this area through a previously awarded grant.

This paragraph need not be long. You want to demonstrate that you have taken the time to research the funding source's interests and that your proposal will address an issue that has been a concern of the grantor's. By doing so, your proposal will command the respect of the reader and warrant the investment of time he or she will make to review it.

Again, you are following Festinger's theory of cognitive dissonance. To keep the reader interested in your proposal, you are going to have to present a proposal that reinforces his or her values and feelings of worth and importance. Seek to align your organization with the values of the grantor by adding something like "It is with our mutual concern for (or commitment to) the welfare of the indigent that we come to you with this proposal."

Needs Paragraph

If you have constructed a proposal development workbook as suggested in chapter 3, you already have gathered statistics, case studies, quotes, and articles to document a compelling statement of need for action. The main difference between stating the need in a letter proposal to a foundation or corporation and stating it in a federal grant application is that you have the opportunity to incorporate the human element in your appeal to the private grantor. While your letter proposal must be based on fact, you can motivate the foundation and corporate funding source with the more human side of the problem. The challenge is to portray a compelling need without overusing either the facts (by quoting too many research articles) or the human-interest aspects of the problem.

Select the components of the need that will most likely convince the grantor that the gap between what is and what ought to be must be closed *immediately*.

To accomplish this you must have done research on the values and perspective of the grantor. Use what you have learned to describe the gap in a manner that is tailored to each particular funding source. In a few paragraphs, your letter proposal must

- include a few well-chosen statistics
- exhibit sensitivity to the geographic perspective of the grantor
- portray the human side of the problem

Whether your proposal is for research, a service model, technology transfer, or product development, your statement of need must be more compelling than your competitor's to keep the reader interested. Readers must want to read the rest of your proposal to discover what you are going to do about closing the gap you have so eloquently and succinctly documented. Many novice grantseekers overlook or underestimate the importance of the needs section of their letter proposal; they assume readers must already know about the need because they have granted funds to this area in the past. This assumption is a mistake. Even if grantors do know about the need, they expect you to command their respect by proving *your* expertise in the field as in the following example:

> The need for cancer prevention and treatment in the United States continues to grow—but not equally for all races. If you were diagnosed with cancer in 1950, you would have had a slightly higher survival rate if you were black. Today, however, the statistics are dramatically reversed. In a study by Stotts, Glynn, and Baquet, African Americans were ranked first among U.S. ethnic groups with the lowest cancer survival rate and first with the highest age-adjusted rates of cancer incidence and mortality.

Solution Paragraph

What will you do to close the gap you have just documented? The solution section of your proposal calls for a brief description of the approach you propose to use to solve the problem. In most cases your approach will not totally eliminate the problem, but you must describe how much of the gap you will close (your objective). While describing how you will close the gap, include the measurement indicator you will use to evaluate the success of your approach.

Depending on the number of pages allowed, you may have to limit this section to one or two paragraphs of five to seven lines. While you need to have a legitimate plan, you must guard against making the methodology too elaborate. Since you are the content expert, you may have difficulty viewing your proposal from the reader's point of view. Ask yourself the following questions:

- How much does the reader really need to know?
- Will the reader understand my plan?
- Will the words used in the description of my solution be familiar to the reader?

- Is all the information included critical to convincing the funder that I have a sound, worthwhile plan, or am I including some of it just for myself?

Remember, while you are concerned with how you will solve the problem, grantors are concerned with what will be different after their money is spent. If possible, use this section to summarize your approach and objectives and refer the funder to your project planner for more information as in the following example:

> What can we do in Smithville to promote the sharing of responsibility for education among schools, parents, and children? At Smithville Elementary School we have developed a program aimed at increasing responsible behavior and encouraging parental involvement in the classroom and at home. Teachers will actually work with parents and students to develop tailored, individual contracts to produce increases in all levels of education and the quality of course work. The attached project planner outlines each objective and the activities that will foster the changes we desire. Through the education and involvement of parents in their children's responsible use of out-of-school time, our program will provide the catalyst for decreasing television viewing of students, increasing the completion of homework assignments, and improving test scores.

Uniqueness Paragraph

In the uniqueness paragraph you want to assure the grantor that your organization is the best choice for implementing the solution. Assuming you have held the reader's interest up to this point, he or she knows

- why you have selected the funding source
- that there is a compelling need
- that you have a plan to address this need

The key question in the grantor's mind at this critical moment is whether your organization is the right one to address the problem.

If you have completed the uniqueness exercise in chapter 6, you already have a list of your organization's uniquenesses and, if appropriate, the unique advantages of your consortia members. Select items from the list to include in this section of your letter proposal. Choose credibility builders that will convince the grantor that you have the commitment, staff, skill, buildings, and equipment to do the job. For example, you could say something like:

> Serving the elderly has been the sole mission of Rock of Ages Home for over 50 years. Since our inception we have continually received superior ratings from the state board. Our staff members represent over 300 years of experience, and their commitment to doing more than

their call of duty is exhibited by their willingness to *volunteer* time to develop this model approach for serving Alzheimer patients.

Request for Funds Paragraph

You must make a precise request for money. If you want to demonstrate that you have done your homework, refer to the fact that your request is (or is close to) the grantor's average-size award for your area of interest.

If your request from this grantor does not cover the entire cost of the project, mention those other sources that have already given support, or list the others you will be approaching. In general it is easier to attract corporate support if you already have one corporate sponsor or at least one other credible grantor. This makes the grantor you are approaching feel as if it is investing in a blue chip stock rather than a risky junk bond.

You can summarize the budget categories that make up your total request, or you can provide prospective grantors with the portion of the budget that you would like them to fund. Since you are working under a severe space limitation, your budget summary should be arranged in paragraph form or in several short columns. If you submit your project planner with your proposal, you can refer to the column subtotals in your planner. For example: "The salary and wages, including fringe benefits, total $24,000. The work of the project director and other employees called for in this proposal is documented on page 3 in columns G, H, and I of the project planner."

To keep the focus on the value of the project and the results that you are seeking, you may want to divide the cost of the project by the number of people who will benefit from it. Consider the effect your project may have over several years, and calculate a cost per person served or affected by the project. For example: "In the next five years the equipment that you provide under this grant will touch the lives of approximately 5,000 students at a cost of $5.63 per person served."

Closing Paragraph

Many grantseekers close their letter proposal with a statement reflecting their willingness to meet with the prospective grantor to discuss their proposal. Unless the prospective grantor is a large foundation with a staff, any reference to such a meeting is usually futile. Instead, use the closing of your proposal to underscore your willingness to provide any further documentation or information the funding source may desire.

This brings up the question of who from your organization will be the best person to communicate with the prospective grantor. While you may have written the proposal, you probably will not be the individual to sign it. Therefore, in your closing paragraph request that the prospective grantor contact you (or the individual responsible for the project) for more information or to answer any questions. For example, "I encourage you to telephone me at my office or to call Ms. Connors directly at _____ to respond to technical questions or for additional information." Be sure to include a telephone number and extension, and test the line that will be used for this purpose to be certain that it is answered by a courteous and knowledgeable representative of your organization.

The closing paragraph is also the appropriate place to include your organization's designation as a 501(c)3 organization.

Signatures

Because this is a grant application and constitutes an agreement between your organization and the grantor if it is accepted, the administrator or officer who holds rank and responsibility should sign it. If the link to the grantor is not your chief operating officer or chief executive officer, there is no reason why two individuals—the link and the administrator—cannot sign the proposal.

Because the board is legally responsible for the consequences of your organization's actions, including a board member's signature along with the chief executive officer's may impress the grantor. Just remember that the purpose of the signature is to provide the proposal with legal commitment and credibility.

Attachments, if Allowed

Most foundations and corporations do not encourage prospective grantees to submit any additional materials with their proposal. This includes attachments as well as videotapes, audio tapes, compact discs, and so on. In some cases you can incorporate a photograph in your proposal, but be aware that this may hurt rather than help your chance for funding.

Whenever possible include your project planner as a page in your proposal rather than as an attachment, and be sure to always refer to it by page number. In general, your proposal should give the impression that you have more information you are willing to give the prospective grantor if desired. Including too much with the proposal, however, may reduce the likelihood that it will be read.

A sample letter proposal to a foundation (see exhibit 22.1) and a sample letter proposal to a corporation (see exhibit 22.2) are included for your review.

The letter proposal follows an orderly progression that focuses on the needs and interests of the funding source. As you gain insight into your prospective grantor, you will develop the ability to write grant-winning foundation proposals.

May 5, 19____

Abraham Donaldson, Executive Director
Foundation for the Terminally Ill
One East Third Avenue
Washington, DC 22222

Dear Mr. Donaldson:

While working with your colleague David Ketchum, I learned of your foundation's efforts to support the hospice movement. Your underwriting of a book on AIDS victim Scott Whittier and your concern for serving AIDS patients have prompted us to write this letter and request your foundation's support of the Central AIDS Hospice Project. This is a unique project that will serve over 1,000 AIDS patients in Georgia over the next five years.

The Central Hospital is located in Smithville and adjoins Central Medical College. A leader in caring for medically underserved minorities, Central has been in the forefront of health promotion since 1904.

The current AIDS epidemic has hit our minority population hard. The enclosed chart illustrates the cumulative number of AIDS patients diagnosed in Georgia and those who were in the active stage as of January 1, 19____. Central Hospital lies in Region I—Middle Georgia as shown on the chart. In addition to serving the 987 known cumulative cases and the 842 active cases in our region, we also serve AIDS patients in the west and central districts, which pushes our totals to 1,129 known cumulative and 906 active cases. Naturally, these figures represent a conservative estimate of the true number of cases.

Some of our AIDS patients have family members and friends to take care of them at home at the onset of their disease. Others are alone and destitute. Because our catchment population consists primarily of the medically underserved, we know many do not enter our treatment system until the later stages of their disease. No matter what the individual situation may be, it is at this final stage of life that our AIDS patients so desperately need an in-patient hospice facility to care for them.

Central Hospital has agreed to provide 20 patient rooms for an AIDS hospice unit. We have the space, we have the patients, and we have the commitment and support of the hospital and the medical college. What we don't have are the funds for furniture (estimated at $16,000), renovations (estimated at $16,000), or special staff training (estimated at $5,000).

The attached project planner outlines our plan of action. (A complete and itemized budget is available upon request.) We will start with a 6-bed unit, then increase it to 8, then to 10, and so on. We forecast that the unit will be self-sufficient by the sixth month of operation.

We feel confident that this project will be a meaningful contribution to the Smithville community and Georgia for many years to come. First, look at our mission. Central Hospital and Central Medical College are unique in their extraordinary and admirable mission to provide medical training *and* patient care to minorities. Second, consider our graduates. Over 75 percent of Central's graduates go on to choose medically underserved urban and rural settings in which to practice medicine. And finally, look at our staff. The hospital staff members responsible for developing this project and for operating it, Dolores Levell and Mel Campo, have over 61 years of cumulative experience in nursing and long-term patient care!

It will take $37,000 to make our AIDS in-patient hospice facility a reality. However, a $15,000 grant from the Foundation for the Terminally Ill would give us the boost we need to solicit the rest of the funds locally. Your foundation's investment in our project would provide us with the positive image and credibility we need to raise the remainder.

SAMPLE LETTER PROPOSAL TO A FOUNDATION

EXHIBIT 22.1

In recognition of your generous and truly caring gift, we would like to dedicate the entire 20-room facility to the Foundation for the Terminally Ill and have you or one of your board members attend our ribbon-cutting ceremony here in Smithville. You will also be proud to know that your foundation's name will be placed on 10 of the rooms and that you and your donors, through a grant of $15,000, made a needed, meaningful contribution to the disadvantaged minority population of Georgia.

Please call Dolores Levell at _____ to discuss this further and to arrange a visit to Central Hospital and Central Medical College.

Sincerely,

Thomas Watkins, Ph.D.
Chief Executive Officer
Central Hospital

Adele Trent, M.D.
President
Central Medical College

SAMPLE LETTER PROPOSAL TO A FOUNDATION *(continued)*

EXHIBIT 22.1

September 8, 19_____

Lawrence Blaine, President
Blaine Corporation
811 Cold Spring Highway
Appleton, OH 25891

Dear Mr. Blaine:

I would like to take this opportunity to invite you to join our school district in initiating an exciting new program. We know your company is particularly interested in education because you generously support elementary and secondary schools, are an enthusiastic partner in the Adopt-A-School Program, and encourage your employees, like Leon Smith and Marilyn Jones, to volunteer at our local schools.

As a matter of fact, Mr. Smith and Ms. Jones are currently involved in helping our district address the problem of declining math and science skills and the growing inability of our students to transfer these skills from the classroom to the work place. Our students rank _____ in the country and score in the _____ percentile on standardized math tests, but we are not the only ones to recognize the problem.

- A 19_____ study conducted by the Educational Testing Center showed that American 13-year-olds placed 14th among 15 industrialized countries on standard math tests.

SAMPLE LETTER PROPOSAL TO A CORPORATION

EXHIBIT 22.2

- A 19_____ Scans Report indicated that the average American high school junior spends 30 hours a week on school work; the average Japanese junior spends 60.

Although there is some evidence that our students' mathematical scores are improving, the demand for mathematical skills is not remaining constant. It is growing, and we have already graduated individuals with inadequate skills.

You may have read about the Will-Burt Corporation of Orrville, Ohio (*Profile*, August 19__). They recently found themselves in a terrible situation. Their company employees were producing inferior products. In fact, they had a 35 percent rejection rate, massive product recalls, and 2,000 hours per month of "re-work." Their employees' lack of basic math skills was found to be one of the main culprits. After setting up a school in the plant to teach math skills, the company's rejection rate decreased to 2 percent, but the Will-Burt Corporation discovered that while remedial training was an effective solution it was also a costly one.

It is estimated that over $25 billion is spent annually on remedial training in this country! We must do better. Our schools must provide our students with the skills necessary to meet the challenges of the year 2000. An April 19__ article in *INC.* magazine reported that even today's modern corporations want employees who can and will think about innovation, quality service, and using advanced techniques such as statistical process control.

Our school district has been developing several solutions to deal with declining math and science skills, including parental involvement in education, less television, and more valuable homework. However, we also need to apply new techniques—techniques we cannot afford in our regular budget. For example, we know that individualized instruction and self-paced learning materials could make a big difference if we only had the funds to provide for and purchase these resources.

Our parents advisory committee, teachers, staff, and volunteers are very excited about implementing SUCCESS-MAKER, a computer-assisted learning program designed to help teachers develop an individualized instructional approach that will allow:

- remedial students to catch up,
- average students to excel, and
- gifted students to leap beyond.

The SUCCESS-MAKER elementary package in math is particularly interesting to us. It would allow our teachers to place students on computers to improve skills in number concepts, computation, problem solving, and math applications in science. The students' progress would be continually recorded and a report would be developed for the student, teacher, and parents. Our objective would be to increase our district's math competency in grades by _____ percent. Other districts that have used this approach have not only documented an improvement in skills but also significant increases in parental involvement.

Our district is ready to accept the challenge that SUCCESS-MAKER offers. Our teachers have already volunteered their time for in-service training, and our district has dedicated $_____ in resources to support the project. Everything is ready, but we need you.

A grant of $_____ from the Blaine Corporation will provide $_____. This equates to an investment of $___ per student who will benefit. I have enclosed a spreadsheet [or project planner] that outlines exactly how your funds will be put to use. I am sure you will agree that we need to move now before another group of students becomes another group of American workers needing remedial training. Your support will be an important catalyst in ensuring the strength of our country's future work force and the growth of companies such as the Blaine Corporation.

SAMPLE LETTER PROPOSAL TO A CORPORATION *(continued)*

EXHIBIT 22.2

We think of this project as an investment with a tremendous return and we hope you will too. We promise to stand accountable and to share all results of the program with you and your company. Please contact my office or [name] at [phone number] with any questions you may have. If you would like, we can provide you with support materials and a videotape that describes SUCCESS-MAKER in greater detail and includes comments from educators who have used this approach.

Sincerely,

Melissa Appleton, Ed.D.
Superintendent, Friendship Heights School District

SAMPLE LETTER PROPOSAL TO A CORPORATION *(continued)*

EXHIBIT 22.2

CHAPTER 23

Proposal Submission
Private Funding Sources

The deadlines set by private funding sources should be taken just as seriously as those of the government. If you cannot meet a deadline, you will appear to be a poor steward of funds, so try to be prompt, or, better yet, early. Private funding sources, unlike the government, have been known to give a few extra days' "grace" period when the prospective grantee has a good explanation for the delay and the benefit of personal contact. However, it still does not look good when you need extra time, especially when the deadline has been published for a year or more.

When you are submitting your request to a large corporation or foundation, you can deliver it in person or have an advocate or board member deliver it for you. Although there is not as much advantage to hand delivery in the private sector as in the public sector, hand delivery makes an impression and helps avoid problems with delivery service. In other words, you can be sure the proposal is there! If you decide to mail your proposal, send it by certified mail with a return receipt requested. You can also obtain a signed receipt when using United Parcel Service (UPS), Federal Express, or the United States Postal Service's overnight service. This way you will have proof that your proposal arrived on time.

In conclusion, make note of the following:

- Send the contacts or people you discovered through the webbing and linkage process a copy of your letter proposal.

- Ask these "friends" to push for your proposal at the board meeting or to contact their friends or other board members to encourage a favorable decision.
- Minimize personal contact once you have submitted your proposal to avoid appearing pushy.

CHAPTER 24

The Decision of Private Funders and Follow-Up

Private funding sources are generally more prompt than public funders at letting you know their decision about your proposal. They will give you a simple yes or no.

If the answer is yes, you should immediately:

- Send a thank-you letter to the funding source. One foundation trustee told me that one of the only records they keep on grantees is whether or not they thank the foundation. She said, "If an organization that receives a grant doesn't thank us, they do not receive another grant from us."
- Find out the payment procedures. Usually the acceptance letter comes with a check. If a check is not enclosed, the letter will at least inform you of when you will receive payment. Due to staff shortages, small foundations will usually grant the entire amount requested in one lump sum. Large foundations with staff may make partial or quarterly payments based on your cash forecast.
- Check on any reporting procedures that the funding source may have.
- Ask the funding source when you might visit to report on the grant, and invite funders to visit you when traveling in your area.
- Ask, or have your link ask, the funding source what was best about your proposal and what could have been better. Although most grantors will not comment on your proposal, it cannot hurt to ask.

Most funding sources feel neglected once they have given away their money. You can get on their list of good grantees by following up. Your follow-up checklist should include

- putting funding sources on your public relations mailing list so that they will receive news or press releases
- keeping your funding source files updated and having a volunteer maintain current lists of grants funded by each of your grantors
- writing to funding sources two years after they have funded you to let them know how successful you are and to thank them again for their farsightedness in dealing with the problem

If the answer is no, make the most of it by learning as much as you can from the experience.

- Send a thank-you letter to the funding source. Express your appreciation for the time and effort spent on reviewing your proposal.
- Remind the funder of what an important source of funds it is.
- Ask for helpful comments on your proposal and whether the funding source would look favorably on resubmission with certain changes.
- Ask whether the funder could suggest any other funding sources who may be interested in your project.

If the foundation has no staff and you have no links, you may not find answers to your questions. However, try again. Successful grantseekers are persistent!

The steps suggested in this final chapter follow the unifying principle of this book; that is, look at everything you do from the perspective of the grantor. From pre-proposal contact, to writing your thank-you letter, to follow-up, consider how you would want to be appreciated and recognized for your contribution now and in the future.

The best approach to grantseeking is to develop a long-term and mutually beneficial relationship among you, your organization, and the grantor. This relationship could be based on honesty and a sincere concern for the grantor's needs. Saying thank you is a crucial element in building such a relationship.

Thank you for purchasing this book, and I am confident that you will be rewarded for practicing the strategies outlined.

LIST OF RESOURCES

Y ou may wish to look at copies of these recommended grant tools before you purchase them. Many of the resources listings include locations where you can find the materials and get assistance from helpful staff. Many institutions have developed joint or cooperative grants libraries to reduce costs and encourage consortium projects.

The list of resources is divided into the following sections:

- Government Grant Research Aids
- Foundation Grant Research Aids
- Corporate Grant Research Aids
- Government, Foundation, and Corporate Grant Resources
- Computer Research Services and Resources

GOVERNMENT GRANT RESEARCH AIDS

Tips

1. Each congressional district has at least two federal depository libraries. Your local college librarian or public librarian will know where the designated libraries are and will advise you on the availability of the resources listed in this section.
2. Many federal agencies have newsletters or agency publications. You can ask to be placed on their mailing lists to receive these publications.
3. Contact federal programs to get the most up-to-date information.
4. All of the government grant publications listed here are available through your congressperson's office.

Government Publications

Catalog of Federal Domestic Assistance (CFDA)

The *Catalog* is the government's most complete listing of federal domestic assistance programs, with details on eligibility, application procedures, and deadlines, including the location of state plans. It is published in June, with supplementary updates in December. Indexes are by agency

program, function, title, applicant eligibility, and subject. It comes in looseleaf form, punched for a three-ring binder.
Price: $72.00 per year
Order from
Superintendent of Documents
P.O. Box 271954
Pittsburgh, PA 15250-7954
(202)512-1800
Available online at http://www.gsa.gov/fdac/default.htm

Commerce Business Daily

The government's contracts publication, published five times a week, CBD announces every government Request for Proposal (RFP) that exceeds $25,000, as well as upcoming sales of government surplus.
Price: $274.00 to $324.00 per year depending on type of postage
Order from
Superintendent of Documents
P.O. Box 271954
Pittsburgh, PA 15250-7954
(202)512-1800
Available online at http://cbdnet.access.gpo.gov

Congressional Record

The *Congressional Record* covers the day-to-day proceedings of the Senate and House of Representatives.
Price: $295.00 per year
Order from
Superintendent of Documents
P.O. Box 271954
Pittsburgh, PA 15250-7954
(202)512-1800
Available online at http://www.access.gpo.gov/su_docs/aces/aces150.html

Federal Register

Published five times a week (Monday through Friday), the *Federal Register* supplies up-to-date information on federal assistance and supplements the *Catalog of Federal Domestic Assistance (CFDA)*. The *Federal Register* includes public regulations and legal notices issued by all federal agencies and presidential proclamations. Of particular importance are the proposed rules, final rules, and program deadlines. An index is published monthly.
Price: $607.00 per year with indexes, $555.00 per year without indexes

Order from
Superintendent of Documents
P.O. Box 271954
Pittsburgh, PA 15250-7954
(202)512-1800
Available online at http://www.nara.gov/fedreg/

National Science Foundation E-Bulletin

Provides monthly news about NSF programs, deadline dates, publications, and meetings as well as sources for more information. The *Bulletin* is available to e-mail subscribers and is posted on the Web site. Print-on-demand copies can also be ordered. There is no cost for this service.
For information contact
National Science Foundation
Office of Legislative and Public Affairs
Arlington, VA 22230
(703)306-1070
To subscribe: http://www.nsf.gov/cgi-bin/ebulletin/mailit.pl
Print-on-demand copies: paperbulletin@nsf.gov

NIH Guide for Grants and Contracts

NIH Guide is published electronically once a week. Subscribers are e-mailed either the table of contents or the entire *Guide*. The weekly *Guide* and its archives can also be viewed on the NIH Web site. There is no subscription fee.
For information contact
National Institutes of Health
The Institutional Affairs Office
Building 1, Room 328
Bethesda, MD 20892
(301)496-5366
http://www.nih.gov/grants/guide/index.html
To subscribe: http://www.nih.gov/grants/guide/listserv.htm

U.S. Government Manual

This paperback manual gives the names of key personnel, addresses, and telephone numbers for all agencies, departments, etc. that constitute the federal bureaucracy.
Price: $41.00 per year
Order from
Superintendent of Documents
P.O. Box 371954

Pittsburgh, PA 15250-7954
(202)512-1800
Available online at http://www.access.gpo.gov/nara/nara001.html

Commercially Produced Publications

Academic Research Information System, Inc. (ARIS)

ARIS provides timely information about grant and contract opportunities, including concise descriptions of guidelines and eligibility requirements, upcoming deadline dates, identification of program resource persons, and new program policies for both government and non-government funding sources. Reports are available in printed and electronic versions.
Prices: Prices vary depending on version and whether it is an institutional or individual subscription.
Biomedical Sciences Report, call for pricing information
Social and Natural Science Report, call for pricing information
Arts and Humanities Report, call for pricing information
All three ARIS Reports and Supplements, call for pricing information
Order from
Academic Research Information System, Inc.
The Redstone Building
2940 16th Street, Suite 314
San Francisco, CA 94103
415-558-8133
e-mail: arisnet@dnai.com
http://www.dnai.com/~arisnet/index.html

Education Grants Alert

This weekly publication gives quick access to federal and private funding opportunities available for education.
Price: $329.00 for 50 issues
Order from
Aspen Publishers, Inc.
7201 McKinney Circle
Frederick, MD 21704
(800)638-8437
http://www.grantscape.com/omaha/grants/catalog/news.html

Federal Directory

The *Directory* includes names, addresses, and phone numbers of federal government agencies and key personnel.
Price: Print $300 per year; CD-ROM $730 per year, online $730 per year
Order from
Carroll Publishing
1058 Thomas Jefferson Street, NW
Washington, DC 20007
(202)333-8620
http://www.carrollpub.com/Info/directories.html

Federal Grants and Contracts Weekly

This weekly contains information on the latest Requests for Proposals (RFPs), contracting opportunities, and upcoming grants. Each issue includes details on RFPs, closing dates for grant programs, procurement-related news, and newly issued regulations.
Price: $389.00 for 50 issues
Order from
Aspen Publishers, Inc.
7201 McKinney Circle
Frederick, MD 21704
(800)638-8437
http://www.grantscape.com/omaha/grants/catalog/news.html

Federal Yellow Book

This directory of the federal departments and agencies is updated quarterly.
Price: $290.00
Order from
Leadership Directories, Inc.
104 Fifth Avenue, 3rd Floor
New York, NY 10011
(212)627-4140
http://www.leadershipdirectories.com

Health Grants and Contracts Weekly

This weekly publication provides early alerts on public and private health-related funding opportunities.
Price: $379.00 for 50 issues
Order from
Aspen Publishers, Inc.
7201 McKinney Circle

Frederick, MD 21704
(800)638-8437
http://www.grantscape.com/omaha/grants/catalog/news.html

Washington Information Directory, 1999/2000

This directory is divided into three categories: agencies of the executive branch; Congress; and private or "nongovernmental" organizations. Each entry includes the name, address, telephone number, and director of the organization, along with a short description of its work.
Price: $110.00
Order from
Congressional Quarterly Books
1414 22nd Street, NW
Washington, DC 20037
(800)638-1710

FOUNDATION GRANT RESEARCH AIDS

Tips

Many of the following research aids can be found through the Foundation Center Cooperating Collections Network. If you wish to purchase any of the following Foundation Center publications contact

The Foundation Center
79 Fifth Avenue, Dept. FJ
New York, NY 10003-3076
(800)424-9836 or in New York state, (212)807-3690
Fax: (212)808-3677
Internet: http://www.fdncenter.org

AIDS Funding: A Guide to Giving by Foundations and Charitable Organizations, 5th edition, 1997, 206 pp.

Over 600 grantmakers who have stated or demonstrated a commitment to AIDS-related services and research are identified here.
Price: $75
Order from
The Foundation Center

Corporate Foundation Profiles, 10th edition, February 1998, 778 pp.

A Foundation Center publication, this book contains detailed analysis of 195 of the largest corporate foundations in the United States. An appendix lists financial data on hundreds of additional smaller grantmakers.

Price: $155.00
Order from
The Foundation Center

Directory of Operating Grants, 4th edition

Profiles on more than 600 foundations receptive to proposals for operating grants are provided.
Price $59.50
Order from
Research Grant Guides
P.O. Box 1214
Loxahatchee, FL 33470
Fax orders to: (561)795-7794
Tel.: (561)795-6129 (no credit card or telephone orders accepted)
http://www.researchgrant.com/

Foundation and Corporate Grants Alert

Price: $297 for 50 issues
Order from
Aspen Publishers, Inc.
7201 McKinney Circle
Frederick, MD 21704
(800)638-8437
http://www.grantscape.com/omaha/grants/catalog/news.html

The Foundation Directory, 1999 edition, 2,640 pp.

The most important single reference work available on grant-making foundations in the United States, this directory includes information on foundations having assets of more than $2 million or annual grants exceeding $200,000. Each entry includes a description of giving interests, along with address, telephone numbers, current financial data, names of donors, contact person, and IRS identification number. Six indexes are included: index to donors, officers, and trustees; geographic index; types of support index; subject index; foundations new to edition index; and foundation name index. The index to donors, officers, and trustees is very valuable in developing links to decision makers.
Price: $215.00 hardcover; $185.00 softcover
Order from
The Foundation Center

The Foundation Directory Part 2, March 1999, 1,200 pp.

This directory provides information on over 5,700 midsize foundations with grant programs between $50,000–$200,000.

Price: $185 *Part 2*; $485 hardcover *Directory, Supplement,* and *Part 2*;
$455 softcover *Directory, Supplement,* and *Part 2*
Order from
The Foundation Center

The Foundation Directory Supplement, September 1999, 626 pp.

The *Supplement* updates the *Directory,* so that users will have the latest
addresses, contacts, policy statements, application guidelines, and finan-
cial data.
Price: $125.00 *Supplement*; $320.00 hardcover *Directory* and *Supplement*;
$290 softcover *Directory* and *Supplement*
Order from
The Foundation Center

Foundation Giving Watch

News and the "how-to's" of foundation giving, are provided in this
monthly newsletter, along with a listing of recent grants.
Price: $149.00 for 12 issues
Order from
The Taft Group
PO Box 9187
Farmington Hills, MI 48333-9187
(800)877-8238
http://www.taftgroup.com/

The Foundation Grants Index, 1999 edition, 2,130 pp.

This is a cumulative listing of over 86,000 grants of $10,000 or more
made by over 1,000 major foundations. A recipient name index, a subject
index, a type of support/geographic index, a recipient category index, and
an index to grants by foundation are included.
Price: $165.00
Order from
The Foundation Center

Foundation Grants to Individuals, 11th edition, 630 pp.

This directory provides a comprehensive listing of over 3,800 indepen-
dent and corporate foundations that provide financial assistance to
individuals.
Price: $65.00
Order from
The Foundation Center

Foundation News

Each bimonthly issue of the *News* covers the activities of private, company-sponsored, and community foundations, direct corporate giving, and government agencies and their programs, and includes the kinds of grants being awarded, overall trends, legal matters, regulatory actions and other areas of common concern.
Price: $48.00 annually or $88.00 for 2 years
Order from
Council on Foundations
PO Box 96043
Washington, DC 20077-7188
(202)466-6512
http://www.cof.org/

The Foundation 1,000, 1998/1999 edition, 3,030 pp.

The 1,000 largest U.S. foundations are profiled by foundation name, subject field, type of support, and geographic location. There is also an index that allows you to target grantmakers by the names of officers, staff, and trustees.
Price: $295.00
Order from
The Foundation Center

Foundations of the 1990s, May 1998, 1,386 pp.

This publication describes more than 9,000 independent, community, and corporate foundations that have incorporated as grantmaking institutions in the United States. after 1990.
Price: $150.00
Order from The Foundation Center

Foundation Reporter

This annual directory of the largest private charitable foundations in the United States supplies descriptions and statistical analyses.
Price: $415.00
Order from
Gale Group
P.O. Box 9187
Farmington Hills, MI 48333-9187
(800)877-8238
http://www.gale.com

Grant Guides

There are a total of 35 *Grant Guides* available in a variety of areas such as children and youth, alcohol and drug abuse, mental health, addictions and crisis services, minorities, the homeless, public health and diseases, and social services. Each guide provides descriptions of hundreds of foundation grants of $10,000 or more recently awarded in its subject area. Sources of funding are indexed by type of organization, subject focus, and geographic funding area. Of the 35 guides, eight are in the field of education, including elementary and secondary education, higher education, libraries and information services, literacy, reading and adult/continuing education, scholarships, student aid and loans, science and technology programs, and social and political programs.
Price: $75.00 each
Order from
The Foundation Center

Guide to Funding for International and Foreign Programs, 4th edition, May 1998, 358 pp.

This guide includes over 800 funding sources that award grants to international nonprofit institutions and projects, as well as over 6,000 grant descriptions.
Price: $115.00
Order from
The Foundation Center

Guide to Grantseeking on the Web, December 1998, 408 pp.

Includes information on hundreds of grantmaker Web sites and a variety of related nonprofit sites of interest.
Price: $19.95
Order from
The Foundation Center

Guide to U.S. Foundations, Their Trustees, Officers, and Donors, April 1998, 2 vols., 4,235 pp.

Includes information on over 40,000 U.S. private, corporate, and community foundations and an index to the individuals who establish, manage, and oversee these foundations.
Price: $215.00
Order from The Foundation Center

National Guide to Funding for Elementary and Secondary Education, 4th edition, May 1997, 725 pp.

Over 2,400 sources of funding for elementary and secondary education and over 6,300 grant descriptions listing organizations that have successfully approached these funding sources are included in this guide.
Price: $140.00
Order from
The Foundation Center

National Guide to Funding for the Environment and Animal Welfare, 4th edition, June 1998, 527 pp.

Includes over 2,000 sources of funding for environment- and animal welfare-related nonprofit institutions and projects, as well as over 4,800 grant descriptions.
Price: $95.00
Order from
The Foundation Center

National Guide to Funding in Arts and Culture, 5th edition, May 1998, 1,138 pp.

This guide includes over 5,200 sources of funding for arts- and culture-related nonprofit organizations and projects, as well as over 12,700 grant descriptions.
Price: $145.00
Order from
The Foundation Center

National Guide to Funding in Health, 5th edition, April 1997, 1,195 pp.

This guide includes over 3,800 sources for health-related projects and institutions and over 12,000 grant descriptions.
Price: $150.00
Order from
The Foundation Center

National Guide to Funding in Higher Education, 5th edition, June 1998, 1,275 pp.

Over 3,900 sources of funding for higher education projects and institutions and over 15,000 grant descriptions are included in this source.
Price: $145.00
Order from
The Foundation Center

National Guides from the Foundation Center are also available in the following areas:

Aging, 1995, $95.00
Children, Youth and Families, 1997, $150.00
Community Development, 1998, $135.00
Information Technology, 1997, $115.00
Libraries and Information Services, 1997, $95.00
Religion, 1997, $140.00
Substance Abuse, 1998, $95.00
Women and Girls, 1997, $115.00

Who Gets Grants, 5th edition, February 1998, 1,469 pp.

This book features over 66,000 grants recently awarded to more than 22,000 nonprofit organizations in the United States and abroad.
Price: $135.00
Order from
The Foundation Center

Private Foundation IRS Tax Returns

The Internal Revenue Service requires private foundations to file income tax returns each year. Form 990-PF provides fiscal details on receipts and expenditures, compensation of officers, capital gains or losses, and other financial matters. Form 990-AR provides information on foundation managers, assets, and grants paid or committed for future payment.

The IRS makes this information available on aperture (microfiche) cards that may be viewed for free at the reference collections operated by the Foundation Center (New York, San Francisco, Washington, DC, Cleveland, and Atlanta) or at the Foundation Center's regional cooperating collections (see chapter 19, exhibit 19.4). You may also obtain this information by writing to the Ogden IRS Service Center, P.O. Box 9953, Mail Stop 6734, Ogden, Utah 84409 [fax: (801)775-4839]. Enclose as much information about the foundation as possible including its full name; street address with city, state, and zip code; employer identification number (EIN, which appears in Foundation Center directories and Infotax, a CD-ROM database); and the year or years for which returns are requested. It generally takes four to six weeks for the IRS to respond and it will bill you for all charges—$1.00 for the first page and $.15 per additional page or $1.00 for the first aperture card and $.18 for each additional card.

Try Web sites http://www.irs.ustreas.gov, http://www.guidestar.org, and http://www.nonprofits.org on the Internet to obtain information from 990s. For historical information on a private foundation contact Indiana University/Purdue University—Indianapolis University Library at (317)278-2329. It has 990-PFs dating from the late 1960s donated by the Foundation Center.

Directories of State and Local Grantmakers

Visit the Foundation Center cooperating collection (see chapter 19, exhibit 19.4) closest to you to determine what directories are available for your state and surrounding region. The following three regional guides are available through the Foundation Center:

- *Guide to Greater Washington, DC, Grantmakers*, 3rd edition, July 1998, 233 pp., $60.00
- *New York State Foundations*, 5th edition, June 1997, 1,095 pp., $180.00
- *Directory of Missouri Grantmakers*, 2nd edition, June 1997, 159 pp., $75.00

Visit the Rural Information Center on the Internet at http://www.nal.usda.gov/ric/ricpubs/funding/funding1.htm for a comprehensive listing of available state directories. Please note that while some directories are updated on a regular basis, many are not.

CORPORATE GRANT RESEARCH AIDS

Corporations interested in corporate giving often establish foundations to handle their contributions. Once foundations are established, their Internal Revenue Service returns become public information, and data are compiled into the directories previously mentioned under Foundation Grant Research Aids.

Corporate contributions that do not go through a foundation are not public information, and research sources consist of

- information volunteered by the corporation
- product information
- profitability information

Corporate Contributions in 1997

Sponsored by the Conference Board and the Council for Financial Aid to Education, this annual survey includes a detailed analysis of beneficiaries of corporate support but does not list individual firms and specific recipients.

Price: $25.00 for associates; $100.00 for non-associates

Order from
The Conference Board
845 Third Avenue
New York, NY 10022
(212)759-0900
http://www.conference-board.org/

Corporate Giving Watch

This newsletter reports on corporate giving developments.
Price: $149.00 for 16 issues
Order from
The Taft Group
P.O. Box 9187
Farmington Hills, MI 48333-9187
(800)877-8238
http://www.taftgroup.com

Directory of Corporate Affiliations, 1999

This five-volume directory lists divisions, subsidiaries, and affiliates of
thousands of companies with addresses, telephone numbers, key persons,
employees, etc.
Price: $1,059
Order from
Reed Elsevier New Providence
P.O. Box 31
New Providence, NJ 07974
(800)323-6772
http://www.reedref.com/index.html

Dun and Bradstreet's Million Dollar Directory, 5 volumes

The five volumes list names, addresses, employees, sales volume, and
other pertinent data for 140,000 of the largest businesses in the United
States.
Price: $1,525.00 print copy; $9,975.00 Internet database
Order from
Dun and Bradstreet Information Services
3 Sylvan Way
Parsippany, NJ 07054
(800)526-0651
http://www.dnb.com/

The National Directory of Corporate Giving, 5th edition, October 1997, 1,092 pp.

Information on over 1,905 corporate foundations, plus an additional 900 direct-giving programs, is provided in this directory. An extensive bibliography and seven indexes are included to help you target funding prospects.

Price: $225.00
Order from
The Foundation Center
79 Fifth Avenue, Dept. FJ
New York, NY 10003-3076
800-424-9836 or in New York state, (212)807-3690
Fax: (212)807-3677
Internet: http://www.fdncenter.org

North American Industry Classification System Manual

Developed for use in the classification of establishments by type of activity in which they are engaged.

Price: printed version $28.50 softcover, $32.50 hardcover; CD-ROM version: $45.00 single user; $120.00 5 or fewer concurrent network users; $240.00 unlimited concurrent network users
Order from
National Technical Information Service
Springfield, VA 22161
(800)553-6847
Internet: http://www.ntis.gov

Standard and Poor's Register of Corporations, Directors, and Executives, 3 volumes

This annual register is made up of three volumes (volume 1, *Corporations*; volume 2, *Directors and Executives*; volume 3, *Indexes*). These volumes are available on a lease-basis only. The volumes provide up-to-date rosters of over 500,000 executives of the 75,000 nationally known corporations they represent, along with their names, titles, and business affiliations.

Price: $795.00 per year for print, $1,095.00 for CD-ROM or Internet, both print and electronic versions include quarterly updates
Order from
Standard and Poor's Corporation
Attn: Sales
65 Broadway, 8th Floor

New York, NY 10006-2503
(212)770-4412

Taft Corporate Giving Directory, 1999

This directory provides detailed entries on 1,000 company-sponsored foundations and includes nine indexes.
Price: $440.00
Order from
Gale Group
P.O. Box 9187
Farmington Hills, MI 48333-9187
(800)877-8238
http://www.gale.com

Who's Who in America, 1998/1999, 53rd edition

Known for its biographic and career data on noteworthy individuals. The 53rd edition has two volumes.
Price: $525.00
Order from
Reed Elsevier New Providence
P.O. Box 31
New Providence, NJ 07974
(800)236-6772
http://www.reedref.com/index.html

GOVERNMENT, FOUNDATION, AND CORPORATE GRANT RESOURCES

Many of the following research aids can be purchased from Oryx Press, 4041 N. Central Avenue, Suite 700, Phoenix, AZ 85012-3397, (800)279-6799, fax: (800)279-4663, Internet: info@oryxpress.com, http://www.oryxpress.com

Administering Grants, Contracts, and Funds, 1999

Provides information on the roles and responsibilities of an effective grants office. Particularly useful for those in the process of setting up a new grants office or evaluating an existing one.
Price: $36.95
Order from
The Oryx Press

The Complete Grants Sourcebook for Higher Education, 3rd edition, 1995, 465 pp.

Provides brief information on grant research and proposal development, plus a directory of funding opportunities in higher education.
Price: $85.00
Order from
The Oryx Press

Directory of Biomedical and Health Care Grants

This directory provides information on biomedical and health care-related programs sponsored by the federal government, foundations, corporations, professional associations, special interest groups, and state and local governments. Published annually.
Price: $84.50
Order from
The Oryx Press

Directory of Building and Equipment Grants, 5th edition

Aimed at aiding in the search for building and equipment grants, this directory profiles more than 800 foundations.
Price: $59.50
Order from
Research Grant Guides
P.O. Box 1214
Loxahatchee, FL 33470
Fax orders to: (561)795-7794
Tel.: (561)795-6129, no credit card or phone orders accepted
http://www.researchgrant.com/

Directory of Computer and High Technology Grants, 3rd edition

This directory provides 500 foundation profiles to help organizations obtain software and computer and high-tech equipment.
Price: $59.50
Order from
Research Grant Guides
P.O. Box 1214
Loxahatchee, FL 33470
Fax orders to: (561)795-7794
Tel.: (561)795-6129, no credit card or phone orders accepted
http://www.researchgrant.com/

Directory of Grants for Organizations Serving People with Disabilities, 10th edition

Profiles on more than 800 foundations that have a history of serving people with disabilities are included.
Price: $59.50
Order from
Research Grant Guides
P.O. Box 1214
Loxahatchee, FL 33470
Fax orders to: (561)795-7794
Tel.: (561)795-6129, no credit card or phone orders accepted
http://www.researchgrant.com/

Directory of Grants in the Humanities

Current data on funds available to individual artists and arts organizations from corporations, foundations, and professional associations as well as from the NEA, NEH, and state and local arts and humanities councils.
Price $84.50
Order from
The Oryx Press

Directory of Research Grants

Information on government, corporate, foundation, and institute funding sources supporting research programs in academic, scientific, and technology-related subjects. Published annually.
Price: $135.00
Order from
The Oryx Press

Funding Sources for Community and Economic Development

Descriptions of programs that offer funding opportunities for quality-of-life projects at the community level are included. Funding programs sponsored by both local and national sources are listed, including state, local, and federal government sources, nonprofit and corporate sponsors, foundations, and advocacy groups. Published annually.
Price: $64.95
Order from
The Oryx Press

Funding Sources for K-12 Education
Descriptions of programs that offer funding opportunities for classroom instruction, teacher education, art in education, general operating grants, and equipment from federal, state, corporate, and foundation sources.
Price: $34.50
Order from
The Oryx Press

Giving USA 98
Annual report on philanthropy for the year 1997.
Price: $49.95 plus $25.00 for each newsletter
Order from
AAFRC Trust for Philanthropy
25 W. 43rd Street, Suite 820
New York, NY 10037
(212)354-5799 X 3001 (customer service)
http://www.aafrc.org/

COMPUTER RESEARCH SERVICES AND RESOURCES

There is a wealth of information available through databases and information retrieval systems. Check with your librarian and your grants office to locate those databases you may already have access to.

Community of Science (COS) Funding Opportunities
COS *Funding Opportunities* database is a comprehensive source of funding information accessed via the World Wide Web.
Price: COS *Funding Opportunities* is included with fee-based membership in the Community of Scholars. Other institutions may purchase access to COS *Funding Opportunities* for a fixed annual subscription fee. Subscription pricing is determined by the amount of external research funding your institution manages.
Sales/Free trial Contact:
Edwin Van Dusen
VP, Information Products
1629 Thames Street, Suite 200
Baltimore, MD 21231
(410)563-5382 X225
Fax: (410)563-5389
E-mail: evd@cos.com
http://www.cos.com

Congressional Information Service Index (CIS Index)

CIS covers congressional publications and legislation from 1970 to date. Hearings, committee prints, House and Senate reports and documents, special publications, Senate executive reports and documents, and public laws are indexed. *CIS Index* includes monthly abstracts and index volumes. Hard copies of grant-related materials are also available from CIS, including *CIS Federal Register Index*, which covers announcements from the *Federal Register* on a weekly basis.

Price: $1,460.00 hardcover 1998 edition; monthly service (including hardbound annual edition) is on a sliding scale depending on your library's annual book, periodical, and microform budget

Order from

Congressional Information Services, Inc.
4520 East-West Highway, Suite 800
Bethesda, MD 20814
800-638-8380
http://www.cispubs.com/

Dialog OnDisc: Federal Register

This is a CD-ROM version of the *Federal Register*.

Price: The price for this service depends on whether your organization is currently a subscriber to other DIALOG searching services.

For more information or to order contact

Dialog, Inc.
11000 Regency Parkway, Suite 10
Cary, NC 27511
(800)334-2564
Fax: (919)468-9890
Internet: http://www.dialog.com

Dialog OnDisc Grants Database

The *Dialog OnDisc Grants Database* lists approximately 10,000 grants offered by federal, state, and local governments; corporations; professional associations; and private and community foundations. Entries include a description; qualifications; and full name, address, and telephone number for each sponsoring organization. Deadlines, amounts available, and Internet addresses are included as available.

Price: $850.00 includes bimonthly updated CD-ROM

Order from

Dialog, Inc.
11000 Regency Parkway, Suite 10
Cary, NC 27511

(800)334-2564
Fax: (919)468-9890
Internet: http://www.dialog:com
For more information contact:
The Oryx Press
4041 N. Central Avenue, Suite 700
Phoenix, AZ 85012-3397
(800)279-6799
Fax: (800)279-4663
Internet: info@oryxpress.com
http://www.oryxpress.com/grants.htm

Federal Assistance Program Retrieval System (FAPRS)

The *FAPRS* provides access to federal domestic assistance program information. All states have *FAPRS* services available through state, county, and local agencies as well as through federal extension services. For further information, call (202)708-5126 or *FAPRS* toll-free answering service at (800)669-8331, or write to your congressperson's office; he or she can request a search for you, in some cases at no charge.
For more information contact
Federal Domestic Assistance Catalog Staff (MVS)
General Services Administration
300 Seventh Street, SW
Reporters Building, Room 101
Washington, DC 20407

FEDIX

FEDIX, or the Federal Information Exchange, is a free online database of federal grant and research opportunities for the education and research communities. Participating federal agencies use *FEDIX* as an outreach tool to enhance communications with colleges, universities, and other educational and research organizations. *FEDIX* also offers *US Opportunities Alert*, a fee-based subscription service of foundation and corporation funding announcements.
Order from
RAMS/FIE
(800)875-2562
http://www.fie.com

Foundation Center Databases

The Foundation Center offers the public two online computer databases—one providing information on grantmakers, the other on the grants they distribute. Both databases are available online through Dialog.

For more information contact
Dialog, Inc.
11000 Regency Parkway, Suite 10
Cary, NC 27511
(800)334-2564
Fax: (919)468-9890
Internet: http://www.dialog.com

GrantScape CFDA

This is an electronic edition of the *Catalog of Federal Domestic Assistance*, including the full text of all federal grant programs included in the CFDA.
Price: $175.00
Order from
Aspen Publishers, Inc.
7201 McKinney Circle
Frederick, MD 21704
(800)638-8437
http://www.grantscape.com/omaha/grants/catalog/news.html

GrantSelect

This database, available on the World Wide Web, provides information on 10,000 funding programs available from over 3600 nonprofit organizations; foundations; private sources; and federal, state, and local agencies in the United States and Canada. Grantseekers can subscribe to the full research database or to any one of five segments offered: children and youth, health care and biomedical, arts and humanities, K-12 schools and adult basic education, and community development. A daily e-mail alert service that notifies grantseekers of any new funding opportunities within their area of interest is also available.
Price: yearly subscription full database $1,000; e-mail alert service only $1,000; full database plus e-mail alert service $1,500; single database segment $350; single segment e-mail alert service only $350; single segment plus e-mail alert service $500. Prices are for one campus/institution only; add 25% for each additional campus; a 25% discount is available for 2-year subscriptions; consortia pricing available on request
Order from
The Oryx Press
4041 N. Central, Suite 700
Phoenix, AZ 85012-3397
(800)279-6799
Fax: (800)279-4663

Internet: info@oryxpress.com
http://www.grantselect.com

Illinois Researcher Information Service (IRIS)

The IRIS database of funding opportunities contains records on over 7,700 federal and nonfederal funding opportunities in the sciences, social sciences, arts, and humanities. It is updated daily and is available in WWW and Telnet versions.

Price: IRIS is available to colleges and universities for an annual subscription fee.

For more information on the subscription policy and/or an IRIS trial period contact

Illinois Researcher Information Service (IRIS)
University of Illinois at Urbana-Champaign
128 Observatory
901 South Mathews Avenue
Urbana, Illinois 61801
(217)333-0284
Fax: (217)333-7011.
E-mail: rso@uiuc.edu

The Sponsored Programs Information Network (SPIN)

This is a database of federal and private funding sources for sponsored research and creative activities.

Price: Ranges from $1,000 to $6,000 depending on the institution's level of research and development expenditures.

For more information or to order contact

InfoEd
2301 Western Avenue
Guilderland, NY 12084
(800)727-6427
Fax: (518)464-0695
Internet: http://www.infoed.org/products.stm

DAVID G. BAUER ASSOCIATES, INC.
Ordering Information

Order the following grantseeking and fund raising materials directly from David G. Bauer Associates, Inc. Prices do not include shipping charges and are subject to change without notice.

Call toll free (800)836-0732, Monday—Friday, 9-5 Pacific Standard Time

GRANTSEEKING MATERIALS

Technology Funding for Schools—Techniques schools can use for obtaining funding for technology and Internet access. Price to be announced.

Creating Foundations in American Schools—Techniques for Creating School Foundations. Price to be announced.

Grants Time Line—Pad of 25 worksheets for developing time lines and cash forecasts. $3.95 per pad. For 10 or more pads, $2.95 per pad.

The Teacher's Guide to Winning Grants—A systematic guide to grantseeking skills that work for classroom leaders. $24.95.

The Principal's Guide to Winning Grants—Strategies principals can apply to support grantseeking at their schools. $24.95.

Project Planner—Pad of 25 worksheets for developing workplans and budget narratives. $8.95 per pad; 10 or more pads $7.95 each.

Proposal Organizing Workbook—Set of 30 Swiss cheese tabs. $9.95 per set; 10 or more sets, $8.95 each.

Successful Grants Program Management—Practical tool for the superintendent or central office administrator to assist in developing a district-wide grants support system. $29.95.

FUND-RAISING MATERIALS

Donor Pyramid—3 fold visual depicting various levels of donor activities and volunteer involvement. $9.95 per pyramid. For 10 or more, $8.95 per pyramid.

Fund Raising Organizer—Pad of 25 spreadsheets for planning and analyzing fund raising events. $8.95 per pad; 10 or more pads, $7.95 each.

Fund Raising Organizer Activity Cards—Pack of 25 cards that summarize resource allocation, costs and net funds. $3.95 per pack; 10 or more packs, $2.95 each.

The Fund Raising Primer—112 pages that provide basic information on various fund raising strategies. $24.95.

VIDEOTAPE PROGRAMS

For more information or to order call (800)228-4630, Monday—Friday

Winning Grants 2—Proven grant winning system on 5 video cassettes. Produced by the University of Nebraska Great Plains Network. $495.00

How To Teach Grantseeking To Others—Two-hour video providing the essential know-how to instruct others in the strategies and techniques of successful grantseeking. Comes with a companion text and computer disk that provide detailed support and supplies all necessary forms and checklists. $189.00

Strategic Fund Raising—Five 60-minute video cassettes designed to help nonprofit organizations increase board and staff involvement and understanding of basic fund raising principles and the development of a funding plan. $495.00.

SOFTWARE PROGRAMS

For more information or to order call (800)836-0732, Monday—Friday, 9-5 Pacific Standard Time.

Grant Winner—IBM-PC or compatible software package that organizes grantseeking techniques and stores four proposals and the worksheets found in *The "How To" Grants Manual.* $189.00.

Winning Links—IBM-PC or compatible software package providing a database that records the contacts of your board members, staff, and volunteers. $139.00

SEMINARS AND CONSULTING

Public Seminars—Call (800)836-0732 for information concerning David Bauer's public seminars held in major cities throughout the United States.

In-House Seminars and Consulting—David Bauer gives seminars at your institution or organization to increase your staff and/or board members' skills and interest in the following areas: federal grantseeking, foundation and corporate grantseeking, fund raising, evaluating your grants and/or fund raising system, and motivation/productivity. For more information on these services call (800)836-0732.

INDEX

by Linda Webster